Narratives of
The American Revolution

GENERAL GEORGE WASHINGTON

Commander-in-chief of the American Revolutionary Armies

A nineteenth-century print from a painting by A. Chapel

The Lakeside Classics

NARRATIVES OF
THE
AMERICAN REVOLUTION

As told by a young sailor,
a home-sick surgeon, a French volunteer,
and a German general's wife

EDITED BY
HUGH F. RANKIN

The Lakeside Press

R. R. DONNELLEY & SONS COMPANY
CHICAGO
Christmas, 1976

PUBLISHERS' PREFACE

NARRATIVES OF THE AMERICAN REVOLUTION is the 1976 edition of *The Lakeside Classics*, the seventy-fourth of an annual series started in 1903 by Thomas E. Donnelley, then president of R. R. Donnelley & Sons Company, to serve as an appropriate Christmas remembrance to friends of our Company. He felt that a simple well-designed book would also reflect favorably on our work. We are pleased to continue the tradition he established.

This year's volume includes four stories of highly individual personal wartime experiences. The first is by a young sailor who ran away to sea at an early age; the second is by a young doctor who was separated from his family and spent the winter of 1777 at Valley Forge; the third is by a hot-blooded young Frenchman who was sent to North America by his father to fight on the side of the Colonists; and the last is by the wife of a German general who, with her children, accompanied her husband to the Revolutionary battlefields and later into custody as prisoners.

The events were all significant in the lives of the narrators and in the progress of the war, but the significance of the authors themselves lies mainly in their close observations and the charm with which they set them down in their journals and memoirs. In order to preserve the spirit of their writings, our editor has made only minor changes in spelling and punctuation.

Professor Hugh F. Rankin, the editor, guided us to a great number of authentic narratives from which we selected these four. Professor Rankin is a widely recognized historian, lecturer, and author, whose scholarly annotations and comments immeasurably add to the enjoyment of NARRATIVES OF THE AMERICAN REVOLUTION. His books and articles are well-researched histories of colonial and Revolutionary War periods and extend into the early history of the United States. He is now working on a military history of the Revolution from the British point of view. His fame as a historian is a reflection of his lifelong research into that subject. He is presently W. R. Irby professor of History at Tulane University in New Orleans. Professor Rankin is active in a great number of historical associations and societies.

For the fifth year, Robert Williams of Chicago has provided the final drawings and calligraphy for the maps which accompany this year's edition of *The Lakeside Classics.* Mr. Williams worked with base maps created by the Donnelley Cartographic Services from sources used in the preparation of *Atlas of Early American History: The Revolutionary Era, 1760–1790,* published by Princeton University Press for the Newberry Library (Chicago) and the Institute of Early American History and Culture.

Typography for this book continues our reliance

on the Donnelley Electronic Graphics* service which generated the complete pages on a cathode ray tube with the use of computerized electronic equipment. Our Crawfordsville (Indiana) Division printed the book by offset lithography and bound the volumes on its high-speed binding lines in complete agreement with Thomas E. Donnelley's philosophy that a machine-made book should be every bit as handsome and easy to read as an entirely handmade book. Design, typographic assistance, and technical editorial services were provided by the Donnelley Creative Services Division.

THIS 74th edition of *The Lakeside Classics* gives us another opportunity to present a brief account of R. R. Donnelley & Sons Company, as viewed in the latter part of 1976.

We entered the year still feeling some effects of the recession. Net sales and net income were not increasing significantly, if at all, after the elimination of inflationary increases. As the year progressed, our volume increased, thanks to aggressive efforts from an expanded decentralized sales organization with several new offices. Our net income advanced at a slower, but encouraging, rate. The printing industry continued to have excess capacity, with resulting pressure on prices. In addition, we are still experiencing significant start-up costs on expan-

*Electronic Graphics is a service mark of R. R. Donnelley & Sons Company.

sion projects at several divisions, notably Old Saybrook, Connecticut, with four additional web offset presses for publications and catalogs, and Lancaster East, Pennsylvania, where an advanced computerized composition facility is being established.

Neither our Gallatin, Tennessee, catalog plant, nor our Elgin, Illinois, composition plant have yet reached their full potential of productivity.

In Crawfordsville the short run book module is now on stream. The Chicago Division, which along with Old Saybrook, suffered a grievous blow with the demise of *Life*, has made an excellent comeback. It shares with other divisions the high activity in both publications and catalogs. Our directory divisions have a reasonable amount of business, but have the capacity for a great deal more. The book divisions, which have suffered most severely from the recent recession, show signs of improvement, but also can handle more work. Financial printing is growing nicely, and some most creditable performances were accomplished.

With inflation moderating, we feel generally optimistic as to the future. Two clouds on the horizon are the continued shortage of natural gas and the renewed anticipation of tight paper supplies. To help alleviate the former, we have some local gas wells dedicated to our use. For the latter, we continue to maintain close relations with paper manufacturers and carefully plan with them our future anticipated needs.

To underscore our present optimism, our Board of Directors approved in July an increase in dividends, for the sixth consecutive year. Dividends have been paid every year since 1911, reflecting a profitable operation every year, even during the depression of the early thirties. Also an expanded Capital Budget was approved, to provide both for work under new contracts and for further penetration of our markets. The largest item was the expansion of our Gallatin, Tennessee Division with the ordering of three new gravure presses and additional building space. Thanks to our conservative dividend policy, we have sufficient retained earnings to do this, and still maintain a strong working capital position. Also by evaluating and availing ourselves of the latest and best technology, we are in a position to serve graphic arts customers better than ever before.

Most important is our great resource in people at every level, unskilled, semi-skilled, craft, staff, sales, and management. There is a remarkable dedication to quality and service, backed up by technical and managerial know-how. New approaches in technology are being tested and applied, and our employees are achieving new records of productivity in many areas.

We warmly and sincerely pay tribute to the thousands of fine people who make up our Company today and those who contributed so much to our past successes.

Shortly after our last year's *Classic* was in distribution, we lost our beloved Vice Chairman, Elliott Donnelley. He devoted most of his life and many abilities to our Company in many capacities. At the same time he gave more than his share of time and talents to leadership in civic, social service, and educational endeavors. We all shall miss his humor and perceptive common sense.

At this season of the year, we are most mindful of the many people and organizations who have contributed so much to our past success and growth, and on whom our future depends so much. We are truly grateful, and sincerely hope that the future will be bright for them all.

Merry Christmas and a Happy New Year.

The Publishers

Christmas, 1976

CONTENTS

xiii

ILLUSTRATIONS

HISTORICAL INTRODUCTION

A WAR, for both soldiers and civilians, is ofttimes the most emotional, and even the most exhilarating experience of a person's lifetime. Misery makes a stronger impression upon the mind than happy times. After a war of exposure to the elements and an enemy, the remainder of a person's life often seems rather dull and mundane.

Considering the state of education in the eighteenth century, it is surprising that so many people kept diaries and journals. Others, in the twilight of their lives, felt compelled to record their great adventure. Sometimes they forgot, sometimes they became confused in their chronology, or sometimes they even added hearsay as a personal experience, so vivid had it become in their memory. Many wanted to remember those things they had attempted to avoid on the battlefield.

Here we have selected four accounts that seem to best give a cross-section of the experiences of those involved in the struggle for independence: a young sailor, a homesick young surgeon, a young Frenchman of blithe spirit, and the charming wife of a German general. In general, we have attempted to steer clear of battle accounts, for however valuable they are to the historian, there is a tendency for a reader not familiar with the American Revolution to become bogged down in details—nay, he may even become bored. And it should be mentioned that all of the accounts selected, except that of Surgeon Waldo, are much longer in the originals, but we have selected only those portions dealing with their revolutionary experiences.

First, there is the lad, Ebenezer Fox, who in the exuberance of youth went dashing off to war and got more than he bargained for, only escaping the miseries of prison life by enlisting in the British army.

Following this there are the musings of Surgeon Albigence Waldo, whose finely-honed temperament allowed him to slide downhill in that slough of despair called Valley Forge.

Then there is the happy-go-lucky Frenchman, the Chevalier de Pontgibaud, who had been something of a hellion in France and had been sent off to the American war by his family to get him out of the way. For Pontgibaud, war was a fascinating experience and one to be enjoyed to the hilt.

Concluding these selections is that delightful journal by Madame von Riedesel, wife of a German general, following her beloved husband through the American wilderness just to be at his side. She too suffered the inconveniences of being a prisoner of war, although as an officer's wife she did not experience the sufferings of Ebenezer Fox, but by contrast with her previous station in life it is to be suspected that she underwent almost as much mental anguish, if not the physical discomfort.

Perhaps one way to get into the spirit of the times
is to repeat an early Chinese history of the young
American nation which first appeared in the old
Historical Magazine in 1867. Between 1844 and
1850 the governor of the Chinese province of Fuh-
Kien was a sometime historian by the name of Sen-
Ki-Yu. During his tenure in office he published, in
Chinese, a work on universal geography which in-
cluded a brief, and quaint, history of the United
States as he knew it—which wasn't very well. As
Sen-Ki-Yu was something of a liberal for his time,
one suspects he wrote the piece as propaganda.
Nevertheless, it was so favorable to the United
States that it was translated into English by the
United States legation at Peking, and the Secretary
of State presented a portrait of George Washington
to him. As it is centered primarily on the era of the
American Revolution, with Washington as the central figure, it seems fitting to reprint most of the
account, but it is here for the pleasure of reading,
not for learning American history.

It was the English people who first discovered and took
North America, and drove out the aborigines. The fertile
and eligible lands were settled by emigrants moved over
there from the three (British) islands, who thus occupied
them. These emigrants hastened over with a force like
that of a torrent running down the gully. Poor people
from France, Holland, Denmark and Sweden also sailed
over to join them, and as they all daily opened up new
clearings, the country grew rich in its cultivated lands.
High English officers held it for their sovereign, and as

cities and towns sprung up all along the coasts, their revenues were collected for his benefit. Commerce constantly increased in extent and amount, so that thus the inhabitants rapidly became rich and powerful.

During the reign of the Kemburg (A.D. 1736–1796) the English and French were at war for several years, during which the former exacted the duties throughout all their possessions, increasing the taxes more than previously. By the old tariff, for instance, the duty on tea was levied when it was sold; but the English now required that another tax should be payed by the buyer.

The people of America would not stand this, and in the year 1776 their gentry and leading men assembled together in order to consult with the (English) Governor how to arrange this matter; but he drove them from his presence, dispersed the assembly, and demanded that the tax be collected all the more strictly. The people thereupon rose in their wrath, threw all the tea in the ships into the sea, and then consulted together how they could raise troops to expel the British.

There was at this time a man named Washington, a native of another colony, born in 1732, who had lost his father at the age of ten, but had been admirably trained by his mother. While a boy he showed a great spirit and aptitude for literary and martial pursuits, and his love for brave and adventurous deeds exceeded those of ordinary men. He had held a military commission under the English, and during the war with France, when the French leagued with the Indians, and made an irruption into the southern provinces, he led on a body of troops and drove them back; but the English general would not report this expeditious operation, so that his worthy deeds were not recorded (for his promotion).

The people of the land now wished to have him to be their leader, but he went home on plea of sickness and shut himself up. When they had actually raised the standard of rebellion, however, they compelled him to become their general.

Though neither troops nor depots, neither arms nor ammunition, stores nor forage, existed at this time, Washington so inspired everybody by his own patriotism, and urged them on by his own energy, that the proper boards and departments were soon arranged, and he was thereby enabled to (bring up his forces) invest the capital. The British general had intrenched some marines outside the city, when a storm suddenly dispersed his ships. Washington improved the conjuncture by vigorously attacking the city, and succeeded in taking it.

The English then gathered a great army, and renewed the engagement. He lost the battle completely, and his men were so disheartened and terrified that they began to disperse. But his great heart maintained its composure, and he so rallied and reassured his army that they renewed the contest, and victory finally turned in their favor. Thus the bloody strife went on for eight years. Sometimes victorious and sometimes vanquished, Washington's determination and energy never quailed, while the English generals began to grow old.

The King of France also sent a general across the sea to strengthen the tottering states. He joined his forces with those of Washington, and gave battle to the British army. The rulers of Spain and Holland likewise hampered their military operations, and advised them to conclude a peace. The English at last could no longer act freely, and ended the strife in the year 1783, by making a treaty with Washington. According to the stipulation, the boundary line was so drawn that they had the desolate and cold regions on the north, while the fertile and genial southern portions were confirmed to him.

Washington having thus established the States, gave up his military command for the purpose of returning to his farm, but the people would not permit him thus to retire, and obliged him to become their ruler. He, however, proposed a plan to them as follows: "It is very selfish for him who gets the power in the State to hand it down to his posterity. In filling the post of the shepherd to the people, it will be most suitable to select a virtuous man."

Each of the old colonies was thereupon formed into a separate State, having its own Governor to direct its affairs, with a Lieutenant Governor to assist him, each of whom hold office for four years. At the general meeting of the people of his State, if they regarded him as worthy, he is permitted to hold his post during another term of four years, but if not, then the Lieutenant Governor takes his place. If, however, the latter does not obtain the approbation of the people, another man is chosen to the dignity when his time has expired. When the head men of the villages and towns are proposed for office, their names and surnames are written on tickets and thrown into a box. When everybody has done so the box is opened, and it is then known who is elected by his having the most votes, and he takes the office. Whether he has been an official or is a commoner, no examination is required of his qualifications; and when an officer vacates his place he becomes in all respects one of the common people again.

From among all the Governors of the separate States one supreme Governor (or President) is chosen, to whom belongs the right to make treaties and carry on war, and whose orders each State is bound to obey. The manner of his election is the same as that for a Governor of a State. He holds his office four years, or, if re-elected, for eight years. . . .

When Washington made peace with the British he dismissed all the troops, and directed the attention of the country entirely to agriculture and commerce. He also issued a mandate saying: "If hereafter a President should covetously plot how he can seize all the forts or lands of another kingdom, or harass and extort the people's wealth, or raise troops to gratify his personal quarrels, let all the people put him to death." He accordingly retained only twenty national war vessels, and limited the army to 10,000 men. . . .

It appears from the above that Washington was a very remarkable man. In devising plans he was more daring than Chin Shing or Hain Kwang. In winning a country he was braver than Tson Tsan or Sin Pi. Wielding his four foot falchion [broad sword], he enlarged the frontier myriads of miles, and yet he refused to usurp regal dignity, or even to transmit it to posterity; but, on the contrary, first proposed the plan of electing men to office. Where in the world can be found a mode more equitable? It is the same idea in fact, that has been handed down to us (the Chinese) from three reigns of San, Shun and Yu. In ruling the State he honored and fostered good usages, and did not exalt military merit, a principle totally unlike what is found in other kingdoms. I have seen his portrait. His mien and countenance are grand and impressive in the highest degree. Oh, who is there that does not call *him* a hero?

Despite Sen-Ki-Yu's infatuation with Washington, the American Revolution was more than a one-man war with the General figuratively slaying the redcoated Philistines with the jawbone of an ass. And because there were others than generals involved, we have deliberately stayed away from the accounts of those of higher rank.

Asterisks are notes made by the original journalist. Arabic numbers indicate my notes. Not all persons were prominent enough to be so identified, and I have likewise omitted identifying notes on such prominent persons as George Washington or

Thomas Jefferson. The narratives as published here are as they were written, with very minor revisions in spelling and punctuation.

I have enjoyed putting this together; I hope the readers will find pleasure in it.

Hugh F. Rankin

Tulane University
New Orleans, Louisiana, 1976

The Original Thirteen Colonies

THE ORIGINAL THIRTEEN COLONIES

St. Johns

Banks of Newfoundland

NEWFOUNDLAND

ST. PIERRE & MIQUELON (Fr.)

CAPE BRETON I.

SABLE I.

GULF OF ST. LAWRENCE

ANTICOSTI I.

ST. JOHN I.

Charlottetown

Halifax

NOVA SCOTIA

St. John • Annapolis

Penobscot Bay

St. John R.

Castine

Penobscot R.

Portland

(MASS)

Kennebeck R.

Manicouagan R.

Saguenay R.

Connecticut R.

N.H.

MASS.

Quebec

Lake Champlain

Ft. Chambly

Hud

N.Y.

L. St. Jean

Three Rivers

Montreal

F. Oswego

Ft. Johnson

F. Stanwix

Lake Mistassini

HUDSON'S BAY COMPANY

St. Lawrence R.

Niagara

ONTARIO

Fort George R.

Ottawa R.

L. Nipissing

L. Simcoe

QUEBEC

HURON

ATLANTIC
BERMUDA
Pittsburgh
Allegh
Valley Forge
Burlington
Philadelphia
New Castle
Baltimore
Dover
Annapolis
DEL.
MD.
Chesapeake Bay
Scioto R.
Ohio R.
Charlottesville
Richmond
James
Williamsburg
Yorktown
R. Roanoke R.
VIRGINIA
Kentucky R.
Wake C.H.
New Bern
Tennessee R.
Charlotte
Pee Dee R.
N.C.
Wilmington
S.C.
Savannah R.
Coosa R.
Augusta
Georgetown
Charlestown
GEORGIA
Savannah
N
WEST FLORIDA
Suwanee
St. Marks
St. Johns R.
St. Augustine
EAST FLORIDA
0 100 200 300
MILES
Crown Point
Ticonderoga
Hubbardton
Skenesborough
Ft. Anne
Concord
Portsmouth
Saratoga
Bennington
Lexington
Boston
Concord
Dorchester
Albany
Roxbury
Walpole
Providence
Hartford
Newport
Stonington
New Haven
Peekskill
LONG I.
New York
Wilkes-Barre
Wallabout Bay
Perth Amboy
Red Bank
Bethlehem
Trenton
0 25 50 75
MILES

1

The Revolutionary Adventures
of
Ebenezer Fox
of
Roxbury, Massachusetts

EBENEZER FOX

At the age of seventy-five

From *The Revolutionary Adventures of Ebenezer Fox*, 1838

Ebenezer Fox

The rebellious American colonies were at a distinct disadvantage at the start of the American Revolution; they had no navy, and the British Navy during this time was the most powerful in the world. In attempting to rectify this weakness, various expedients were tried. Not only did the Continental Congress create a regular navy, but nearly every state had a state navy, although in some instances their vessels were little more than oversized rowboats. Most seamen, however, preferred to serve aboard privateers whose primary mission was to prey upon the shipping of the enemy. A shipowner, or owners, would arm a vessel, recruit a crew, and secure a Letter of Marque and Reprisal, making it an official warship of the government. Profits from the sale of captured prizes were distributed in shares to the owners, officers, and crew. Although the seamen of the Continental and state navies shared in prize money, they were often engaged against enemy warships and the prize was often so battered that its value was not so great.

The "Protector," the ship of the Massachusetts state navy in which Ebenezer Fox sailed, was considered the largest and finest frigate of that fleet. The total number of vessels in the Massachusetts navy from the beginning to the war's end was at least thirty-four. The keel of the "Protector" was laid at Salisbury, Massachusetts, in 1778 and her maiden voyage took place in 1779. The "Protector's" finest hour came when she engaged and defeated an English privateer, the "Admiral Duff." Perhaps such successes played a role in persuading Massachusetts to engage in one of the boldest and most foolhardy expeditions of the war.

The Penobscot expedition of 1779 was the result of the British occupying what is now modern Castine. At this time Massachusetts claimed the territory that was to become, in 1820, the state of Maine, and she undertook an expedition to drive the enemy from the Penobscot. Although a sizable army and navy were sent upon the expedition, the whole disintegrated into a confused mass of milling ships and men when they were bottled up in Penobscot Bay by a British fleet sent out from New York. One peripheral result was the capture of the "Protector," and young Ebenezer Fox becoming a prisoner of war. In his memoirs, Fox says little about the Penobscot expedition but it is to be suspected that recalling his sufferings aboard the "Jersey" prison ship cast other experiences into the shadow of his memory.

Neither side provided particularly good pris-

on facilities during the war. The British, outside
of New York, Quebec in Canada or Halifax in
Nova Scotia, had no permanent bases nor adequate jails to incarcerate large prisoner hauls. In
New York sugar houses, the churches of dissent-
ing sects, the hospital, and King's College (Co-
lumbia University) were all pressed into service
as prisons.

Because of the lack of facilities the British,
particularly after the great New York City fire of
1776, resorted to the employment of prison hulks,
warships that had outlived their usefulness.
These were used on the assumption that these old
ships would provide more security and would be
healthier than conventional prisons. Time proved
them wrong on both counts. Any good swimmer
could escape from a ship easier than from a jail
on land. And with as many as 1,000 prisoners
crowded below decks, along with the general poor
administration, poor sanitation, and inadequate
food these floating prisons became veritable death
traps.

It has been stated that more Americans died in
British prisons than as a result of British muskets. This has the ring of truth. Howard Peckham in his "Toll of Independence" states that in
the 1,331 military engagements there were 5,992
killed, while the 215 naval engagements took a

toll of 832 deaths for a total of 6,824 killed in battle. The dead from the New York prison ships were buried in shallow graves along the edge of Wallabout Bay. In 1808, when the bones were collected for reinterment they were counted, and from that count the estimate suggested that as many as 11,500 men died aboard the New York prison hulks.

On the other hand, Peckham's more modern estimate gives a figure of 8,500 for those who died in all prisons. And the bones of young Ebenezer Fox might have been among them had he not been so young and healthy.

Equally important insofar as young Fox was concerned was that the urge for self-preservation ran so strong within him that he was willing to enlist in the British army to save his hide, but only with the proviso that he would not have to fight against his fellow countrymen. So eager was he to escape the horrors of the prison ship that his reasoning did not consider that the British would be able to detach the soldiers from the West Indies that he replaced to fight on the mainland. And it should be mentioned that his enlistment with the British was not unique, for prisoners and deserters from both sides often chose to fight within the ranks of their former enemies. In fact, Major General Nathanael Greene has been quoted as saying, *"At the close of the war, we fought the enemy with British soldiers, and they fought us with those of America."*

When he was an old man of seventy-five, a grandchild came to Ebenezer Fox asking him, *"Grandfather, I wish you would relate to us all your revolutionary stories. You have told us a great many stories, but we wish to hear the whole at once."* To gratify the young folks, Fox rose early every morning and wrote several pages before breakfast. These memoirs were published in Boston in 1838.

This is his story as he remembered it.

The Caribbean of Ebenezer Fox

ATLANTIC OCEAN

FLORIDA

BAHAMA ISLANDS

Abaco
Eleuthera
New Providence
Andros
Cat I.
Watling
Exuma
Long I.
Crooked I.
Caicas
Inagua
Turks Is.
Little Inagua
Puerto Príncipe

Havana
San Juan de los Remedios
Pinar del Río
Isla de Pinos
Trinidad

C U B A

GREATER ANTILLES

Santiago de Cuba
Great Cayman
Jamaica
Kingston
Port Royal
Port-au-Prince
St. Domingo
Cap Français
Santo Domingo
Santo Domingo
Hispaniola

Santa Domingo

Virgin Is.
San Juan
Puerto Rico

LEEWARD IS.

Anguilla
St. Eustatius
St. Christopher
St. Croix
Nevis
Barbuda
Antigua
Montserrat
Guadeloupe
Marie Galante
Dominica
Martinique

LESSER ANTILLES

St. Pierre
St. Lucia
Barbados
St. Vincent
Grenada
Tobago
Trinidad

WINDWARD IS.

Margarita
Port of Spain
Caracas
Santa Ana de Coro
Tortuga

Aruba
Curaçao
Bonaire

VENEZUELA
Maracaibo

CARIBBEAN SEA

ANTILLES

Santa Marta
Cartagena

Old Providence
St. Andrews

Trujillo
Mosquito Coast
Lake Nicaragua
S. Juan de Nic

HONDURAS
NICARAGUA
NEW SPAIN
COSTA

GULF OF MEXICO

N

MILES
0   100   200   300

The Revolutionary Adventures
of Ebenezer Fox

I

I WAS BORN in the East Parish of Roxbury, State of Massachusetts, January 30th, 1763. Nothing out of the ordinary course of human events occurred, of which I have any recollection, until I arrived to the age of seven.

My father, who was a tailor, being poor and having a large family, thought that my physical powers were adequate, at this time of life, to my own maintenance; and placed me under the care of a farmer named Pelham. The house in which that gentleman resided was situated in what was then called Roxbury-Street.

With him I continued five years, performing such services in the house and upon the farm as were adapted to my age and strength. I imagined however that I suffered many privations and endured much hardship; which was undoubtedly true, were my situation compared with that of many other boys of my age at that time, or in this more refined period. Boys are apt to complain of their lot, especially when deprived of the indulgences of home. They do not estimate their advantages or disadvantages by comparison; but view them in the abstract, and judge their circumstances as the results of positive evil, when they might be considered as comparative blessings.

I had for some time been dissatisfied with my situation, and was desirous of some change. I had made frequent complaints of a grievous nature to my father; but he paid no attention to them, supposing that I had no just cause for them, and that they arose merely from a spirit of discontent which would soon subside.

Expressions of exasperated feeling against the government of Great-Britain, which had for a long time been indulged and pretty freely expressed, were now continually heard from the mouths of all classes; from father and son, from mother and daughter, from master and slave. A spirit of disaffection pervaded the land; groans and complaints, and injustice and wrongs were heard on all sides. Violence and tumult soon followed.

Almost all the conversation that came to my ears related to the injustice of England and the tyranny of government.

It is perfectly natural that the spirit of insubordination, that prevailed, should spread among the younger members of the community; that they, who were continually hearing complaints, should themselves become complainants. I, and other boys situated similarly to myself, thought we had wrongs to be redressed; rights to be maintained; and, as no one appeared disposed to act the part of a redresser, it was our duty and our privilege to assert our own rights. We made a direct application of the doctrines we daily heard, in relation to the oppression of the mother country, to our own circumstances; and thought that we were more oppressed than our fathers were. I thought that I was doing myself great injustice by remaining in bondage, when I ought to go free; and that the time was come, when I should liberate myself from the thraldom of others, and set up a government of my own; or, in other words, do what was right in the sight of my own eyes.

In all great undertakings a friend is needed, with whom we can advise and consult. Men experience this want, and seldom is any remarkable achievement effected alone and unaided. I felt the necessity of acting in unison with some one, who should be actuated by the same motives as myself, and have a similar object in view.

I sought a friend, and found one in a companion with whom I had long associated, John Kelley, who was a little older than myself. To him I imparted my views and wishes in regard to future operations.

We held many consultations in secret, and, mutual confidence being established, we came to the sage conclusion, that we were living in a state of servitude that ought to be scorned by the sons of freemen.

In our opinion we were abundantly capable of providing for our own wants; of assuming all the responsibilities of life; and needed no protectors.

Our plan was soon formed, which was nothing less than to furnish ourselves with whatever we thought indispensable for our undertaking, to leave home privately, and take the most direct route to Providence, R.I. where we expected to find employment as sailors on board of some vessel.

Our greatest trouble was to raise the means for the expedition. Having collected what few articles we possessed and securing them in two small bundles, we secreted them in a barn at some distance from our habitation.

The place for our meeting was the steps of the church, which stood where the Rev. Mr. Putnam's now stands.* According to appointment, I found my friend Kelley on the spot at eight o'clock in the

*The Rev. Mr. Adams was the pastor then. Deacon Crafts, grandfather of Mr. E. Crafts of Roxbury, used to read aloud one verse at a time of the psalm or hymn, which the choir would sing, and then wait till he had read another.

Hymn-books were not in general use; they were, some time after, in the pews of the wealthy part of the congregation.

At a subsequent period, a kind of music, called *Fugueing tunes,* was introduced; and they had a literally *fugueing* effect upon the elder people, the greater part of whom went out of church as soon as the first verse was sung.

I very well remember the first sabbath that the first bass-viol was used, as an accompaniment to the singing. The old pious people were horror-struck at what they considered a sacrilegious innovation, and went out of meeting in high dudgeon. One old church member, I recollect, stood at the church-door, and showed his contempt for the music by making a sort of caterwauling noise, which he called *"mocking the Banjo."*

evening on the eighteenth of April, the night before the memorable battle of Lexington.

Kelley's first question to me was, "How much money have you got?" I replied, "A half a dollar." "That is just what I have got," said Kelley, "though I might have taken as much as I wanted from the old tory; but I thought I would not take any more than what belonged to me."

I know not whether this proceeded from Kelley's principle of honesty, or from a fear of pursuit, in case he had embezzled any thing which would render him an object worth pursuing. Kelley had lived with a gentleman named Winslow, who was highly esteemed for his benevolence and other virtues; but, being a friend to the royal government, he was stigmatised with the epithet of "Tory," and considered an enemy to his country, and was finally obliged to leave the place when the British troops evacuated Boston. After spending some time in making arrangements, we started about nine o'clock at night, and travelled till we arrived at Jamaica-Plain and stopped on the door-steps of the Rev. Dr. Gordon's church to rest ourselves and hold a consultation.

We concluded to continue on our route, and directed our course to Dedham, where we arrived shortly after ten the same night.

As I have observed, this was on the night previous to the battle of Lexington. At that time, much excitement prevailed in the public mind. Great anxiety was manifested in the country in the vicinity of Boston to know what was going on there. People were out in all directions to hear the "news from town." As we were too young to be very well informed in regard to coming events, and were ignorant of the great plans in agitation, our fears induced us to think that the uncommon commotion that appeared to prevail must have some connexion with our escape, and that the moving multitudes we saw were in pursuit of us. Our consciences reproved us a little for the step we had taken, and our fears magnified the dangers to which we were exposed.

After making some cautious inquiries at Dedham, we directed our course to Walpole with the intention of reaching it that night.

About eleven o'clock, finding ourselves excessively fatigued, we determined upon taking up our night's lodging on the ground by the side of a stone wall.

With feelings of despondence I stretched myself upon the earth, with my bundle for a pillow, and observed to my companion, "This is hard lodging, Kelley, but we may have harder;" little anticipating the hardship and suffering I was to endure in some succeeding years. After a cold and uncomfortable night's rest, we started before day, and reached Walpole about ten o'clock in the morning.

Before we entered the village, we stopped at a tavern and called for a bowl of bread and milk, the price of which was three pence; but the kind-hearted landlord refused to take any compensation. We now were constantly meeting with people, who, anxious to hear the news from Boston, frequently interrogated us respecting whence we came and whither we were going, &c.; in answering which we adhered as nearly to the truth as our fears of discovery would permit.

We stopped at Mann's tavern in Walpole, and here a multitude of people collected, having apparently some great object in agitation. Being seen coming in the direction from Boston, we were again assailed with more questions than we knew how to answer consistently with our safety. The tavern-keeper excited our apprehensions by abruptly asking us whither we were going?

"To seek our fortunes," we replied.

"You have taken hard times for it," and he advised us to return home.

During this conversation, the stagecoach from Boston arrived at the tavern, where the passengers were to dine. They brought the news of the Lexington battle, with an exaggerated account of a loss on the side of the British of two hundred men, and on that of the American of only thirty. This was received with loud shouts of exultation, while the militia marched off full of ardor and zeal.[1]

By this time, my companion and myself felt the

[1] British losses on the nineteenth of April were seventy-three killed, one hundred ninety wounded, and twenty-two taken prisoner. American casualties numbered forty-nine killed, thirty-nine wounded, and five missing.

need of some refreshment; but our funds would not permit us to indulge our appetites with the luxury of a dinner; we therefore contented ourselves with a simple luncheon.

Tired of walking, our next object was to drive a bargain with the coachman for a ride to Providence. The price demanded was one and sixpence for each of us, and that upon condition that one should ride with the coachman and the other on the baggage.

The coachman's seat on stagecoaches in those days was not the comfortable place which it now is; and the baggage used to be fastened directly upon the hind axle-tree. Racks and such-like conveniences are the improvements of modern times. To sit upon the baggage, then, could not be considered a great privilege, and it required not a little exertion to keep one's position.

For such accommodations one and sixpence each we considered an exorbitant price; and, after a great deal of haggling, a bargain was made to carry us both for two and eight-pence. We left Walpole about one o'clock, and arrived in Providence about sunset.

Any one, who has experienced the forlorn and destitute feelings that arise in the mind when he feels himself alone in a strange city, may easily imagine what ours were at this time. The moving multitudes were returning to their homes, after their daily occupations were over, to meet their families and their friends and to spend the quiet night. But we, two poor boys, had no home to receive us, no friends to welcome us.

Solitary and desolate, we felt as it were "strangers in a strange land." We wandered about the streets, without seeing or expecting to see any one who would afford us any assistance, or sympathize in our distress. Hungry and weary, with but thirty coppers in our pockets, it would be, we thought, unjustifiable extravagance to indulge our appetites with the luxuries which a tavern might afford; we accordingly, seated upon the steps of a church, attempted to appease the cravings of hunger upon some provisions in our bundles, with which we had the precaution to provide ourselves before leaving Roxbury. Having finished our scanty meal, we found night approaching, and that it was necessary to obtain lodgings somewhere at a small expense.

Our design in coming to Providence naturally led us to the part of the town where the shipping lay. We found a vessel at a wharf, which appeared to have no person on board.

We went on to her deck, and, finding the cabin doors open, entered, took possession of two vacant berths, in which we slept soundly till morning, when we left the vessel without meeting with any person belonging to her.

We strolled about the town with spirits considerably depressed, and breakfasted upon what remained of the cold food on which we had supped the night previous.

I and my companion then thought it best to separate, for the purpose of seeking employment, in different directions; and we parted without thinking to fix upon any time or place for a subsequent meeting. I have since ascertained, that Kelley found employment on board of a vessel, and went to sea. What was his fate I know not; for after that day I never saw him, nor to the present time have I ever heard any more respecting him than what I have related. Should he meet with these pages, he is informed that I reside in the town from which we absconded sixty-three years ago. He would find me altered in the appearance I presented to him in our last interview. But probably he has long since gone to that world "from whose bourne no traveller returns," and to which my age and infirmities admonish me that I must soon repair.

In the course of my perambulations I went into the market-house, and while there I saw a gentleman who was addressed by the name of Curtis. He was habited according to the fashion of gentlemen in those days; a three-cornered hat, a club wig, a long coat of ample dimensions that appeared to have been made with reference to future growth; breeches with large buckles, and shoes fastened in the same manner, completed his dress.

His face appeared familiar to me, and, feeling some interest in him, I was induced to make some inquiries respecting him, and found that his Christian name was Obadiah; and that he had lately removed to Providence from Boston. With this gentleman an aunt of mine, a sister of my mother, had lived in Boston, and I thought it probable that she might have removed to Providence with his family.

With this impression I followed Mr. Curtis to his house, and to my great joy found my aunt. She expressed some surprise at seeing me so far from home; and I had to exercise not a little art, and to depart not a little from the truth to account for my unexpected visit. My aunt however extracted enough from the answers to her many questions to satisfy herself that I had left home without the knowledge of my parents. After satisfying my appetite with an abundance of good things, to which I had been some days a stranger, she endeavored to persuade me to give up my project of going to sea, and to return to Roxbury. This I obstinately refused, and finding it useless to remonstrate with me any more, she dropped the subject, after warning me of many evils which might ensue if I persisted in my undertaking. To this good woman was I indebted for sustenance while I remained in Providence, and for many articles of clothing of which I was in great need.

II

AFTER seeking for a situation on board of some vessel for several days, I at length found one in the service of Capt. Joseph Manchester, who was in the employ of Nathaniel Angier. I shipped in the capacity of cabin boy, for a compensation of twenty-one shillings per month, to go to Cape François in the island of St. Domingo. The wages of the sailors were forty-two shillings per month.

By the assistance of my good aunt, in a few days I was tolerably well equipped for the voyage. The vessel was hauled off into the stream, and shortly after we sailed for our destined port. This being the first time I ever was at sea, I experienced a considerable amount of that mental and bodily prostration called "sea-sickness;" but in a few days I became accustomed to the motion of the vessel, and recovered my usual health and spirits.

Being what is termed a "green hand," I had every thing to learn that belonged to my duties; and of course made some blunders for which I received more curses than thanks.

Among other misfortunes, I unluckily placed a large pot of butter in the larboard locker, without the precaution to fasten it in its place. It rolled out in the course of the night, and the fragments of the pot together with the contents were scattered about near the foot of the cabin steps. At the time of the accident the captain was upon deck, and having occasion to go below, he stepped into the midst of the greasy particles and measured his length upon the floor. The butter received a stamp of considerable magnitude in the form of a head, which, although it served to protect the captain's from any lamentable damage, did not shield mine from a volley of oaths and threats arising from the irritation of the moment at the awkward predicament in which he found himself placed.

After a pleasant voyage of about fourteen days, we arrived in sight of our destined port. That part of St. Domingo in which Cape François is situated was then in possession of the French; and, in regard to certain articles, trade was prohibited between the inhabitants and the American colonies. Some management was therefore necessary to obtain the cargo we wanted. A boat was sent ashore to inform certain merchants, who were expecting us, of our arrival. In the morning a pilot came to our assistance, and we were soon anchored in the harbor of Cape François.

We carried out staves and hoops in a state of preparation to be converted into hogsheads; and I worked at coopering till we were ready to receive our cargo. Having filled the hogsheads with molasses, which was apparently all our cargo, we set sail, and afterwards took on board a quantity of coffee, a prohibited article, which was conveyed to us by vessels employed for that purpose.

Our loading being thus completed, we directed

our course for Providence, and after a passage of about fifteen days we arrived at Stonington, Connecticut.

During our absence from home, the Revolutionary war had commenced, and we found that the British had begun their depredations upon our commerce and maritime towns.

We left Stonington in the night, entertaining the hope, that, with a favorable wind, we might get into Providence without being discovered by the British cruisers, which we knew were cruising somewhere between Newport and Providence.

If the breeze had continued favorable, we should have effected our object; but, unfortunately, the wind subsided a little before daylight, and in the morning we found ourselves close by the enemy, consisting of two ships of war, and a small vessel called a tender between them and the land. The American commander, Commodore Whipple,[2] with a naval force greatly inferior to the British, was seen by us, higher up the bay, out of reach of the enemy,

[2]Abraham Whipple (1733–1819) of Rhode Island was appointed commodore of the Rhode Island State Navy in 1775. He had been active in privateering in 1759–1760. He was one of the first captains commissioned in the Continental Navy. He was responsible, in 1779, for capturing eleven ships out of a British convoy, the largest single capture of the war. With four Continental vessels, he was responsible for the naval defense of Charleston, South Carolina, and became a prisoner of war when that city surrendered to the British May 12, 1780. Around 1786 he migrated to Marietta, Ohio.

making signals for us to press all sail and approach. But unluckily we were ignorant of the meaning of the signals, and did not know whether they came from a friend or an enemy. As the cruisers were to the windward of us, we tacked one way and the other, hoping that we should be able to beat up the bay; but, finding that the tender was about to intercept our progress in one direction while the cruisers approached us in the other, and, no chance of escape appearing, we bore away and ran our vessel ashore.

Preparations were hastily made for leaving the vessel, our captain having given permission to all, who were disposed to run the risk, to make their escape. The mate and crew jumped overboard and swam for the shore, where they all arrived safe, although fired upon by the British tender.

Captain Manchester, supposing that I should be unable to reach the shore by swimming kindly advised me to remain on board with him and be taken prisoner.

I hesitated a short time about taking his advice, but finally concluded to run the risk of being drowned; and with nothing on but a shirt and a pair of trousers, I plunged into the sea and swam for the shore, where I arrived without injury, but nearly exhausted with fatigue and fear, not a little augmented by the sound of the bullets that whistled around my head while in the water. In dread of pursuit, I ran into a cornfield, and finding my wet clothes an incumbrance, I stripped them off and ran with all speed through the field.

At a little distance in advance of me I could discover a number of men, whom I soon found to be our ship's crew, who had landed before me. My appearance among them in a state of entire nakedness excited not a little mirth. "Holloa! my boy," exclaimed one of them, "you cut a pretty figure; not from the garden of Eden, I can swear for it, for you have not even an apron of fig-leaves to cover you with: you were not born to be drowned, I see, though you may live to be hanged." But after a few jests at my expense, the mate took off one of the two shirts, with which he had taken the precaution to provide himself before he left the vessel, and gave it to me. This garment answered all the purposes of a covering, as it effectually covered my person from my shoulders to my feet. After travelling about half a mile, we came to a house, where the good woman, taking pity on my grotesque and unique condition, gave me a decent suit of clothes.

I immediately proceeded to Providence, where I arrived the same day, and lost no time before visiting my good aunt, although I had great doubts and fears of the reception I should meet with. She was glad to see me again, but did not lose the opportunity of giving me a long lecture upon the folly of my conduct in leaving home; and appealed to my candor to acknowledge the justice of her reproof, by comparing my present condition with what it formerly was. The anxiety and distress of my parents, too, were described to me in all the eloquence of female affection, as an additional inducement to return to them.

The misfortunes I had thus far experienced, she alleged, I ought to consider as judgments against any more attempts to be separated from my friends: and concluded with advising me, in the kindest manner, to return home, and with many generous offers to assist me and to produce a reconciliation, should her assistance be found necessary.

I felt conscious that the result of this voyage did not fill my mouth with arguments in favor of a second. I went away tolerably well clothed, and returned *stark* naked, but I could not however see the force of her reasoning, nor make a proper application of it to my circumstances. . . .

Finding me obstinately resolved upon undertaking another voyage, to obtain, as I thought, some remuneration for the misfortunes experienced in the first, my aunt showed a disposition to assist me as readily as before; and I was soon comfortably fitted out for a second expedition.

Four days after my arrival in Providence, I fortunately met with a ship-master, named Thomas, and engaged in his employ for a voyage to Cape François, the port to which I sailed on my former voyage. We had a short passage, and arrived at our destined port without anything having transpired worthy of notice during the voyage.

We took in a cargo similar to the one we received on my former voyage, and set sail for Providence, where we arrived after a pleasant passage of eighteen or twenty days. I worked on board the vessel several days, assisting to unload her, and then received my wages, which had been stipulated at four dollars per month.

With my money in my pocket, the largest sum I ever before possessed, and much elated with my success, I visited my good aunt once more, who received me with much joy. She assisted me with her advice in purchasing some articles of clothing, that I might make a respectable appearance among my friends.

I now thought I could consistently return to my native place; and was willing to comply with the desire of my aunt and my own inclinations, to visit my parents, who, I knew, must have suffered much anxiety at my absence, a wanderer they knew not where, at a time when the country was in such a state of commotion as to render it somewhat hazardous for a youth like me to be without a guide or protector.

After securing my clothing in a small pack, I slung it on my back, and started on foot for home, from which I had been absent about six months. This was the latter part of November, 1775.

My finances being rather low, after deducting the expense of my clothing, I found it necessary to exercise economy on my journey, and not indulge

myself in entertainment at public houses. I found a
ready welcome at the dwellings of the farmers on
the road, and was treated with an abundance of
bread and milk without compensation. I was hospitably received at a respectable farm-house the first
night on my journey; and on the second, arrived at
the American camp in Roxbury, on Saturday evening. Ascertaining that my parents had, during my
absence, removed to Dorchester, a distance of about
three miles, I felt too much fatigued to seek their
residence that night, and found comfortable accommodations in one of the barracks.

Early on Sunday morning I started for Dorchester, and soon to my great joy and satisfaction found
my parents in the enjoyment of good health, excepting my father, who was afflicted with a bad cold
and was lying asleep on the bed when I entered the
house. My good mother gazed at me with the amazement of one who had seen a spectre. She had long
before given up all hopes of ever seeing me again,
having heard nothing respecting me during my absence; and, as she was well aware of my inclination
for a sailor's life, she had concluded that I had gone
to sea, and that, in her estimation, was equivalent to
being lost.

As soon as she had recovered from the shock
caused by my sudden and unexpected appearance,
and recovered her self-possession, she aroused my
father with a scream of joy and the exclamation
"Our son is returned!" The disposition of my father

was more equable than that of my mother, and his feelings were less excitable than hers; consequently he exhibited less astonishment at sight of me, though he felt as much pleasure on the occasion. Neither had he yielded to those fears for my safety which had taken possession of my mother's mind; or else he had endeavored to conceal his apprehensions in order to pacify hers; constantly encouraging her with the hope that I "should, no doubt, be taken care of."

My mother was about commencing an endless train of questions respecting my adventures, but, intimating that I was hungry, having had no breakfast, she postponed the gratification of her curiosity to attend to my animal wants.

While impatiently watching the progress of my mother in her culinary operations, my father, with much gravity and solemnity of manner, addressed me as follows:—"My son, I am much surprised and grieved that you should have left home in the manner you did, without giving us any means to ascertain your fate, or what your intentions were. If you had any cause for complaint, and thought yourself ill-treated, why did you not inform me, and I would have seen justice done?" With the sense of wrongs, either real or imaginary, still rankling in my breast, I replied that I had done so, repeatedly, but no attention had been paid to my complaints; and that I had often told my mother that I intended to go forth into the world for the purpose of improving my condition. "Since you have been preserved from any serious disaster," continued my father, "and no evil consequences have resulted from the imprudent steps you have taken, I hope you will abandon all such schemes in future. You can remain at home until you are old enough to learn a trade, and then choose one for yourself.

At this time my father found abundance of employment in working at his trade for the soldiers in the American camp. During the winter I improved the time in attending a school, and making myself useful in various ways to my parents. I often visited the American camp, and endeavored by conversing with the soldiers to ascertain what plans were formed for their future operations. My father having a large family to maintain by his industry, I felt unwilling to remain at home, a burden upon him, and was desirous of supporting myself. My brother James, who was two years older than myself, had likewise been at home during the preceding winter; and it was thought expedient that both of us should learn some useful trade.

III

UNINTERRUPTED intercourse being now established between the country and the town, my
brother and myself were sent into Boston[3] to choose
our trades and seek our employers. James found a
situation in the bakery of Mr. Edward Tuckerman
in the south part of the town, as an apprentice upon
probation; and I found employment in the shop of
Mr. John Bosson, a barber and manufacturer of
wigs, upon the same conditions.

After we had been in these situations long
enough for all parties to be satisfied, we were bound
by my father in regular form as apprentices.

The trade of a barber in those days was very different from what it now is. My principal employment was in the preparation of hair for the purposes
of wigs, crape-cushions, &c.; being occasionally allowed to scrape the face of some transient customer,
who might be reasonably expected never to call
again for a repetition of the operation.

In Mr. Bosson's service I continued until I was
sixteen years old, and made laudable progress in
the mysteries of his art.

The war at this time was fiercely maintained between the United States and Great-Britain; and as
soldiers were wanted, a draught was made upon the
militia of Massachusetts for a quota of men to march
to New-York, to reinforce the American army then

[3]The British evacuated Boston March 17, 1776.

in the vicinity of that city. My master was unfortunately among the number draughted for that service. As he did not possess a great degree of military spirit, he was much distressed at the demand thus suddenly made upon his patriotism. One day, while my fellow apprentice and myself were at work, Mr. Bosson entered the shop laboring under great agitation of mind. It was evident that something had happened to discompose his temper, which was naturally somewhat irritable. He walked rapidly about, occasionally stopping, and honing several razors that he had put in perfect order previous to his going out; and attempting to sharpen a pair of shears that at the time bore the keenest edge; he furnished us with much food for conjecture as to the cause of his strange conduct. At length, from various ejaculations, and now and then a half-smothered curse upon his ill luck, we gathered the fact, that he was enrolled among the soldiers who were soon to take up the line of march for New-York. This was an unfortunate business for him; a reality he had not anticipated. The idea of shouldering a musket, buckling on a knapsack, leaving his quiet family, and marching several hundred miles for the good of his country, never took a place in his mind. Although a firm friend to his country, and willing to do all he could to help along her cause, as far as expressing favorable opinions and good wishes, yet there was an essential difference in his mind between the theory and the art of war; between acting the soldier, and triumphing at the soldier's success.

The reality of his position operated as a safety-valve to let off the steam of his patriotism, and to leave him in a state of languor well calculated to produce in him a degree of resignation for remaining at home. But what was to be done? A substitute could not be obtained for the glory that might be acquired in the service; and as for money, no hopes could be entertained of raising sufficient for the purpose.

Mr. Bosson continued to fidget about, uttering such expressions as his excited feelings prompted, allowing us to catch a disconnected sentence, such as: "Hard times—don't need two apprentices any more than a toad needs a tail;"—"If either of you had the spunk of a louse, you would offer to go for me." With this last remark he quitted the shop apparently in high dudgeon.

The truth was now evident, that he wanted somebody to take his place.

To provide ways and means of payment was the principal obstacle in the way of hiring a substitute. Gold and silver had scarcely a physical existence in the country, and the want of a circulating medium was attempted to be supplied by the legislative acts of government in issuing an excessive quantity of paper money, which, as it never had any intrinsic value, soon degenerated from its nominal worth with progressive rapidity. . . .

Patriotism, more than a love of gain, prompted men to join the army. More were willing to enlist voluntarily than to serve in the capacity of substitutes for an uncertain compensation. My master therefore had but little hope of finding any one willing to serve in his stead.

The spirit of adventure had been suppressed, but not destroyed, within me. The monotonous duties of the shop grew irksome, and I longed for some employment productive of variety. The opportunity seemed favorable to my desires; and, as my elder fellow apprentice was fearful that he might be called upon, he encouraged me in the project, and I resolved upon offering my services.

Mr. Bosson accepted my proposition to act as his substitute with a great degree of satisfaction and gratitude, which he evinced by a liberal supply of clothing and equipments for the service. He did not suffer my zeal to cool, but immediately gave directions to have me enrolled and enlisted for three months, in a company commanded by Capt. William Bird of Boston, in a regiment under Colonel Thomas Proctor.

Early in the month of September, 1779, being not quite sixteen, the age required at that time for the militia service, our company was paraded on Boston common, and with a heavy knapsack on my back, and a gun on my shoulder, superior in weight to those carried by soldiers at the present time, we took up the line of march.

We halted at Roxbury to take under our protection six baggage wagons of ammunition, and commenced our march for Peeks-Kill, in the state of New-York.

During our march, several little events transpired, which serve to show to what losses and vexations the inhabitants of a country are exposed when troops are moving through their territories.

One afternoon some geese were discovered enjoying themselves in a pond near the road; and one of the soldiers, thinking that a little poultry would not be an unacceptable addition to our bill of fare, threw a stone among them and killed one of the largest of the flock.

The prize was secured and concealed by taking off the head of a drum and putting the goose into it, and then restoring the instrument to its former appearance. The owner of the poultry followed and complained to the commanding officer of this depredation on his property. We halted long enough to have the wagons searched, but the goose was not found; and we were allowed to march on. When the camp fires were kindled at night, the goose was roasted, and our captain did not hesitate to eat a leg, wing, and a piece of the breast without troubling us with any questions respecting our right of possession.

A few days subsequent to this event, we halted one evening, after a tiresome day's march, at a well-provided farming establishment belonging to an old

Quaker. Permission was asked to allow us to lodge in some of his spacious barns, but the old man would not give his consent, alleging that his principles were opposed to the spirit of war, and that he could not aid those who were engaged in mortal contests. We urged him to consider our fatigue, our wants, and the perils to which we were exposed for the good of the country: but these appeals produced no change in his purpose.

Finding that solicitation and intreaty were vain, we changed our tone, and peremptorily demanded accommodations. As refusal would have been useless to men tired and hungry as we were, and possessing the physical force to exact compliance, he reluctantly consented to our sleeping in an old building, that seemed to have been erected for some mechanical purpose. This was all we could obtain, for he refused to sell us bread, or milk, or any eatable; and even to permit our commander to lodge in his house.

Such inhospitable treatment was rare in those days. The wants of the soldiers, the defenders of their country, were generally cheerfully supplied; and they, who were not engaged in active service, were willing to contribute all in their power to the comfort and sustenance of the soldier.

In the building, to which we were admitted, we found a large kettle or boiler, which we filled with water, and made a fire under it. Late at night a party was sent out to search the premises and to seize whatever could be found capable of being converted to our benefit, or of contributing to our physical wants.

In an orchard belonging to the Quaker a large number of fowls were found quietly roosting upon the trees, little dreaming of the murderous attack about to be made upon them. Between thirty and forty were captured, to whom no quarters were given, and brought into the camp. The feathers were quickly plucked, and the bodies were scalded in the kettle. Afterwards they were stowed away in our knapsacks, and a party sufficient to carry the plunder were sent on in advance.

We started early the next morning, and, after a march of about fifteen miles, we overtook the party in advance with the half-cooked poultry. The inhospitable spirit, manifested by the Quaker, was the cause of a much greater loss to him than he would have suffered, had he showed a disposition to afford us some trifling accommodations.

We halted at a farm house, and, having borrowed a large brass kettle, emptied the contents of the knapsacks into it, combining therewith a goodly quantity of onions, potatoes, and carrots, and soon converted the heterogeneous mass into what we called a chicken soup, which, though it might not have been very palatable to an epicure, was not to be despised by a company of hungry soldiers.

After a fatiguing march of five or six days, we arrived at Peeks-Kill, and delivered to the commander there our wagons of ammunition, and then marched to Albany.

While we remained at Albany, we were quartered in what was then called the "old French fort." We remained here about six weeks, when, General Washington having changed his plan of operations, and abandoned his design of attacking New-York, and our services being no longer needed, we were discharged, to get home in the best way we could.

When we left Boston, each of us received three thousand dollars in Continental money; of the value of which the reader may have already formed some idea, and it had not risen since our departure, for we found on our return that from one hundred to one hundred and fifty dollars of it were required for a simple repast. In addition to this compensation, our monthly pay was forty shillings, in the same valuable currency.

My clothes were much worn and damaged in the service, and upon our return were found in a very shabby condition, especially my shoes. Of these I had two pair, but the good judgment of a thief was shown by stealing the better pair one night while I was asleep, leaving me no other alternative but to go barefoot, or secure the remaining ones to my feet by winding rope-yarn around them in the form of bandages.

My feet were covered with blisters while I marched over the frozen ground and snow; and thus, almost crippled, and worn down with fatigue,

I arrived at my father's in Roxbury, whither he had returned, after an absence of about two months.

After resting a few days at home, and recovering my strength and spirits, I returned to Mr. Bosson, abundantly satisfied with the specimen I had experienced of a soldier's life, assuring him that nothing would again induce me to officiate as a substitute for him or anybody else.

IV

I CONTINUED to perform my duties in the shop, and
was contented with my employment till I was
about seventeen years of age, when a spirit of roving
once more got possession of me; and I expressed a
desire to go to sea. The condition of the country
was at this time distressing: and, as my master had
not more business than he and one apprentice
could perform, he expressed a willingness to consent, upon condition that he should receive one half
of my wages and the same proportion of whatever
prize money might fall to my share.

Our coast was lined with British cruisers, which
had almost annihilated our commerce; and the state
of Massachusetts judged it expedient to build a government vessel, rated as a twenty-gun ship named
the *"Protector,"* commanded by Captain John Foster Williams. She was to be fitted for service as soon
as possible, to protect our commerce, and to annoy
the enemy. A rendezvous was established for recruits at the head of Hancock's wharf, where the
national flag, then bearing thirteen stripes and stars,
was hoisted.[4] All means were resorted to, which ingenuity could devise, to induce men to enlist. A
recruiting officer, bearing a flag and attended by a
band of martial music, paraded the streets, to excite
a thirst for glory and a spirit of military ambition.

[4] The stars and stripes were designated as the national flag
by the Continental Congress on June 14, 1777.

The recruiting officer possessed the qualifications requisite to make the service appear alluring, especially to the young. He was a jovial, good-natured fellow, of ready wit and much broad humor. Crowds followed in his wake when he marched the streets; and he occasionally stopped at the corners to harangue the multitude in order to excite their patriotism and zeal for the cause of liberty.

When he espied any large boys among the idle crowd around him, he would attract their attention by singing in a comical manner the following doggerel:

> All you that have bad masters,
> And cannot get your due;
> Come, come, my brave boys,
> And join with our ship's crew.

A shout and a huzza would follow, and some would join in the ranks. My excitable feelings were roused; I repaired to the rendezvous, signed the ship's papers, mounted a cockade, and was in my own estimation already more than a half of a sailor. The ship was as yet far from being supplied with her complement of men; and the recruiting business went on slowly. Appeals continued to be made to the patriotism of every young man to lend his aid, by his exertions on sea or land, to free his country from the common enemy. Promises of gain were held out, which set truth at defiance, and offers as tempting as the most impoverished state of the finances of government could promise. About the last of February the ship was ready to receive her crew, and was hauled off into the channel, that the sailors might have no opportunity to run away after they were got on board.

Upwards of three hundred and thirty men were carried, dragged, and driven on board, of all kinds, ages, and descriptions, in all the various stages of intoxication; from that of "sober tipsiness" to beastly drunkenness, with the uproar and clamor that may be more easily imagined than described. Such a motley group has never been seen since Falstaff's ragged regiment paraded the streets of Coventry.

The wind being fair, we weighed anchor and dropped down to Nantasket roads, where we lay till about the first of April; and then set sail for a cruise of six months. Our course was first directly eastward; and, while keeping along the coast, we espied two English ships of war, each carrying sixteen or eighteen guns. We immediately gave chase; but to our surprise and regret they avoided an engagement, and made all sail from us. In consequence of having coppered bottoms, the sloops were better sailors than our ship, which was not coppered, and they made their escape. Their conduct was inexplicable to us, as each, without co-operation, was of force sufficient to be a match for us; and both, acting in concert, might have given us cause to repent, had we come in contact with them.

We continued to cruise along the coast for a few weeks, without meeting with any of the enemy, when, some indications of tempestuous weather appearing, our captain judged it expedient to steer for the banks of Newfoundland; that he might have more sea room in case of a gale. We arrived off the banks, where we cruised for nearly eight weeks, most of the time in a dense fog, without meeting with friend or foe.

On the morning of June 9th, 1780, the fog began to clear away; and the man at the mast head gave notice that he saw a ship to the westward of us. As the fog cleared up, we perceived her to be a large ship under English colours to the windward, standing athwart our starboard bow. Our relative position gave us an opportunity to escape, but our valiant captain did not see fit to avail himself of it.

As she came down upon us, she appeared as large as a seventy-four; and we were not deceived respecting her size, for it afterwards proved that she was an old East-Indiaman, of eleven hundred tons burden, fitted out as a letter-of-marque[5] for the West-India trade, mounted with thirty-two guns, and furnished with a complement of one hundred and fifty men. She was called the *Admiral Duff*, commanded by Richard Strang, from St. Christopher* and St. Eustatia, laden with sugar and tobacco, and bound to London. I was standing near our first lieutenant,

*Commonly called St. Kitts.

[5] A Letter of Marque and Reprisal was a document that made a merchant vessel a legitimate war vessel of the nation she represented and authorized her to prey upon the commerce of the enemy.

Mr. Little, who was calmly examining the enemy, as she approached, with his spy-glass, when Captain Williams stepped up and asked his opinion of her. The lieutenant applied the glass to his eye again and took a deliberate look in silence, and replied, "I think she is a heavy ship, and that we shall have some hard fighting; but of one thing I am certain, she is not a frigate; if she were, she would not keep yawing, and showing her broad sides as she does; she would show nothing but her head and stern: we shall have the advantage of her, and the quicker we get alongside the better."

Our captain ordered English colours to be hoisted, and the ship to be cleared for action. The shrill pipe of the boatswain summoned all hands to their duty. The bedding and hammocks of the sailors were brought up from between decks; the bedding placed in the hammocks, and lashed up in the nettings: our courses hauled up; the top-gallant sails clewed down; and every preparation was made, which a skilful officer could suggest, or active sailors perform.

The enemy approached till within musket shot of us. The two ships were so near to each other that we could distinguish the officers from the men; and I particularly noticed the captain, on the gangway, a noble looking man, having a large gold-laced cocked hat on his head, and a speaking trumpet in his hand. Lieutenant Little possessed a powerful voice, and he was directed to hail the enemy; at the same time the quarter-master was ordered to stand ready to haul down the English flag and to hoist up the American. Our lieutenant took his station on the after part of the starboard gangway, and, elevating the trumpet, exclaimed, "Hallo! whence come you?"—"From Jamaica, bound to London," was the answer. "What is the ship's name?" inquired the lieutenant. "The *Admiral Duff*," was the reply.

The English captain then thought it his turn to interrogate, and asked the name of our ship. Lieutenant Little, in order to gain time, put the trumpet to his ear, pretending not to hear the question. During the short interval, thus gained, Captain Williams, called upon the gunner to ascertain how many guns could be brought to bear upon the enemy. "Five," was the answer. "Then fire, and shift the colours," were the orders. The cannons poured forth their deadly contents, and, with the first flash, the American flag took the place of the British ensign at our mast-head.

The compliment was returned in the form of a full broadside, and the action commenced. I was stationed on the edge of the quarter-deck, to sponge and load a six-pounder: this position gave me a fine opportunity to see the whole action.* Broadsides

*After these pages were written, I ascertained that Mr. Frederick Lane, of Boston, a relative of Captain John Foster Williams, had in his possession the original log-book of the ship *Protector*. Mr. Lane had the politeness to send it to me, and I have made the following extracts verbatim from one of its pages.

were exchanged with great rapidity for nearly an hour; our fire, as we afterwards ascertained, produced a terrible slaughter among the enemy, while our loss was as yet trifling.

I happened to be looking for a moment towards the main deck, when a large shot came through our ship's side and killed Mr. Benjamin Scollay, a very promising young man, who was, I think, a midshipman. At this moment a shot from one of our marines killed the man at the wheel of the enemy's ship, and, his place not being immediately supplied, she was brought alongside of us in such a manner as to bring her bowsprit directly across our forecastle. Not knowing the cause of this movement, we supposed it to be the intention of the enemy to board us. Our boarders were ordered to be ready with their pikes to resist any such attempt, while our guns on the main deck were sending death and

---

"June 9th, 1780.

"At 7 A.M. saw a ship to the Westward, we stood for her under English Colours, the Ship standing athaught us, under English Colours, appeared to be a large ship. At 11 came along side of her, hailed her, she answered from Jamaica. I shifted my colours and gave her a Broadside, she soon returned us another, the action was very heavy for near three Glasses, when she took fire and blew up—got out the Boats to save the men, took up 55 of them, the greatest part of them wounded with our shot and Burnt when the ship Blew up, she was called the *Adml. Duff* of 32 Guns, Comman'd by Richard Strang from St. Kitts and Estatia, Ladened with Sugar and Tobacco bound to London. We Lost one man, Mr. Benja. Scollay and 5 wounded. Rec'd several Shot in our Hull, and several of our shrouds and stays shot away."

destruction among the crew of the enemy. Their principal object now seemed to be to get liberated from us, and by cutting away some of their rigging, they were soon clear, and at the distance of a pistol shot.

The action was then renewed with additional fury; broadside for broadside continued with unabated vigor; at times so near to each other that the muzzles of our guns came almost in contact, then again at such a distance as to allow of taking deliberate aim. The contest was obstinately continued by the enemy, although we could perceive that great havock was made among them and that it was with much difficulty that their men were compelled to remain at their quarters.

A charge of grape-shot came in at one of our port-holes, which dangerously wounded four or five of our men, among whom was our third lieutenant, Mr. Little, brother to the first.

His life was despaired of, but by the kind attention he received from his brother, and the surgeon, he finally recovered, though he bore evidence of the severity of his wounds thro' life.

While Captain Williams was walking the quarter deck, which he did during the whole action, a shot from the enemy struck the speaking trumpet from his hand, and sent it to a considerable distance from him. He picked it up with great calmness of manner, and resumed his walk, without appearing to have been at all disturbed by the circumstance.

The battle still continued with unabated vigor on both sides, till our marksmen had killed or wounded all the men in the fore, main, and mizen tops of the enemy. The action had now lasted about an hour and a half, and the fire from the enemy began to slacken, when we suddenly discovered that all the sails on her mainmast were enveloped in a blaze. The fire spread with amazing rapidity, and, running down the after-rigging, it soon communicated with her magazine, when her whole stern was blown off, and her valuable cargo emptied into the sea. All feelings of hostility now ceased, and those of pity were excited in our breasts for the miserable crew that survived the catastrophe.

Our enemy's ship was now a complete wreck, though she still floated, and the survivors were endeavoring to save themselves in the only boat that had escaped the general destruction. The humanity of our captain urged him to make all possible exertion to save the miserable, wounded, and burnt wretches, who were struggling for their lives in the water. The ship of the enemy was greatly our superior in size, and lay much higher out of the water.

Our boats had been much exposed to his fire, as they were placed on spars between the fore and main masts during the action, and had suffered considerable damage. The carpenters were ordered to repair them with the utmost expedition, and we got them out in season to take up fifty-five men, the greater part of whom had been wounded by our shot, or burned when the powder magazine exploded. These men exhibited a spectacle truly heart-rending to behold. Their limbs were mutilated by all manner of wounds, while some were burned to such a degree that the skin was nearly flayed from their bodies. Our surgeon and his assistants had just completed the task of dressing the wounds of our own crew, and then they directed their attention to the wounded of the enemy. Several of them suffered amputation of their limbs, while the wounds of the others were treated in a skilful manner, and every attention was paid to them which our circumstances would allow. Five of them died of their wounds, and were committed to their watery graves. From the survivors we learned, that the British commander had frequently expressed a desire to come in contact with a "Yankee frigate," during his voyage, that he might have a prize to carry to London. Poor fellow! he little thought of losing his ship and his life in an engagement with a ship so much inferior to his own—with an enemy upon whom he looked with so much contempt.

We ascertained that the loss of the enemy was prodigious, compared with ours. This disparity however will not appear so remarkable, when it is considered that, although their ship was larger than ours, it was not so well supplied with men; having no marines to use the musket, they fought with their guns alone, and, as their ship lay much higher out of the water than ours, the greater part of their shot went over us, cutting our rigging and sails, without injuring our men. We had about seventy marines, who did great execution with their muskets, picking off the officers and men with a sure and deliberate aim.[6]

After the action was over, I found that I was so deaf as to cause me to fear that I had totally lost the sense of hearing. I attributed this to the noise of the cannon, which I had been employed in loading and spunging for such a period of time. It was nearly a week before my hearing was restored, and then but partially; and, ever since, I have experienced great inconvenience from this deafness. . . .

Our sailors were busily employed in picking up the various articles that were floating and getting them on board, while the carpenters and riggers were engaged in repairing the damages we had received. The ship was soon in good order and prepared again to meet the enemy, and we continued on our cruise.

The weather growing warm, sails were suspended between the decks, for the purpose of ventilating and purifying the atmosphere by their motion; but little benefit resulted from the experiment.

Our captain, finding that sickness was increasing among the crew, and that the wounded were suffering greatly, judged it expedient to leave our cruising

[6] Marines aboard naval vessels were customarily stationed in the tops or high in the rigging with instructions to pick off officers and those men manning the enemy guns.

ground, and to steer for some Eastern port, that we might obtain a supply of wood and water.

Some repairs likewise were necessary, which we could not conveniently make at sea, previous to a short cruise which our captain intended we should make before our return to Boston.

About the twentieth of the month we sailed from the banks of Newfoundland, and arrived at Penobscot bay in seven or eight days. Having found a good harbor, we dropped anchor, and made immediate preparations to get our sick and wounded men on shore. Captain Williams made a contract with a farmer, who was friendly to the American cause, in comfortable circumstances, having good buildings, to provide for the sick and wounded, and to furnish accommodations for our surgeon's mate, who was left on shore with medicines and other things proper for a hospital.

There was now a constant communication kept up between the ship and the shore, and it was necessary for our officers to exercise great vigilance to protect the property of our friendly farmer from depredation. An attempt on the part of some of our crew to steal from him was detected in a singular manner.

A copper-coloured fellow, half Indian and half negro, had seen a fatted calf in the farmer's barn, which he coveted to such a degree as to induce him to make a desperate attempt to make it a prize. The graceless rascal found another of the crew, whose appetite for veal overcame what little moral sense he possessed, ready to second him in the undertaking.

Late at night, after all hands had retired, Cramps, for that was the name of the principal adventurer, took a boat, went on shore, secured the calf, and returned to the ship without discovery. He came with great caution under the ship's bows, and hailed his fellow worker in iniquity, whom he expected to find ready with a rope to hoist the calf on board.

It so happened that, just at this time, our first lieutenant, Mr. Little, had occasion to come on deck, and the fellow, who had been watching for the arrival of Cramps, dodged out of sight and secreted himself. Cramps, mistaking the lieutenant for his coadjutor, hailed him in a low tone, requesting him to lower a rope as quick as possible. The lieutenant, suspecting some mischief, did as he was directed.

Cramps soon fixed a noose round the calf's neck, and then cried out, "Now haul away, blast your eyes! my back is almost broke with carrying the creature so far down to the boat." The lieutenant obeyed, and a strong pull on his part, with some boosting by Cramps in the rear, soon brought the animal upon deck. Cramps immediately followed his prize, and found, to his no small consternation, not only the calf, but himself in the powerful grasp of the lieutenant. The calf was alive and uninjured, although Cramps had carried him a considerable distance from the barn to the boat, and came very near choking him when hoisting him up the side of the ship.

The calf enjoyed more comfortable quarters that night than his captor; for the latter was handcuffed, and secured below for farther punishment the next day. In the morning, the calf and the culprit were sent on shore, and, when landed, Cramps was ordered to shoulder the calf and march to the farmer, confess, and ask his forgiveness; and then to return on board with the consolation that he should receive fifty lashes for his fault, and the assurance that he should be hung at the yard-arm if he was detected in such an undertaking again.

The result of this expedition proved Cramps to be the greater calf of the two.

The fifty lashes were remitted at the solicitation of the kind-hearted farmer.

V

OUR REPAIRS being completed, and all things ready for sea, we weighed anchor about the last of June and steered once more for the banks of Newfoundland, where we cruised three or four weeks, without meeting any thing excepting a brig from the West-Indies bound to Boston, commanded by Capt. Thomas Parker. The provisions of the ship beginning to fail, and no prospect of making captures appearing, our captain, with the advice of his officers, concluded to steer for Boston. We hove to, and caught a considerable quantity of cod-fish, then directed our course for Halifax, off which we cruised for several days.

At noon of the fourth day after our arrival, the man on the look-out at the mast-head gave notice of a sail on our larboard quarter.

Mr. Little ascended to the mizen top to examine the object of the sailor's report with his spy-glass. He ascertained to his satisfaction that the strange sail was a ship directing her course towards us. All hands were piped on deck; the ship was put about, and we made sail for the strange sail. The two ships approached each other rapidly; and it was soon evident to our officers that she was a frigate of large burthen. We afterwards ascertained that these conjectures were true, as she was a frigate from Halifax bound to New-York.

Captain Williams thought it would be imprudent

to risk an action with an enemy so much his superior in force; he therefore gave orders to put the ship about, and crowd all sail, that we might get from the enemy as fast as possible. The enemy gained upon us rapidly, as she was fresh from port, and her bottom coppered; while ours, not having any copper, was extremely foul, in consequence of our long cruise, and our progress was greatly retarded.

At five o'clock in the evening, the enemy had approached so near as to give us several salutes with her bow guns, which compliment we did not hesitate to return with two eighteen pounders from our cabin windows, and a couple of sixes from the quarter deck.[7] An eighteen pound shot was lodged in our main-mast; this was all the damage we received. We resorted to all the usual methods to increase our progress, such as wetting the sails, shifting the position of the guns, &c.; not forgetting to make all the use we could of our stern chases, lest the enemy might think we slighted the compliments they sent us from the bow guns.

About sun-set, the enemy rounded to, and gave us two broadsides, by way of parting; for which we paid due acknowledgements from our cabin windows and quarter-deck, and she gave up the chase. For this last act of courtesy we felt more grateful than for any she had shown us; and we immediately got our guns into their proper places, and every

[7]Guns were usually placed in the stern cabin, often the captain's quarters, to discourage pursuit.

thing in readiness for an action which we anticipated having the next morning.

We continued to crowd sail all night, and the next morning could just discern the enemy at a great distance, steering in an opposite direction.

We thought at the time we were fortunate in escaping; but we afterwards felt some regret that we had avoided an action; for, although she was a six-and-thirty-gun frigate, she was poorly manned, and was bound to New-York to complete her number of men; and the result of an action would probably have been in our favor. Had she been fully manned, she would have persevered in the chase, and we should probably have been taken, as many of our men were sick.

In a few days we came in sight of Boston light-house, and anchored in Nantasket roads, where we remained a short time, then stood up the harbor, and hauled in at Hancock's wharf. The sails were unbent, the sick landed, the ship unloaded, and all hands, who were not disposed to enlist for a second cruise, were paid off and discharged.

Thus ended my first cruise in the *Protector*. And, although I had not added to my wealth, I had gained some knowledge of a sailor's life, and felt disposed to try my fortune a little more in the like manner by enlisting for a second voyage.

During the short interval between my first and second cruise, while I was at home, my father was taken sick and died. The loss of a kind parent is under any circumstances a melancholy bereavement, and this was particularly so to my mother and her eight children, some of whom were very young.

Though unwilling to leave her in her affliction, I felt the necessity of exerting myself, that I might contribute something to the maintenance of the family, who were left very destitute. I knew of no way in which there was a prospect of my being so useful to them, as that of engaging for another cruise.

A rendezvous was opened; a recruiting party paraded the streets under the American flag, accompanied by a band of martial music, and the excitement usual on such occasions. Amid loud huzzas for liberty and independence, sailors fell rapidly into our ranks, and our complement of men was obtained in a short time.

In the mean time, our ship was thoroughly overhauled, her bottom scraped, rigging repaired, and every thing was done to put her into perfect order.

Wood and water, and various kinds of stores necessary for a cruise of six months, were taken on board; and, having recruited about two hundred men, preparations were made for our immediate departure.

About the last of October, our boats were hoisted on deck and secured, and we dropped down into Nantasket roads, where we remained a few days, and then set sail upon our second cruise. We cleared Cape Cod the first of November; directed our course for Halifax, off which we cruised a few days, then steered for the Grand Banks. We arrived there, and cruised about for three weeks, and, not discovering any of the enemy's vessels, we directed our course to the West-Indies, and arrived off the islands, where we cruised for some time.

Finding it necessary to obtain a supply of water, we put into St. Pierre, in the island of Martinico, for that purpose; after which we steered towards Dominica, an island north of Martinico. The next morning we espied an English sloop sailing to leeward of us close under the land. We gave chase, and soon came up with her. Our captain sent an officer and some men on board, and took possession of her.

We then bore away with our prize for St. Juan in the island of Porto Rico, where our captain disposed of the sloop and cargo, part of which consisted of fourteen Negroes, who were sold to the Spaniards.

We then continued our cruise; and in a few days fell in with an English schooner, which we took, putting some men and a prize-master on board, ordered her for Boston, where she arrived in safety.

After cruising for some time and not falling in with any thing, our captain concluded to leave the West-India seas and steer for the southern coast of the United States.

We arrived off the bar of Charleston, South Carolina; and in the course of a few days fell in with a ship called the *Polly*, a letter-of-marque, of twenty guns, bound to London. We gave chase late in the afternoon, and, as it soon grew dark, we lost sight of her.

A thunder storm came on, and all hands were watching for her; and by the flashes of the lightning we at length discovered her, standing in a different direction from what we had at first seen her pursuing. We accordingly shifted our course, and crowded sail in pursuit. By the aid of the lightning, we kept in her course, and soon came up with her.

"What ship is that, and where from?" roared our lieutenant through his trumpet, in a voice that bore no slight resemblance to the thunder which rolled above our heads.

"The ship *Polly*, from Charleston, bound to London," was the reply. The lightning, flashing upon her colours, showed that they were English; while the enemy had the same means of seeing the American flag flying at our mast-head.

We were completely prepared for action; the matches were lighted; the lanterns burning fore and aft; and all anxiously waiting for the commands of the officers. One shot was fired, and our captain ordered the enemy to "Haul down his colours, or he would blow him out of the water."

The appearance of our ship being formidable, our captain's demand was instantly complied with. Our boat was lowered, and a prize-master and crew put on board, who took possession of the ship, and she was ordered for Boston.

Shortly after, we steered for New-York, and arrived off Sandy Hook in the spring. After cruising here nearly a week, one morning the man at mast-head cried out, "A sail upon the larboard quarter." Mr. Little ascended to the top, and, after examining her with his glass, declared her to be a brig standing in for New-York. We immediately gave chase, came up with her, and ordered her to heave-to till we could send a boat alongside. She complied, and, taking her crew on board of our ship, put a prize-master and crew on board of the brig, and ordered her for Boston.

While we were manning the prize, the man at the mast-head gave notice of "A sail on the larboard bows."[8]

We lost no time in commencing the pursuit, and soon came alongside of her.

She proved to be a schooner going into New-York. We took from her a quantity of bread, cheese, and porter.

Captain John Foster Williams held consultation with his officers respecting what course it was best to pursue; and they came to the conclusion, that it would not be prudent to remain any longer cruising off Sandy Hook, lest we should meet some of the British frigates, of too great force for us to contend with. Our prizes being in sight, signals were made for them to approach. The brig we took in tow and ordered the schooner to keep in company. We now

[8]The left, or port side of the ship, looking forward.

made sail for Boston with a fair wind and anticipated the pleasure of sharing a considerable sum of prize money on our arrival.

VI

OUR CRUISE thus far had been prosperous, and we thought the "evil day was afar off." We continued merrily on our course, without seeing friend or foe, during the next day; but, the following morning, the man at mast-head cried out, "Two sail to the leeward."

Mr. Little ascended to the main top with his glass, and soon ascertained that they were two large ships, closely hauled upon the wind, in full chase of us.

The brig we had in tow was quickly cast off, and she and the schooner were ordered to make the best progress they could. Our yards were braced, and all sail crowded that the ship could carry.

The chase continued, without gaining much upon us till about noon, when, the wind shifting, they fell into our wake, and gained upon us very fast.

A few days previous to this, we had fallen in with a brig from Havana for Boston, commanded by Captain Cunningham, having a large quantity of specie on board.

Captain C., thinking that the money would be more safe on board of an armed ship, requested it as a favor of Captain Williams to receive it on board. Captain Cunningham arrived with his brig in safety; but, to his regret as well as ours, his money fell into the hands of the enemy.

The ships in pursuit showed French colours, while we had the American flag flying.

They appeared to gain upon us, and the prospect was, that they would soon overtake us.

Our captain, calling all the hands aft on the quarter deck, expressed his opinion, that the ships in pursuit of us were English, and that we should be captured.

He then distributed among us the money which he had received for safe keeping, in sums of fifteen dollars to each of us, upon condition that it should be returned to him if we were so fortunate as to escape.

It was now nearly sun-set, and the enemy were gaining upon us rapidly. They had exchanged their French for English colours, thus ending our hopes and doubts respecting their character. Our capture was now considered no longer problematical; and, being unwilling that the stores, especially of crackers, cheese, and porter, should fall a prey to the appetite of the enemy, and not knowing when we should have an opportunity of enjoying such luxuries again, I invited about a dozen of my friends into the store room, where we exerted ourselves to diminish the quantity of this part of the prize which we thought would shortly be in possession of the enemy.

The porter made us cheerful if not happy, and having eat and drank to our satisfaction, we shook hands as friends soon to part, uncertain when we should meet again, and returned on deck without our absence having been noticed.

We found that the two ships had got up with us. They proved to be the *Roe-Buck*, a forty-gun ship with a double deck, and the *May-Day*, of twenty-eight guns.

They had been upon the look-out for us for three or four weeks; having received information from the Tories in Boston that we were expected to return from our cruise about this time.

The *Roe-Buck* took her station on our larboard quarter, the *May-Day* on our larboard bow, and sent an eighteen-pound shot over our quarter-deck. We were then ordered to strike our colours, or a broadside would be sent to enforce compliance with the demand.

To attempt resistance against a force so much our superior would have been unjustifiable; and the flag of thirteen stars and stripes, under which we had sailed with much satisfaction and success, was reluctantly pulled down; and this was the unfortunate end of our second cruise.

The boats of the enemy were manned, and sent alongside of our ship. Our crew were now permitted by our officers to collect their clothing and their little property together, and secure them in the best manner they could.

By this time, the boats had arrived alongside, and the enemy had ascended the deck.

Their first exploit was to strike or kick all sailors

that came into their way, bestowing a variety of opprobrious epithets, among which "damned rebels" was of the most frequent recurrence; then they commenced searching in every part of the ship for articles of value.

Our crew were ordered to pass down the side of the ship into the enemy's boats; but were forbidden to carry any thing with them. Some of our crew fastened their bedding upon their backs, and tumbled themselves head foremost down into the boats; and, as it was quite dark, they would unperceived get into the cuddy with their bedding, trusting to future circumstances for opportunity to use or secrete it.

We arrived alongside, and were ordered on to the quarter-deck of our captors. Some English sailor among our crew, to recommend himself to the favor of the British captain, had given information respecting the money we had secreted about our persons. The sergeant of arms was ordered to search every one of us till the sum of fifteen dollars was found upon each of us.

Such was the art which some had exercised in hiding the money, that they were stripped entirely naked before it was found. One fellow had secreted his share so effectually, that it baffled all the searching operations to find it; and the officer, being confident that the fellow had it about him, took the satisfaction of giving him a tremendous kick in the rear by way of conclusion, roaring out at the same time, "Away with you, you damned rebel,* into the hold."

In the capacity of cabin steward I was most of the time in the cabin, and had recommended myself to the favorable notice of the American captain by performing my duties to his satisfaction: and, when the money was distributed among our crew, the captain gave me a double share. I put fifteen dollars in the crown of my hat, which I pressed down upon my head as closely as possible; the remaining fifteen I placed in my shoes, between the soles.

At length my turn to be searched came; and I, as the rest of my fellow prisoners had done, denied having any money. This assertion however did not avail; I was seized by the collar, and shaken so violently that my hat fell off, and the dollars rolled out upon the deck. The sum of fifteen dollars being found, it was concluded that I had no more, and I was sent into the ship's hold, where I found those of the crew who had been previously searched.

A considerable number of us contrived by various stratagems to save our money, for dollars were found to be quite plentiful among us for some time after our capture; and they proved a great convenience, as money generally does among friends or foes.

*My apology for occasionally repeating such profane expressions is, that the young readers may know to what insulting and contemptuous language their forefathers were exposed while contending, with a haughty foe, for liberty and independence.

Our accommodations in the hold were not very desirable, especially to those who had not succeeded in getting their bedding into that place. We found nothing to lie upon softer than the ship's ballast, consisting of stones of all shapes and sizes, with here and there a lump of pig iron by way of variety; and the water casks, which afforded a surface rather uneven for the comfort and convenience of our wearied limbs.

Here we spent the first night, and were not allowed to go on deck till the next morning.

The *Roe-Buck* had the charge of the prisoners, while the *May-Day* was sent in pursuit of the two prizes we had in possession at the time of our capture.

Greatly to our satisfaction, however, she was unable to over-haul them, and they both arrived in safety in Boston a few days after.

VII

SHORTLY AFTER, we anchored off Sandy Hook, and preparations were made to examine the prisoners, to ascertain what part of them were Englishmen; or rather who among them would carry the appearance of able-bodied seamen.

We were called up from the hold; ordered to the larboard side of the quarter-deck; thence marched, in single file, past a number of British officers on the starboard side; after that to the gangway, and down again into the hold. The object of thus moving in procession before the officers was, to give them an opportunity to select such as they chose, to serve on board of their ships. With fear and trembling we passed through this examination. Whenever a healthy, athletic-looking man passed by, he was hailed, and accused of being an Englishman. In vain would his comrades attest to the fact of his being a native-born American; tell the place of his birth and the circumstances of his youth, detailed with all the consistency and connexion which belong to truth: it was all to no purpose. Sailors they wanted, and have them they would, if they set law and gospel at defiance. In this manner was many an American citizen, in the morning of life, dragged from his country, his friends, and his home; forced on board a ship of war; compelled to fight against his own country; and, if he lived, to fight in battle with other nations, against whom he had no feelings of hostility. Many a one spent his whole life in foreign service, far from his native land, while his relatives were ignorant of his fate, till, worn out with toil and wounds, a shadow of his former self, he dropped into the grave unpitied and unknown.

About a third part of our ship's crew were taken on board of their vessels, to serve in the capacity of sailors, without regarding their remonstrances; while the remainder of us were put on board of a wood coaster, to be conveyed on board the noted prison ship called the "*Jersey*." The idea of being incarcerated in this floating Pandemonium filled us with horror; but the idea we had formed of its horrors fell far short of the realities which we afterwards experienced. We wished if possible to avoid the hard fate that awaited us; and conceived the design of rising upon the guard, and seizing upon the sloop and running her aground upon the Jersey shore.

The plan could have been easily executed had there been any one among us to act as a leader in the enterprise. Our captain with his officers were confined in the cabin, under the watchful care of a number of British officers well armed; while a guard of soldiers stood at the head of the companion way, to prevent any communication with the prisoners upon the deck. Sailors and soldiers have the courage to execute, but not the skill to plan.

Had our captain, in whom we had been in the habit of placing the utmost confidence, been with us, I have no doubt we should have obtained our freedom.

As the deck was loaded with wood, we could in a moment have obtained weapons sufficient for our purpose, and, had any one amongst us been disposed to act as a leader, we should soon have had possession of the vessel. We afterwards regretted exceedingly that we did not make the attempt.

We proceeded slowly up the river towards our much-dreaded place of confinement, and at doubling a point we came in sight of the gloomy-looking hulk of the old *Jersey*, aptly named by the sailors, "The hell afloat."

The *Jersey* was originally a seventy-four gun ship, and, at the commencement of the American revolution, being found in a state of decay and unfit for service at sea, she was dismantled, moored in the East-river at New-York, and used as a store-ship. In the year 1780, she was converted into a prison-ship, and continued to be used for that purpose during the remainder of the war.

In consequence of the fears that were entertained that the sickness, which prevailed among the prisoners, might spread to the shore, she was removed, and moored with chain cables at the Wallabout, a lonely and unfrequented place on the shore of Long-Island. Her external appearance was forbidding and gloomy. She was dismantled; her only spars were the bowsprit; a derrick, that looked like a gallows, for hoisting supplies on board; and also a flagstaff at the stern. Port-holes were closed and secured. Two tiers of holes were cut through her sides, about two feet square and about ten feet apart, strongly guarded by a grating of iron bars.

Such was the appearance of the *Jersey*, as we approached it; an appearance well calculated to excite the most gloomy forebodings of the treatment we should receive after we should have become its inmates. The idea of being a prisoner in such a place was sufficient to fill the mind with grief and distress. The heart sickened, the cheek grew pale with the thought. Our destiny was before us, and there was no alternative but to submit.

The sloop anchored at a little distance from the *Jersey*; two boats were sent alongside to receive us.

The boats passed and re-passed several times before all of us got on board; and lastly the captain's barge was sent to convey our officers to their place of confinement. Not a great while after we were imprisoned our captain, together with the lieutenants and the sailing-master, Mr. Lemon, were sent to England; the latter, being an Englishman, had the comfortable assurance, that he should be hanged as soon as he arrived.*

---

* How long our officers remained in England I have no means for information. Captain Williams I found in Boston when I returned.

On the adoption of the federal constitution by Massachusetts, February, 1788, the event was celebrated in Boston by a civick procession, in which, I believe, the great mass of the citizens participated, classed into trades and occupations.

After being detained in the boats alongside a little while, we were ordered to ascend to the upper deck of the prison ship. Here our names were registered, and the capacity in which we had served previous to our capture. Each of us was permitted to

---

Each profession or art on this occasion was headed by appropriate flags and banners, bearing its respective coat of arms and emblems, accompanied in most cases with implements of agricultural, manufacturing, and mechanical industry and skill in full operation. Among the most conspicuous of these, the mariners had mounted a ship on wheels, which was drawn through the streets by 13 white horses, the then number of the United States. The ship was manned by veteran sea-captains and weather-beaten sailors, throwing the lead, reefing the sails, waving the thirteen stripes and stars, and at intervals firing salutes from a 3-pounder, under the command of John Foster Williams, our late captain, who, as I have heard, stood on the quarter-deck with a speaking-trumpet in his hand, dressed in continental regimentals. A song, to the tune of "Yankee Doodle," appeared among other poetical productions in the newspapers of the day, one verse of which was in these words:—

> "John Foster Williams in a ship,
> Join'd with the social band, sir,
> And made the lasses dance and skip,
> To see him sail on land, sir.
>   Yankee Doodle," &c.

I believe it was at this time, whilst the procession was passing thro' High-street, between Summer-street and Federal-street (till then called Long-lane), the ship was interrupted and entangled by a tree in the street, which was finally cut down to give free passage to the tars and their novel vehicle.

Captain Williams was appointed by Gen. Washington to the command of a revenue cutter in 1790, which office he held to the time of his death.

He died in Williams-street, Boston, June 24th, 1814, aged 71.

retain whatever clothing and bedding we had brought, after having been examined to ascertain that they contained no weapons nor money; and then we were directed to pass through a strong door, on the starboard side, down a ladder leading to the main hatchway. I now found myself in a loathsome prison, among a collection of the most wretched and disgusting-looking objects that I ever beheld in human form.

Here was a motley crew, covered with rags and filth; visages pallid with disease, emaciated with hunger and anxiety, and retaining hardly a trace of their original appearance. Here were men, who had once enjoyed life while riding over the mountain wave or roaming through pleasant fields, full of health and vigor, now shriveled by a scanty and unwholesome diet, ghastly with inhaling an impure atmosphere, exposed to contagion and disease, and surrounded with the horrors of sickness and death.

Here, thought I, must I linger out the morning of my life, in tedious days and sleepless nights, enduring a weary and degrading captivity, till death shall terminate my sufferings, and no friend will know of my departure. A prisoner on board of "the old *Jersey!*" The very thought was appalling. I could hardly realize my situation.

The first thing we found it necessary to do after our captivity was to form ourselves into small parties, called "messes," consisting of six men each; as, previous to doing this, we could obtain no food. All

The JERSEY *Prison Ship*

From Albert C. Greene's, *Recollections of the Jersey Prison Ship*, 1829

the prisoners were obliged to fast on the first day of their arrival; and seldom on the second could they procure any food in season for cooking it. No matter how hungry they were, no deviation from the rules of the ship was permitted. All the prisoners fared alike; officers and sailors received the same treatment on board of this old hulk. Our keepers were no respecters of persons. We were all "Rebels." The quantity and quality of our fare was the same for all. The only distinction known among us was made by the prisoners themselves, which was shown in allowing those, who had been officers previous to their capture, to congregate in the extreme after-part of the ship, and to keep it exclusively to themselves as their places of abode.

The various messes of the prisoners were numbered; and nine in the morning was the hour, when the steward would deliver from the window in his room, at the after-part of the ship, the allowance granted to each mess. Each mess chose one of their company to be prepared to answer to their number when it was called by the steward, and to receive the allowance as it was handed from the window. Whatever was thrust out must be taken; no change could be made in its quantity or quality. Each mess received daily what was equivalent in weight or measure, but not in quality, to the rations of four men at full allowance: that is, each prisoner received two-thirds as much as was allowed to a seaman in the British navy.

Our bill of fare was as follows:

On Sunday, one pound of biscuit, one pound of pork, and half of a pint of peas. Monday, one pound of biscuit, one pint of oat-meal, and two ounces of butter. Tuesday, one pound of biscuit, and two pounds of salt beef. Wednesday, one and a half pounds of flour, and two ounces of suet. Thursday was a repetition of Sunday's fare, Friday of Monday's, and Saturday of Tuesday's.

If this food had been of a good quality and properly cooked, as we had no labor to perform, it would have kept us comfortable, at least from suffering. But this was not the case. All our food appeared to be damaged.

The bread was mouldy, and filled with worms. It required considerable rapping upon the deck before the worms could be dislodged from their lurking places in a biscuit.

As for the pork, we were cheated out of it more than half of the time: and, when it was obtained, one would have judged from its motley hues, exhibiting the consistence and appearance of variegated fancy soap, that it was the flesh of the porpoise, or sea-hog, and had been an inhabitant of the ocean rather than of the sty. But, whatever doubts might arise respecting the genera or species of the beast, the flavor of the flesh was so unsavory that it would have been rejected as unfit for the stuffing even of Bologna sausages.

The peas were generally damaged, and, from the

imperfect manner in which they were cooked, were about as indigestible as grapeshot. The butter the reader will not suppose was the real "Goshen;" and had it not been for its adhesive properties to retain together the particles of the biscuit, that had been so riddled by the worms as to lose all their attraction of cohesion, we should have considered it no desirable addition to our viands.

The flour and the oat-meal were often sour, and when the suet was mixed with it, we should have considered it a blessing to have been destitute of the sense of smelling before we admitted it into our mouths: it might be nosed half the length of the ship.

And last, though not the least item among our staples in the eating line—our beef. The first view of it would excite an idea of veneration for its antiquity, and not a little curiosity to ascertain to what kind of an animal it originally belonged. Its colour was of dark mahogany; and its solidity would have set the keen edge of a broad-axe at defiance to cut across the grain, though like oakum, it could be pulled into pieces one way in strings, like rope-yarn. A streak of fat in it would have been a phenomenon, that would have brought all the prisoners together to see and admire. It was so completely saturated with salt, that, after having been boiled in water taken from the sea, it was found to be considerably freshened by the process. It was no uncommon thing to find it extremely tender; but then this peculiarity was not owing to its being a prime cut from a premium ox, but rather owing to its long keeping—the vicissitudes of heat and cold, of humidity and aridity it had experienced in the course of time: and of this disposition to tenderness we were duly apprized by the extraordinary fragrance it emitted before and after it was cooked. It required more skill than we possessed to determine whether the flesh, which we were obliged to devour, had once covered the bones of some luckless bull that had died from starvation; or of some worn-out horse that had been killed for the crime of having outlived his usefulness.

Such was our food: But the quality of it was not all that we had reason to complain of. The manner in which it was cooked was more injurious to our health, than the quality of the food; and, in many cases, laid the foundation of diseases, that brought many a sufferer to his grave, years after his liberation.

That cooking for the prisoners was done in a great copper vessel, that contained between two and three hogsheads of water set in brick work. The form of it was square, and it was divided into two compartments by a partition.

In one of these, the peas and oatmeal were boiled; this was done in fresh water: in the other, the meat was boiled, in salt water, taken up from alongside of the ship.

The *Jersey*, from her size and lying near the

shore, was imbedded in the mud; and I do not recollect seeing her afloat during the whole time I was
a prisoner.*

All the filth that accumulated among upwards of
a thousand men was daily thrown overboard, and
would remain there till carried away by the tide.
The impurity of the water may be easily conceived;
and in this water our meat was boiled.

It will be recollected too that the water was salt,
which caused the inside of the copper to become
corroded to such a degree that it was lined with a
coat of verdigris. Meat thus cooked must in some
degree be poisoned; and the effects of it were manifest in the cadaverous countenances of the emaciated beings, who had remained on board for any
length of time.

The persons, chosen by each Mess to receive
their portions of food, were summoned by the
cook's bell to receive their allowance, and, when it
had remained in the boiler a certain time, the bell
would again sound, and the allowance must be immediately taken away: whether it was sufficiently
cooked, or not, it could remain no longer.

The food was generally very imperfectly cooked;
yet this sustenance, wretched as it was, and deficient
in quantity, was greedily devoured by the half-
starved prisoners.

No vegetables were allowed us. Many times since,

*The tides in New-York do not generally rise or fall
above two or three feet.

when I have seen in the country, a large kettle of potatoes and pumpkins steaming over the fire to satisfy the appetites of a farmer's swine, I have thought of our destitute and starved condition, and what a luxury we should have considered the contents of that kettle on board the *Jersey*.

The prisoners were confined in the two main decks below. The lowest dungeon was inhabited by those prisoners who were foreigners, and whose treatment was more severe than that of the Americans.

The inhabitants of this lower region were the most miserable and disgusting-looking objects that can be conceived. Daily washing with salt water, together with their extreme emaciation, caused their skin to appear like dried parchment. Many of them remained unwashed for weeks; their hair long and matted, and filled with vermin; their beards never cut, excepting occasionally with a pair of shears, which did not improve their comeliness, though it might add to their comfort. Their clothes were mere rags, secured to their bodies in every way that ingenuity could devise.

Many of these men had been in this lamentable condition for two years, part of the time on board other prison-ships; and, having given up all hope of ever being exchanged, had become resigned to their situation. These men were foreigners, whose whole lives had been one continual scene of toil, hardship, and suffering. Their feelings were blunted, their dispositions soured; they had no sympathies for the world; no home to mourn for; no friends to lament for their fate.

But far different was the condition of the most numerous class of the prisoners, composed mostly of young men from New-England fresh from home. They had reason to deplore the sudden change in their condition. The thoughts of home, of parents, brothers, sisters, and friends, would crowd upon their minds; and, "brooding on what they had been, and what they were, their desire for home became a madness." The dismal and disgusting scene around; the wretched objects continually in sight, and "hope deferred, which maketh the heart sick," produced a state of melancholy, that often ended in death—the death of a broken heart. . . .

In the morning, the prisoners were permitted to ascend the upper deck, to spend the day, till ordered below at sunset. A certain number, who were for the time called the "Working Party," performed in rotation the duty of bringing up hammocks and bedding for airing, likewise the sick and infirm, and the bodies of those who had died during the night: of these there were generally a number every morning. After these services, it was their duty to wash the decks. Our beds and clothing were allowed to remain on deck till we were ordered below for the night; this was of considerable benefit, as it gave some of the vermin an opportunity to migrate from the quarters they had inhabited.

About two hours before sun-set, orders were given to the prisoners to carry all their things below; but we were permitted to remain above till we retired for the night into our unhealthy and crowded dungeons. At sun-set, our ears were saluted with the insulting and hateful sound from our keepers, of "Down, rebels, down," and we were hurried below, the hatchways fastened over us, and we were left to pass the night amid the accumulated horrors of sighs and groans, of foul vapor, a nauseous and putrid atmosphere, in a stifled and almost suffocating heat. The tiers of holes through the sides of the ship were strongly grated, but not provided with glass; and it was considered a privilege to sleep near one of these apertures in hot weather for the pure air that passed in at them.

But little sleep however could be enjoyed even there; for the vermin were so horribly abundant, that all the personal cleanliness we could practise would not protect us from their attacks, or prevent their effecting a lodgement upon us.

When any of the prisoners died in the night, their bodies were brought to the upper deck in the morning, and placed upon the gratings. If the deceased had owned a blanket, any prisoner might sew it around the corpse, and then it was lowered with a rope, tied round the middle, down the side of the ship into a boat. Some of the prisoners were allowed to go on shore, under a guard, to perform the labor of interment. Having arrived on shore, they found in a small hut some tools for digging, and a hand-barrow on which the body was conveyed to the place for burial.

Here in a bank near the Wallabout, a hole was excavated in the sand, in which the body was put, and then slightly covered; the guard not giving time sufficient to perform this melancholy service in a faithful manner. Many bodies would, in a few days after this mockery of a burial, be exposed nearly bare by the action of the elements. . . .

This was the last resting place of many a son and brother; young and noble-spirited men, who had left their happy homes and kind friends to offer their lives in the service of their country; but they little thought of such a termination to their active career, they had not expected to waste their energies in this dreadful prison. . . .

It was a painful task for the prisoners to carry, to this unconsecrated burial place, the bodies of those who had been their companions for months perhaps, and who were endeared to them by their love for the same glorious cause, and the same feeling of resentment toward their unmanly oppressors.

The fate of many of these unhappy victims must have remained forever unknown to their friends; for, in so large a number, no exact account could be kept of those who died, and they rested in a nameless grave; while those, who performed the last sad rites, were hurried away before their task was half completed, and forbidden to express their horror and indignation at this insulting negligence toward the dead.

But the emotions, thus suppressed, only glowed the more intensely within their bosoms, and contributed as much as any other cause to keep alive the hatred and animosity toward their enemies.

VIII

THE REGULAR CREW of the *Jersey* consisted of a captain, two mates, a steward, a cook, and about a dozen sailors. There was likewise on board a guard of ten or twelve old invalid marines, who were unfit for active service; and a guard of about thirty soldiers, from the different regiments quartered on Long Island, who were relieved by a fresh party every week.

The physical force of the prisoners was sufficient at any time to take possession of the ship; but the difficulty was to dispose of themselves after a successful attempt. Long Island was in possession of the British, and the inhabitants were favorable to the British cause.

To leave the ship, and land upon the island, would be followed by almost certain detection; and the miseries of our captivity would be increased by additional cruelties heaped upon us from the vindictive feelings of our oppressors.

Yet, small as was the chance for succeeding in the undertaking, the attempt to escape was often made, and in not a few instances with success.

Our sufferings were so intolerable, that we felt it to be our duty to expose ourselves to almost any risk to obtain our liberty. To remain on board of the prison ship seemed to be certain death, and in its most horrid form; to be killed, while endeavoring to get away, could be no worse.

American prisoners are proverbial for their ingenuity in devising ways and means to accomplish their plans, whether they be devised for their own comfort and benefit, or for the purpose of annoying and tormenting their keepers.

Although we were guarded with vigilance, yet there did not appear much system in the management of the prisoners; for we frequently missed a whole "mess" from our number, while their disappearance was not noticed by our keepers. Occasionally a few would be brought back, who had been found in the woods upon Long Island, and taken up by the "Tories."

Our mess one day noticed, that the mess that occupied the place next to them were among the missing. This circumstance led to much conjecture and enquiry respecting the manner in which they had effected their escape. By watching the movements of our neighbors, we soon found out the process necessary to be adopted. Any plan, which a mess had formed, they kept a secret among their number, in order to insure a greater prospect of success. In this way, we were kept ignorant for a long time of the manner in which the undertaking was accomplished.

For the convenience of the officers of the prison ship, a closet, called the "round house," had been constructed under the forecastle, the door of which was kept locked. This room was seldom used, there being other conveniences preferable to it.

Some of the prisoners had contrived to pick the lock of the door; and, as it was not discovered, the door remained unfastened.

After we had missed our neighboring prisoners, and had ascertained to our satisfaction their mode of operation, the members of our Mess determined to seize the first opportunity offered to attempt our escape.

We selected a day, about the fifteenth of August, and made all the preparations in our power for ensuring us success in our undertaking.

At sun-set, when the usual cry from the officer of the guard, "Down, rebels, down," was heard, instead of following the multitude down the hatchways, our mess, consisting of six, all Americans, succeeded in getting into the "round house," excepting one. The round house was found too small to contain more than five; and the sixth man, whose name, I think, was Putnam, of Boston, concealed himself under a large tub, that happened to be lying near the place of our confinement.

The situation of the five, as closely packed in the "round house" as we could stand and breathe, was so uncomfortable as to make us very desirous of vacating it as soon as possible.

We remained thus cooped up, hardly daring to breathe, for fear that we should be heard by the guard. The prisoners were all below, and no noise was heard above, saving the tramp of the guard as he paced the deck.

It was customary, after the prisoners were secured below, for the ship's mate every night to search above: this however was considered a mere form, and the duty was very imperfectly executed. While we were anxiously waiting for the completion of this service, an event transpired, that we little anticipated, and which led to our detection.

One of the prisoners, an Irishman, made his arrangements to escape the same evening, and had not communicated with any one on the subject, excepting a countryman of his, whom he persuaded to bury him up in the coal hole, near the forecastle. Whether his friend covered him faithfully or not, or whether the Irishman thought that if he could not see any body, nobody could see him, or whether, feeling uncomfortable in his position, he turned over to relieve himself, I know not; but, when the mate looked into the coal-hole, he espied something rather whiter than the coal, which he soon ascertained to be the Irishman's shoulder. This discovery made the officer suspicious, and induced him to make a more thorough search than usual. We heard the uproar that followed the discovery, and the threats of the mate that he "would search every hole and corner." He soon arrived at the round house, and we heard him ask a soldier for the key. Our hopes and expectations were a little raised, when we heard the soldier reply, "there is no need of searching this place, for the door is kept constantly locked." But the mate was not to be

diverted from his purpose, and ordered the soldier
to get the key.

During the absence of the soldier, we had a little
time to reflect upon the dangers of our situation;
crowded together in a space so small as not to admit
of motion, with no other protection than the thickness of a board; guarded on the outside by about a
dozen soldiers, armed with cutlasses; and the mate,
considerably drunk, with a pistol in each hand,
threatening to fire through, every moment, our feelings may be more easily conceived than described.
There was but little time for deliberation; something must be immediately done. We knew, that, as
soon as we should be compelled to quit our hiding-
place, our destination would be the quarter-deck
for the night; the luxury of sleeping below would
not be granted to prisoners detected in the heinous
crime of attempting their escape.

In a whispering consultation of a few moments,
we concluded that the safest course we could pursue
would be to break out with all the violence we
could exercise, overcome every obstacle, and reach
the quarter-deck. By this time, the soldier had arrived with the key, and upon applying it, the door
was found to be unlocked. We now heard our last
summons from the mate, with imprecations too horrid to repeat, and threatening us with instant destruction if we did not immediately come out.

To remain any longer where we were would have
been certain death to some of us; we therefore car-

ried our hastily-formed plan into operation. The door opened outwards, and, forming ourselves into a solid body, we burst open the door, rushed out pell-mell, and, making a brisk use of our fists, knocked the guard heels over head in all directions, at the same time running with all possible speed for the quarter-deck. As I rushed out, being in the rear, I received a wound from a cutlass on my side, the scar of which remains to this day.

As nearly all the guard were prostrated by our unexpected sally, we arrived at our destined place, without being pursued by any thing but curses and threats.

The mate exercised his authority to protect us from the rage of the soldiers who were in pursuit of us as soon as they had recovered from the prostration into which they had involuntarily been thrown; and, with the assistance of the captain's mistress, whom the noise had brought upon deck, and whose sympathy was excited when she saw we were about to be murdered: she placed herself between us and the enraged guard, and made such an outcry as to bring the captain up, who ordered the guard to take their station at a certain distance and watch us narrowly. We were all put in irons, our feet being fastened to a long bar, a guard placed over us, and in this manner we were left to spend the night.

During the time of the transactions related, our fellow prisoner, Putnam, remained quiet under the tub, and heard the noise around his hiding place. He was not suffered to remain long in suspense. A soldier lifted up the tub, and, seeing the poor prisoner, thrust his bayonet into his body just above his hip, and then drove him to the quarter-deck to take his station in irons among us. The blood flowed profusely from his wound, and he was soon after sent on board of the hospital ship, and we never heard any thing respecting him afterwards.

With disappointed expectations, we passed a dreary night. A cold fog, followed by rain, came on; to which we were exposed, without any blankets or covering to protect us from the inclemency of the weather.

Our sufferings of mind and body during that horrible night exceeded any that I have ever experienced. We were chilled almost to death, and the only way we could preserve heat enough in our bodies to prevent our perishing was to lie upon each other by turns. Morning at length came, and we were released from our fetters. Our limbs were so stiff that we could hardly stand. Our fellow prisoners assisted us below; wrapping us in blankets, we were at length restored to a state of comparative comfort.

For attempting to escape we were punished by having our miserable allowance reduced one-third in quantity for a month; and we had found the whole of it hardly sufficient to sustain life. This diminution in our fare was the only variety we experienced in our monotonous lives for several weeks.

One day a boat came alongside, containing about sixty firkins[9] of grease, which they called butter. The prisoners were always ready to assist in the performance of any labor necessary to be done on board ship, as it afforded some little relief to the tedious monotony of their lives. On this occasion, they were ready to assist in hoisting the butter on board. The firkins were first deposited upon the deck, and then lowered down the main hatchway. Some of the prisoners, who were the most officious in giving their assistance, contrived to secrete a firkin, by rolling it forward under the forecastle, and afterwards carrying it below in their bedding.

This was considered as quite a wind-fall; and, being divided among a few of us, proved a considerable luxury. It helped to fill up the pores in our mouldy bread, when the worms were dislodged, and gave to the crumbling particles a little more consistence.

Several weeks after our unsuccessful attempt to escape, another one, attended with better success, was made by a number of the prisoners. At sunset the prisoners were driven below, and the main hatchway was closed. In this there was a small trapdoor, large enough for a man to pass through, and a sentinel was placed over it with orders to permit one prisoner at a time to come up during the night.

[9]A firkin is a cask equal to about one-fourth of a barrel.

The plan that had been formed was this: One of the prisoners should ascend, and dispose of the sentinel in such a manner that he should be no obstacle in the way of those who were to follow.

Among the soldiers was an Irishman, who, in consequence of having a head of hair remarkable for its curly appearance, and withal a very crabbed disposition, had been nicknamed "Billy the Ram." He was the sentry on deck this night, for one was deemed sufficient, as the prisoners were considered secure when they were below, having no other place of egress saving the trap-door over which the sentinel was stationed.

Late in the night, one of the prisoners, a bold, athletick fellow, ascended upon deck, and in an artful manner engaged the attention of "Billy the Ram," in conversation about the war; lamenting that he had ever engaged in so unnatural a contest; expressing his intention of enlisting in the British service; and requesting Billy's advice as to the course necessary to be pursued to obtain the confidence of the officers.

Billy happened to be in a mood to take some interest in his views, and showed an inclination, quite uncommon for him, to prolong the conversation. Unsuspicious of any evil design on the part of the prisoner, and while leaning carelessly on his gun, "Billy" received a tremendous blow from the fist of his entertainer, on the back of his head, which brought him to the deck in a state of insensibility.

As soon as he was heard to fall by those below, who were anxiously waiting the result of the friendly conversation of their pioneer with "Billy," and were satisfied that the final knock-down argument had been given; they began to ascend, and, one after another, to jump overboard, to the amount of about thirty.

The noise aroused the guard, who came upon deck, where they found "Billy," not sufficiently recovered from the stunning effects of the blow he had received, to give any account of the transaction. A noise was heard in the water; but it was so dark that no object could be distinguished. The attention of the guard however was directed to certain spots, which exhibited a luminous appearance, which salt water is known to assume in the night when it is agitated; and to these appearances they directed their fire, and, getting out the boats, picked up about half of the number that attempted to escape, many of whom were wounded, though no one was killed. The rest escaped.

During the uproar overhead, the prisoners below encouraged the fugitives and expressed their approbation of their proceedings in three hearty cheers; for which gratification we suffered our usual punishment—a short allowance of our already short and miserable fare.

For about a fortnight after this transaction, it would have been a hazardous experiment to approach near to "Billy the Ram," and it was a long time before we ventured to speak to him, and finally to obtain from him an account of the events of that evening.

Not long after this, another successful attempt to escape was made, which for its boldness is perhaps unparalleled in the history of such transactions.

One pleasant morning, about ten o'clock, a boat came alongside, containing a number of gentlemen from New-York, who came for the purpose of gratifying themselves with a sight of the miserable tenants of the prison-ship: influenced by the same kind of curiosity that induces some people to travel a great distance to witness an execution.

The boat, which was a beautiful yawl, and sat like a swan upon the water, was manned by four oarsmen, with a man at the helm. Considerable attention and respect was shown to the visitors, the ship's side being manned when they showed their intention of coming on board, and the usual naval courtesies extended. The gentlemen were soon on board; and the crew of the yawl, having secured her to the fore-chains on the larboard side of the ship, were permitted to ascend the deck.

A soldier as usual was pacing with a slow and measured tread the whole length of the deck, wheeling round with military precision when he arrived at the end of his walk; and, whether upon this occasion any one interested in his movements had secretly slipped a guinea into his hand, not to *quicken*, but to retard his progress, was never known; but it was evident to the prisoners that he had never occupied so much time before in measuring the distance with his back to the place where the yawl was fastened. At this time, there were sitting in the forecastle, apparently admiring the beautiful appearance of the yawl, four mates and a captain, who had been brought on board as prisoners a few days previous, taken in some vessel from a southern port.

As soon as the sentry had passed these men, in his straight-forward march, they in a very quiet manner lowered themselves down into the yawl, cut the rope, and the four mates taking in hand the oars, while the captain managed the helm, in less time than I have taken to describe it, they were under full sweep from the ship. They plied the oars with such vigor, that every stroke they took seemed to take the boat out of the water. In the mean time, the sentry heard nothing and saw nothing of this transaction, till he had arrived at the end of his march, when, in wheeling slowly round, he could no longer affect ignorance, or avoid seeing that the boat was several times its length from the ship. He immediately fired; but, whether he exercised his best skill as a marksman, or whether it was on account of the boat going ahead its whole length at every pull of the rowers, I could never exactly ascertain: but the ball fell harmless into the water. The report of the gun brought the whole guard out, who blazed away at the fugitives, without producing any diminution in the rapidity of their progress.

By this time, the officers of the ship were on deck
with their visitors; and, while all were gazing with
astonishment at the boldness and effrontery of the
achievement, and the guard were firing as fast as
they could load their guns, the captain in the yawl
left the helm, and, standing erect in the stern, with
his back to the *Jersey*, bending his body to a right
angle, he exhibited the broadest part of himself to
their view, and with a significant gesture directed
their attention to it as a proper target for the exercise of their skill. This contemptuous defiance
caused our captain to swell with rage; and when the
prisoners gave three cheers to the yawl's crew as
expressive of their joy at their success, he ordered
all of us to be driven below at the point of the
bayonet, and there we were confined the remainder
of the day.

These five men escaped, greatly to the mortification of the captain and officers of the prison ship.
After this, as long as I remained a prisoner, whenever any visitors came on board, all the prisoners were
driven below, where they were obliged to remain
till the company had departed.

IX

THE MISERIES of our condition were continually increasing: the pestilence on board spread rapidly, and every day added to our bill of mortality. The young, in a particular manner, were its most frequent victims. The number of the prisoners was continually increasing, notwithstanding the frequent and successful attempts to escape: and when we were mustered and called upon to answer to our names, and it was ascertained that nearly two hundred had mysteriously disappeared without leaving any information of their departure, the officers of the ship endeavored to make amends for their past remissness by increasing the rigor of our confinement, and depriving us of all hope of adopting any of the means for liberating ourselves from our cruel thraldom, so successfully practised by our comrades.

With the hope that some relief might be obtained to meliorate the wretchedness of our situation, the prisoners petitioned Gen. [Henry] Clinton, commanding the British forces in New-York, for permission to send a memorial to General Washington, describing our condition, and requesting his influence in our behalf, that some exchange of prisoners might be effected.[10]

[10] It was customary for the armies of the day to arrange cartels for the exchange of prisoners. Usually prisoners were exchanged rank for rank, but sometimes a ratio would be established, i.e., one colonel for three majors, etc.

Permission was obtained, and the memorial was sent. In a few days, an answer was received from Gen. Washington, containing expressions full of interest and sympathy, but declaring his inability to do any thing for our relief by way of exchange, as his authority did not extend to the marine department of the service, and that soldiers could not consistently be exchanged for sailors. He declared his intention however to lay our memorial before Congress, and that no exertion should be spared by him to mitigate our sufferings.

Gen. Washington at the same time sent letters to Gen. Clinton, and to the British Commissary of Prisoners, in which he remonstrated against their cruel treatment of the American prisoners, and threatened, if our situation was not made more tolerable, to retaliate by placing British prisoners in circumstances as rigorous and uncomfortable as were our own: that "with what measure they meted the same should be measured to them again."

We experienced after this some little improvement in our food, but no relaxation in the severity of our confinement. The interposition of Divine Providence, or removal from our loathsome prison, seemed the only preservative from the pestilence which "walked in darkness and destroyed at noonday."

The long detention of American sailors on board of British prison-ships was to be attributed to the little pains that were taken by our countrymen to retain British subjects, who were taken prisoners on the ocean during the war. Our privateers captured many British seamen; who, when willing to enlist in our service, as was generally the case, were received on board of our ships. Those, who were brought into port, were suffered to go at large; for, in the impoverished condition of the country, no state or town was willing to subject itself to the expense of maintaining prisoners in a state of confinement: they were permitted to provide for themselves. In this way, the number of British seamen was far too small for a regular and equal exchange. Thus British seamen, after their capture, enjoyed the blessings of liberty, the light of the sun, and the purity of the atmosphere, while the poor American sailors were compelled to drag out a miserable existence amid want and distress, famine and pestilence. As every principle of justice and humanity was disregarded by the British in the treatment of their prisoners, so likewise every moral and legal right was violated in compelling the prisoners to enter into their service.

We had obtained some information in relation to an expected draught that would soon be made upon the prisoners to fill up a complement of men that were wanted for the service of his majesty's fleet.

One day, in the latter part of August, our fears of the dreaded event were realized. A British officer with a number of soldiers came on board. The prisoners were all ordered on deck, were placed on the larboard gangway, and marched in single file round to the quarter-deck, where officers stood to inspect them and select such ones as suited their fancies, without any reference to the rights of the prisoners, or considering at all the duties they owed to the land of their nativity, or the government for which they had fought and suffered.

The argument was, "Men we want, and men we will have." We continued to march around, in solemn and melancholy procession, till they had selected from among our number about three hundred of the ablest, nearly all of whom were Americans; and they were directed to go below under a guard, to collect together whatever things they wished to take belonging to them.

They were then driven into the boats, waiting alongside, and left the prison-ship, not to enjoy their freedom, but to be subjected to the iron despotism, and galling slavery of a British man-of-war; to waste their lives in a foreign service; and toil for masters whom they hated. Such, however, were the horrors of our situation as prisoners, and so small was the prospect of relief, that we almost envied the lot of those who left the ship to go into the service even of our enemy. . . .

In December, 1776, the American board of war, after procuring such evidence as convinced them of the truth of their statement, reported: "That there were nine hundred privates, and three hundred officers, of the American army, prisoners in the city of

New-York, and five hundred privates and fifty officers, in Philadelphia. That, since the beginning of October, all these prisoners, both officers and privates, had been confined in prison-ships or the provost. That, from the best evidence the subject could admit of, the general allowance of the prisoners did not exceed four ounces of meat per day, and that often so damaged as not to be eatable. That it has been a common practice with the British, to keep their prisoners four or five days without a morsel of meat, and then tempt them to enlist, to save their lives."[11]

Many were *actually starved to death*, in hope of making them enrol themselves in the British army.

The American sailors, when captured, suffered even more than the soldiers; for they were confined on board prison-ships in great numbers, and in a manner which showed that the British officers were willing to treat fellow human beings, whose only crime was love of liberty, worse than the vilest animals; and indeed, in every respect, with as much cruelty, as is endured by the miserable inhabitants of the worst class of slave ships.

The prisoners were so crowded in these ships, and so brutally treated, that in consequence of bad food and impure air, diseases broke out among them, which destroyed immense numbers.

[11] Here Fox seems confused as to his dates, as the reference to prisoners in Philadelphia would suggest that this was in 1777–1778 when the British occupied that city.

In the course of the war, it has been asserted on good evidence, that *eleven thousand persons* died on board the *Jersey*, one of the largest of the prison-ships, stationed in East-river, near New-York.

These unfortunate beings died in agony in the midst of their fellow sufferers, who were obliged to witness their tortures, without the power of reliev-ing their dying countrymen, even by cooling their parched lips with a drop of cold water, or a breath of fresh air; and, when the last breath had left the emaciated body, they sometimes remained for hours in close contact with the corpse, without room to shrink from companions death had made so horri-ble. And when at last the dead were removed, they were sent in boats to the shore, and so imperfectly buried, that, long after the war was ended, their bones lay whitening in the sun on the beach of Long-Island, a lasting memorial of British cruelty, so entirely unwarranted by all the laws of war, of even common humanity.

They could not even pretend they were retaliat-ing; for the Americans invariably treated prisoners with kindness,[12] and as though they were their fel-

[12] Here Fox is allowing his patriotism to overwhelm him. Prisoners of war in the hands of the Americans suffered as much as did those in British custody. This was especially true with regard to loyalists, some of whom were kept in prison ships at Esopus on the Hudson. Other loyalists were confined in the abandoned Simsbury copper mines in Con-necticut, while others were crowded under the court house in Kingston, New York.

low men. All the time that these cruelties were performed, those, who were thus deprived of every comfort and necessary, were constantly entreated to leave the American service, and induced to believe, while kept from all knowledge of publick affairs, that the republican cause was hopeless; that all, engaged in it, would meet the punishment of traitors to their king; and that all their prospect of saving their lives, or escaping from an imprisonment worse than death to young and high-spirited men, as most of them were, would be in joining the British army, where they were sure of good pay and quick promotion.

These were the means employed by our enemies to increase their own forces, and discourage the patriots, and it is not strange that they were successful in many instances. . . .

In the midst of our distress, perplexities, and troubles at this period, we were not a little puzzled to know how to dispose of the vermin that would accumulate upon our persons, notwithstanding all our attempts at cleanliness. To catch them was a very easy task, but to undertake to deprive each individual captive of life, as rapidly as they could have been taken, would have been a more herculean task for each individual daily, than the destruction of the three thousand Philistines by Samson of old. To throw them overboard would have been but a small relief; as they would probably add to the impurities of the boiler, by being deposited in it the first time it was filled up for cooking our unsavory mess. What then was to be done with them? A general consultation was held, and it was determined to deprive them of their liberty.

This being agreed upon, the prisoners went to work immediately, for their comfort and amusement, to make a liberal contribution of those migratory creatures, who were compelled to colonize for a time within the boundaries of a huge snuff-box appropriated for that purpose. There they lay, snugly ensconced, of all colours, ages, and sizes, to the amount of some thousands, waiting for orders.

British recruiting officers frequently came on board, and held out to the prisoners tempting offers to enlist in his Majesty's service; not to fight against their own country, but to perform garrison duty in the island of Jamaica.

One day an Irish officer came on board for this purpose, and, not meeting with much success among the prisoners who happened to be on deck, he descended below to repeat his offers. He was a remarkably tall man, and was obliged to stoop as he passed along between the decks. The prisoners were disposed for a frolick, and kept the officer in their company for some time, flattering him with expectations, till he discovered their insincerity, and left them in no very pleasant humor. As he passed along, bending his body, and bringing his broad shoulders to nearly a horizontal position, the idea occurred to our minds to furnish him with some recruits from the colony in the snuff-box. A favorable opportunity presented, the cover of the box was removed, and the whole contents discharged upon the red-coated back of the officer. Three cheers from the prisoners followed the migration, and the officer ascended to the deck, unconscious of the number and variety of recruits he had obtained without the formality of an enlistment. The captain of the ship, suspicious that some joke had been practised, or some mischief perpetrated, from the noise below, met the officer at the head of the gangway, and, seeing the vermin crawling up his shoulders and aiming at his head with the instinct peculiar to them, exclaimed, "Hoot, mon, wha' is the matter with yer bock?" The captain was a Scotchman. By this time many of them, in their wanderings, had travelled around from the rear to the front, and showed themselves, to the astonishment of the officer. He flung off his coat in a paroxysm of rage, which was not allayed by three cheers from the prisoners on the deck. Confinement below, with a short allowance, was our punishment for this gratification.

From some information we had obtained, we were in daily expectation of a visit from the British recruiting officers; and, from the summary method of their former procedure, no one felt safe from the danger of being forced into their service. Many of the prisoners thought it would be better to enlist voluntarily, as it was probable that afterwards they would be permitted to remain on Long-Island, preparatory to their departure for the West-Indies, and during that time some opportunity would be offered for their escape to the Jersey shore.

To remain an indefinite time as prisoners, enduring sufferings and privations beyond what human nature could sustain, or to make a virtue of necessity, and with apparent willingness to enlist into a service, into which we were satisfied that we would soon be impressed, seemed to be the only alternatives.

There was a hope too, that, by voluntarily enlisting, we should obtain a degree of confidence, which would result in affording us an opportunity of deserting, and thereby regaining our liberty.

While prisoners on board of the *Jersey*, we could obtain no accurate knowledge of the success of the American cause. The information we had, came from our enemies, whose interest it was to deceive us. They magnified our disasters, and kept us in ignorance of our success, and constantly represented the cause as hopeless. Cold weather was approaching, and we had no comfortable clothing to protect us from the rigors of an inclement season.

Situated as we were, there appeared to us to be no moral turpitude in enlisting in the British service, especially since we considered that it was almost certain we should soon be impressed into the same. Our moral discernment was not clear enough to perceive, that it was not safe "to do evil that good may come." We thought the end justified the means, and, in despair of any improvement being in prospect for our liberation, we concluded that we would enlist for soldiers, for the West-India service, and trust to Providence for finding an opportunity to leave the British for the American service.

Soon after we had formed this desperate solution, a recruiting officer came on board to enlist men for the eighty-eighth regiment, to be stationed at Kingston, in the island of Jamaica. We had just been trying to satisfy our hunger upon a piece of beef, which was so tough that no teeth could make an impression on it, when the officer descended between decks, and represented to us the immense improvement that we should experience in our condition, if we were in his Majesty's service: an abundance of good food, comfortable clothing, service easy, and in the finest climate in the world, were temptations too great to be resisted by a set of miserable, half-starved, and almost naked wretches as we were, and who had already concluded to accept of the proposition even had it been made under circumstances less enticing.

The recruiting officer presented his papers for our signature. We stared at each other, and felt that we were about to do a deed of which we were ashamed, and which we might regret. Again we heard the tempting offers, and again the assurance that we should not be called upon to fight against our government or country; and, with the hope that we should find an opportunity to desert, of which it was our firm intention to avail ourselves when offered—with such hopes, expectations, and motives, we signed the papers, and became soldiers in his Majesty's service.

How often did we afterwards lament that we had ever lived to see this hour! how often did we regret that we were not in our wretched prison-ship again, or buried in the sand at the Wallabout!

X

WE SHORTLY AFTER, twelve in number, left the *Jersey*, and were landed upon Long-Island and marched under a guard about a mile to an old barn, where we were quartered. We had formed our plan to desert that night; but great was our disappointment and surprise to find, that the barn was surrounded by a strong guard, as though our design was suspected and means were taken to prevent it. Though our lodgings seemed a palace compared with our prison-ship, yet sleep was a stranger to us during that night. Under various pretexts, we frequently went out to reconnoitre; but were satisfied that there was no chance for escape then, and must trust to Providence for some more favorable opportunity. The next morning, after we had partaken of, what appeared to us, a luxurious repast, we were paraded for drill, and then marched down to the shore under a guard of twenty soldiers, whom the officer called, in compliment to us, as escort; an honor with which we could very well have dispensed. In our march, we passed the *Jersey;* and this gloomy hulk, with all the horrible associations connected with it, seemed a desirable resting-place, compared with the melancholy prospect before us.*

* The reader may have some curiosity to know what became of the *"Old Jersey."* The prisoners, who were on board of her at the conclusion of the war in 1783, were liberated. The prison-ship was then abandoned, and the dread of contagion prevented any one visiting her. Worms soon

Disappointed in all our hopes and expectations of escape, we were hurried on board of a vessel ready to sail for Jamaica, only waiting for a favorable wind. We entertained a faint hope, that, during our voyage, we might be taken by some American privateer, and consequently obtain our freedom.

In the course of six or eight days, we weighed anchor, and hoisted our sail for Jamaica. I placed myself upon the quarter-deck, to prolong my view of my beloved native land, which I was leaving I feared for ever. The winds were propitious, and our progress was rapid.

We had in company a small schooner, a Virginia-built vessel, and a rapid sailer. Our captain occasionally put on board of her twelve or fifteen men, whom he generally selected from among those who had enlisted as soldiers, as they had for the most part experienced a sea service. We captured a small French vessel during the voyage, after we had come in sight of land and were running down to leeward of it under French colours.

We suddenly formed a plan to take possession of

destroyed her bottom; she afterwards sunk. It is said that her planks were covered with the names of the captives, who had been immured there; a long and melancholy catalogue, as it is supposed that a greater number of men perished on board of her, than history informs us of in any other place of confinement in the same period of time.

In the year 1803, the bank at the Wallabout was removed, as preparatory to building a Navy Yard. A vast quantity of bones were found, which were carefully collected and buried under the direction of the Tammany Society of New-York.

the schooner, of which we composed the greater part of the crew, and run into some Spanish or Portuguese island. Our ship was a good way ahead of us; and as she was a very dull sailer, we thought there would be no difficulty in escaping from her. It was necessary for us to be prompt and decided in our operations. The crew was composed of various nations, and great caution must be used in our consultations. We finally agreed upon our plan, and were about putting it in execution, when the courage of one of our party failed. He was a Scotchman; and, from the manner in which he expressed his fears and doubts, we had great reason to apprehend that he had or would betray us. During this time, we were running to the leeward, and, in case we succeeded, we should be obliged to beat up to the windward again, to recover the distance we had lost, and be exposed to the danger of meeting with English cruisers under the land. The attempt seemed too desperate to risk, and we reluctantly abandoned it, although it was our last and forlorn hope.

The next day we anchored in the harbor of Port-Royal, where we lay one day, and sailed for Kingston. "Kingston is on the south coast of the island of Jamaica, and on the north side of a beautiful harbor, in which vessels of the largest burden may anchor in safety. It is built on a plain which commences on the shore, and rises with a gradual ascent to the foot of the Liguanea mountains, a distance of about six miles. Port-Royal stands at the extremity of the long and narrow peninsula which bounds Kingston harbor on the south, about ten miles south-west of Kingston. It has an excellent harbor, in which a thousand ships could anchor with convenience. It contains the royal navy-yard, the navy hospital, and barracks for a regiment of soldiers. The fortifications are remarkably strong, and are kept in excellent order." Our vessel was hauled up to a wharf; we remained on board till a British sergeant came and took our names.

The captain of our ship then informed us, that he was not ignorant of the design we had formed of taking possession of the ship during the voyage; and although it was in his power to have us tried for our lives by a court-martial for an intended mutiny, yet he was actuated by feelings of compassion, and was more desirous of doing us good than evil, and was willing to forgive us. He then gave us some salutary advice respecting our future conduct, and bid us farewell. This magnanimous conduct on his part produced in us a heart-felt expression of gratitude.

We then landed, and with the sergeant at the head marched in single file through Kingston to a place called "Harmony-hall," where the regiment was quartered, and were placed under the care of a drill sergeant. The next morning we were ordered out for drill, and received our uniform and arms, which we were ordered to keep bright and in good order for service. We had but little employment, excepting being drilled to our hearts' content by the sergeant, trying to make good soldiers of us to serve His Majesty, King George the Third. The life of a soldier in a garrison is an idle one at the best; and, though the duties are not laborious, there is a monotony in them which is extremely irksome to the active mind of youth. But we could not reasonably expect to spend our lives in a garrison, if such a thing were desirable: after having had our share of it, we were aware that we should be called upon to perform some foreign service, we knew not where, perhaps to bear arms against our beloved country. With the fear of this in view, and the reluctance we experienced in serving what we still considered the cause of our enemy; our minds were constantly employed in devising ways and means to effect our escape.

It appeared to be the object of our officers to reconcile us to the service, by making our duties easy and agreeable. We were often indulged with the privilege of leaving our quarters to visit the town or wander about the country adjacent. Harmony-Hall, our quarters, was enclosed by a high fence, having two gates in front and one in the rear, at each of which a sentry was stationed. When a soldier wished to leave the Hall, it was necessary for him to obtain a written order called a "pass," to show to the sentry when he went out, and to give up when he returned. Several of us thought it a practicable thing to get on board some of the British merchant vessels in the harbor, which were in need of men, and whose captains would not hesitate to receive and secrete us, as they were frequently deprived of their hands by impressment on board of the ships of war. We availed ourselves of every opportunity we could obtain to get information respecting English vessels, their time of sailing, their destined ports, &c.; thinking that, if we could once get to England, we should find some means to get thence to France, whence we could return to our own country.

In our rambles about the town and country, we visited the grog-shops and taverns, places where sailors generally resort, and had got considerably acquainted with the keepers of these establishments. Our "passes" were signed by a commissioned officer, and they gave us permission to carry our side-arms, that is, a bayonet, and to be absent two hours at a time.

While I and one of my comrades were wandering about the town one day, we stepped into a house, where liquors and refreshments were to be obtained. We found one of the seats occupied by an English sailor, to whom we, rather too frankly for prudence, communicated our intentions; or more correctly speaking, gave him some cause for suspecting our designs from the questions we asked him respecting the probability of obtaining employment on board of some merchant vessel, in case we could get released from our present engagements. The sailor was inclined to be very sociable, and discovered no objections to drinking freely at our expense; telling us that he belonged to an English ship that would sail in a few days; that his captain was in want of hands; that, at his intercession, he would undoubtedly take us on board.

He appeared so friendly, and his manners were so insinuating, that he completely won our confidence. He asked us, how we could obtain liberty to leave the garrison, and to pass in and out when we pleased?

Taking my "pass" out of my pocket, I showed it to him, and told him that was our authority. He took it into his hand apparently with an intention of reading it; and, after looking at it for some time, in a sort of careless manner, he put it into his pocket. I felt a little surprised when I saw him do it, and my companion expressed his fears by whispering into my ear, "Blast his eyes, he means to keep the pass."

Having allowed the fellow to get possession of the paper, I felt myself responsible for it, and that it was necessary for me to recover it, even if I were obliged to resort to violent measures. I therefore said to him, "My friend, I must have that paper, as we cannot return to our quarters without it." He replied, "You had better be peaceable about it, for I mean to see your commanding officer."

Matters had now come to a crisis. I saw that it was the sailor's object to inform against us, and to carry the "pass" as an evidence of our conference with him. I immediately drew my bayonet from its scabbard, and, thrusting it against his side with force sufficient to inflict a slight wound, put my hand into his pocket and took out the "pass"; and then giving him a blow upon the head with the butt end of my bayonet, dropped him senseless on the floor. The noise of this conflict brought the landlord into the room, followed by his wife, with whom a previous acquaintance had made me somewhat of a favorite. The rascal had by this time recovered his senses and had got upon his legs, and began to represent the matter in a light the most favorable to himself.

We vehemently contradicted his assertions, and were stoutly backed up by the landlady, who was a considerable of a termagant, and declared that "the sailor was a quarrelsome fellow; that he had made a difficulty once before in the house; and that her husband would be a fool if he did not kick him out of doors."

The landlord, to prove that he was "*compos mentis,*" and to appease the wrath of his wife, which waxed warm, complied with her kind wishes, and the sailor was, without much ceremony, hurried through the door, his progress not a little accelerated by a brisk application of the landlord's foot in the manner prescribed by the good woman. We were then advised by our friends to return to our quarters as quick as possible, lest the fellow might make some trouble for us. We paid our bill, and gave the landlord many thanks, not forgetting the landlady, to whose kind interference we owed our fortunate escape. This circumstance made me more cautious in future of communicating my designs to strangers how friendly soever they might appear.

About this time, I was unexpectedly released from the duties of a soldier. One day I attracted the attention of an officer, by the exercise of my skill as a barber in the act of shaving a comrade; and was forthwith promoted to the high station of hairdresser and shaver for the officers.

This was very agreeable to me, as it gave me an opportunity of obtaining much information respecting the town and country around, and likewise much leisure time, and many indulgences not granted to the soldiers.

I was assiduous in my attentions to my superiors, and thereby gained their confidence, and could, almost whenever I wished, procure a pass to go out when I desired.

But although my duties were light and I experienced much kind treatment, I still felt myself in a state of servitude,—a prisoner, as it were, among the enemies of my country—in a thraldom, from which I was desirous of being released. I was willing to incur any hazard to obtain my liberty, and to breathe once more the air of freedom.

To visit my dear native land, my friends, and the scenes of my childhood, was the prevailing wish of my mind; to accomplish this desire I was willing to hazard my life.

Many difficulties were to be surmounted before this could be effected. Friends were to be found, in whom confidence could be placed.

It was difficult to tell whom to trust. To impart my views to others might expose me to treachery; and, if betrayed, the consequences would be fatal. It was necessary to proceed with great caution in obtaining the opinions of those who were likely to embark in the undertaking I had in contemplation. Several must be found, possessing similar views and intentions, alike in courage and determination to carry through whatever plan might be formed. To desert from a military force, in an enemy's country, and that an island, seemed to be a desperate undertaking with little prospect of success. But I was resolved upon the attempt, and my thoughts were continually employed in devising ways and means to effect it.

I gained upon the confidence of the officers daily, and was indulged with opportunities of leaving the garrison whenever I chose.

Availing myself of this privilege, I became acquainted with all the avenues from the town as far as Rock-fort, which was situated at the distance of two miles from Kingston, on the right-hand side of the road.

I ascertained that it was the custom to place a number of sentries on the left-hand side of the road, about the eighth of a mile from the fort, in the road to Rock-fort, at a place called the "Plum-tree."

Deserters, who were ignorant of this circumstance, were often taken up by the sentries, and brought back to the garrison. The night before we escaped, five soldiers were caught in the act of deserting, and brought back in the morning while the regiment were on parade. The poor fellows looked the very objects of despair when they were delivered up, and put under guard to await their trial by a court-martial.

I had become acquainted with five soldiers, who had been released from military duty, because they were mechanicks, and could make themselves more useful in the performance of various mechanical services.

They enjoyed considerable liberty, but did not possess the confidence of the officers in so great a degree as I did, having made myself useful and agreeable to them by personal attention in contributing to their comfort and convenience. My knowledge of the town and its environs rendered me a valuable coadjutor, and gave me more consequence in the estimation of my comrades, than I should otherwise have had, and made me a sort of leader in the enterprise, though I was then but about nineteen years of age.

We had frequent opportunities of being together to digest our plan, and to make arrangements for putting it into execution.

About this time, I had the good fortune to obtain a high degree of confidence, and to find great favor in the sight of the commanding-officer by the exercise of my professional skill in making him wonderfully satisfied with himself upon the occasion of a military ball. He was so much pleased with the improvement I made in his personal appearance, that, in the fulness of his heart, he gave me a "pass to go out whenever I chose till further orders."

This was a great privilege, and I derived great advantages from the use of it.

The five comrades, with whom I had associated, as I have observed, were mechanicks, two of whom were armorers; and they had obtained from the arsenal two pistols and three swords, which were all the weapons we had: these, together with some articles of clothing, we had deposited in the hut of an old negro, whom we had bribed to secrecy. The regiment, stationed at Rock-fort, was designated as "Lord Montague's men," or the American Rangers, and had been recruited in North and South Carolina. Their uniform was a short blue jacket with white facings. Having made all the preparations in our power, we appointed the time to commence the attempt.

Our plan was, to travel across the island, and trust to circumstances, which might providentially be thrown in our way, to escape to the island of Cuba. Our fears were not a little excited, when we saw the poor fellows brought back on the morning preceding the night we had fixed for our undertaking; especially when we heard the commanding-officer declare, "that, whatever might be their fate, the next, who should undertake to desert, should be hung."

I had a general pass, as I have before observed, for myself to go out at pleasure; but it was necessary to obtain a special one for my companions, and this duty devolved on me.

In the afternoon, soon after dinner, I asked the commanding-officer to grant me the favor of a pass for five of my acquaintance to go out to spend the evening, upon condition of returning before nine o'clock. The officer hesitated for a moment; and then, as he signed the pass, said, "I believe I can trust you; but remember that you must not come back without them." This I readily promised, and I faithfully fulfilled the obligation.

XI

ABOUT the middle of the week, in the month of July, 1782, our little party of six, five Americans, and one Irishman, an active, courageous fellow, left the town, and proceeded to the negro's hut, where we received our weapons and clothing and some little store of provisions which we had deposited. That afternoon, a soldier had been buried at Rock-fort, and part of the regiment had been out to attend the funeral.

Seeing these soldiers upon their return at a distance, and fearing that our bundles might excite their suspicion, we concluded to separate and meet again as soon as the soldiers had passed. We escaped their notice, and fortunately met together a little time after, all but one who was missing. We waited some time, and looked in various directions for him, without success. We were afraid to remain where we were any longer, as it was now past eight o'clock; and we knew, if we did not return by nine, a party would be sent in search of us.

The man, whom we missed, was somewhat intoxicated, and the probability was that he had lain down and fallen asleep; or perhaps his courage had failed, and he had given up the undertaking, and might have gone back and given information against us. We were satisfied that we could wait no longer for him without exposing ourselves to great danger, and therefore concluded to proceed without him.

What was his fate I have never been able to ascertain.

We pushed rapidly forward till we had got about a mile from Kingston, when we entered a small piece of wood-land, and divested ourselves of our uniform, which we had worn with much reluctance, and had never ceased to regret having exposed ourselves to the necessity of putting on; clothed ourselves in the sailor garments, which we had taken care to provide; cut the white binding from our hats; and were soon metamorphosed into much better sailors, than we had ever been soldiers.

Having loaded our pistols, we again proceeded. We had advanced but a few rods, when we met a sergeant, belonging to a regiment called the Liverpool Blues, who had been to Rock-fort to see some of his acquaintance, and was then upon his return. It was near the time for stationing the guard, as usual, at the place called the "Plum-tree." The sergeant hailed us with, "Where are you bound, my lads?" We answered, "To Rock-fort."

He replied, "I have just come from there, and found all well: how goes on the recruiting at New-York? and what is the news?"

A ship had arrived the day previous, from New-York, and he supposed that we were some of the recruits that she had brought over.

We perceived his mistake, and adapted our answers to his questions, so as to encourage his delusion. We told him that the recruiting went on bravely, and we were going to join our regiment at Rock-fort.

The fellow seemed to be in a very happy mood, and immediately declared his intention of turning back to show us the way to the fort.

Our situation was rendered very embarrassing by this kind offer; and to refuse it, we feared, would excite suspicion. Our generous guide thought he was doing us service, when he was leading us directly to destruction; and the idea of killing him, while he imagined that he was performing a good service for us, was very unpleasant; but it was our only alternative.

In a few moments the deed would have been done; self-preservation made it necessary: but, fortunately for the poor fellow, and very much to our satisfaction, he suddenly recalled that his pass required him to be back to Kingston by nine o'clock, and, bidding us good-night, and telling us that we could not miss the way, he left us, and pursued his route to Kingston at a rapid pace.

We thought it important that we should get as far from Kingston that night as possible, as we should undoubtedly be pursued in the morning; and the sergeant, from whom we had just parted, would give information of us, as soon as he arrived and ascertained that we were deserters. The danger, to which we had been exposed by our recent interview, cast a gloom over our spirits, and gave us a realizing sense of the difficulties and hazards with which we must contend. But go forward we must, for to go back would be death.

We proceeded at a rapid pace for about half of a mile farther, when we met with an old negro, who hailed us, saying*, "Where be you going, massa buckra men? there be a plenty of soldiers a little way a-head; they will take you up, and put you on board of man-of-war." We told him that we had got a pass. The negro replied, "Dey no care for dat, dey put you on board a man-of-war." He mistook us for sailors, who were deserting from some ship.

I had become acquainted with several negroes in Kingston, and always found them kind and willing to give any information that was in their power to furnish. They appeared to feel a sort of sympathy for the soldiers and sailors; seeing some resemblance between their own degraded condition and that of the miserable military and naval slaves of British despotism. Whatever might be the cause, I always found the negroes in and about Kingston ready to give every facility to a soldier or sailor who wished to desert. We soon agreed with the old fellow for a dollar to guide us into a path through the woods, by following which we should avoid the guard at the "Plum-tree," in whose vicinity we then were. I had reconnoitred the ground sufficiently, previous to this, to be aware of the necessity of taking this path and knew about where it was; but we

---

* "Buckra man" was the common name among the Negroes for a white man.

were sensible that a faithful guide, who had a perfect knowledge of the ground, would be of great service to us, especially in the night.

After we had entered the woods, we had no fear of treachery on the part of our guide, as his life was in our hands. The fate that awaited him, should he attempt to jeopardize our safety, was clearly understood by him; but, from the earnest and simple manner in which he declared the sincerity of his intentions in serving us, put at rest in our minds all doubts of his fidelity. We followed our guide about a mile, when he told us that we had got past the guard, and, giving us directions as to our future course, he left us, after having called God to witness that he never would inform against us. We had no reason to doubt that he faithfully kept his promise.

Our anxiety to escape pursuit determined us to use all the expedition we could through the night. About midnight, we came to one of the many rivulets, with which Jamaica abounds. As we were unable to determine what its width or depth was in the darkness, it was necessary to proceed with caution. The tallest of our party was sent forward to try to wade across. The rest followed in a single file, according to respective heights; I, being the shortest, brought up the rear. Holding our arms and provisions and part of our clothing above our heads, we soon arrived on the opposite shore. When I was in the middle of the river, I found the water up to my chin, and was fearful at one time that I should be obliged to abandon my bundle, and resort to swimming. We traveled in our wet clothes the remainder of the night, and, towards day-light, we looked round for some retired spot, where we could secrete ourselves during the day, as we considered that it would expose us to great hazard, if not to certain detection, to travel by day-light at so little distance from Kingston as we then were. We soon found a secluded spot on the side of a hill thickly set with brushwood, well calculated for concealing us from the view of any who might pass that way.

In the course of the forenoon we saw, from our place of concealment, a number of negroes pass by, carrying to the market at Kingston various articles of country produce upon their heads in baskets. We had provided for our sustenance a small quantity of bread and dried herring, sufficient to last three days, the time we thought requisite to travel across the island: of this provision we eat sparingly, but suffered much for want of water, as we were afraid of being seen if we ventured from our hiding-place till night, when we cautiously, one at a time, crept down to the foot of the hill, and quenched our thirst from a small rivulet.

As soon as it was dark enough to prevent discovery, we left our place of concealment, and proceeded on our second night's journey.

We had been exposed to considerable danger the preceding night and day, and had suffered much from hunger, and more from thirst: our spirits were depressed, and we experienced the wearisomeness that arises from a want of sleep. Gloomy forebodings assailed us; and we moved on in melancholy silence. After having traveled three or four hours, we unexpectedly found ourselves near a hut, and were alarmed at hearing a negro female voice exclaim, "Here come a whole parcel of Buckra man." We immediately started from the spot, and proceeded with all practicable speed till we had traveled three or four miles, when we sat down to rest, and to refresh ourselves with some of our bread and dried herring.

After resting about half an hour, we renewed our journey with all the speed we could exercise; we then proceeded without interruption till day-light approached, when we thought it necessary to find a place for concealment during the day. We entered the woods at a short distance from the road, where we spent the day, partially satisfying our hunger with a scanty portion of bread and herring, and some berries, which we found, of various kinds; and amusing ourselves with the relation of the dangers we had passed through, and speculations upon the nature of those which we might be called upon to encounter. The day passed without any alarm, and, as night approached, we prepared to re-commence our journey. Soon after dark, we issued from the woods, entered upon the road, and proceeded for several hours without meeting with any thing to molest or make us afraid. We occasionally rested,

eat sparingly of our nearly-exhausted stores, and
drank water when we could find it, and traveled
without interruption till morning. A place for concealment during the day was again selected; and, as
we had slept but little since we left Kingston, we
concluded to get all the rest we could, and spent
the greater part of the day in sleep, each one of us
in succession keeping watch while the others slept.
After several hours' rest, we found ourselves considerably refreshed; and as our small stock of provisions was nearly exhausted, and we had consumed
nearly the time we had anticipated would be required to arrive on the opposite side of the island;
we concluded that we would venture to travel by
day-light.

We took the precaution to divide our party, three
taking one side of the road, a little in advance, and
two on the other side; keeping a vigilant look-out,
in every direction. One of our men in advance gave
notice, some time in the forenoon, that he discovered an object at a distance apparently approaching. We thought it prudent to retire from the road
to a neighboring thicket, till we could ascertain
what the object was. It proved to be a gentleman on
horseback, who, by his dress, appeared to be an
officer of high rank, followed by a servant.

The officer wore a large, gold-laced, three-cornered hat, and was richly dressed: both he and his
servant were well armed. As soon as they had
passed and were out of sight, we left our retreat

with the intention of proceeding; but, finding ourselves in need of more rest, we penetrated farther into the woods to find a place of repose.

Our strength began to fail for want of food, and we found it necessary to take more frequent opportunities for rest and sleep.

We gathered a few berries, and, having enjoyed a few hours of uninterrupted sleep, we felt refreshed, and returned to the road to pursue our journey. We traveled without interruption till about three o'clock in the afternoon, and, while ascending a hill, we were alarmed by hearing the sound of voices. We stopped, and collected together to consult upon what course to adopt. In a few moments, we saw coming over the hill three stout negroes, armed with muskets, which they immediately presented to us, and ordered us to stop.

Our arms, as I have formerly observed, consisted of two pistols and three swords: upon the pistols we could place but little dependence, as they were not in good order; and the swords were concealed under our clothes: to attempt to draw them out would have caused the negroes instantly to fire upon us.

They were about ten rods before us, and stood in the attitude of taking a deliberate aim at us. To run would be certain death to some of us; we therefore saw no alternative but to advance. One of our number, a man named Jones, a tall, powerful fellow, took a paper from his pocket, and, holding it up before him, advanced with great apparent confidence in his manner, and the rest of us imitated his example. As we approached, Jones held out the paper to one of them, telling him that it was our pass, giving us authority to travel across the island. The negroes, as we very well knew, were unable to read; it was therefore immaterial what was written upon the paper,—I believe it was an old letter,—as manuscript or print was entirely beyond their comprehension. While we were advancing, we had time to confer with each other; and the circumstances of the moment, the critical situation, in which we were placed, naturally led our minds to one conclusion, to obtain the consent of the negroes that we might pursue our journey; but that if they opposed our progress, to resort to violence, if we perished in the attempt.

There was something very exciting to our feelings in marching up to the muzzles of these fellows' guns; to have our progress interrupted when we were, as we supposed, so near the end of our journey. Our sufferings had made us somewhat savage in our feelings; and we marched up to them with that determination of purpose which desperate men have resolved upon, when life, liberty, and every thing they value is at stake:—all depended upon prompt and decisive action.

This was a fearful moment. The negroes stood in a row, their muskets still presented, but their attention was principally directed to the paper which Jones held before them; meanwhile our eyes were constantly fixed upon them, anxiously watching their motions, and designing to disarm them as soon as a favorable opportunity should be offered.

The negroes were large and powerful men, while we, though we outnumbered them, were worn down by our long march, and enfeebled by hunger. In physical power we were greatly their inferiors. But the desperate circumstances in which we were placed inspired us with uncommon courage, and gave us an unnatural degree of strength.

We advanced steadily forward, shoulder to shoulder, till the breasts of three of us were within a few inches of the muzzles of their guns. Jones reached forward and handed the paper to one of the negroes. He took it, and, turning it round several times and examining both sides, and finding himself not much the wiser for it, shook his head and said, "We must stop you." The expression of his countenance, the doubts which were manifested in his manner of receiving the paper, convinced us, that all hope of deceiving or conciliating them was at an end.

Their muskets were still presented, their fingers upon the triggers. An awful pause of a moment ensued, when we made a sudden and desperate spring forward, and seized their muskets: our attack was so unexpected, that we wrenched them from their hands before they were aware of our intention. The negro, whom I attacked, fired just as I seized his gun, but I had fortunately turned the direction of it, and the ball inflicted a slight wound upon my side, the scar of which remains to this day. This was the only gun that was discharged during this dreadful encounter.

As soon as it was in my possession, I exercised all my strength, more than I thought I possessed, and gave him a tremendous blow over the head with the breech, which brought him to the ground, from which he never rose.

I had no sooner accomplished my work, when I found my companions had been equally active, and had despatched the other two negroes in the same space of time. None of our party received any injury but myself, and my wound I considered as trifling.

The report of the gun we were fearing would alarm some of our enemies' comrades, who might be in the vicinity, and bring them to the spot. We accordingly dragged the bodies to a considerable distance into the woods, where we buried them under a quantity of leaves and brush. In their pockets we found a few biscuit, which were very acceptable to us in our famished condition.

The best gun was selected, as we did not think it necessary to burden ourselves with the others, as they had been injured in the conflict. We took what ammunition we thought necessary, and then sought a place of rest for the remainder of the day.

The negroes, whom we had encountered, belonged to a class called "Cudjoe men," who were free, in consequence of some services, which their ancestors, the Maroons,[13] agreed to render to the government; and were permitted to inhabit the mountains and the northern part of the island. They were encouraged to exercise their vigilance by the promise of receiving a certain sum of money for every fugitive slave they restored to his master, or soldier whom they should arrest as a deserter. We had been apprized of the existence of these beings before we left Kingston, and were in constant fear of meeting with some of them. Their huts were scattered along the three roads from Kingston, viz.: Rock-fort road, the County road, and the Spanish-town road.

We avoided as much as possible all of these roads, and traveled circuitous paths in the woods; and, having no guide and an imperfect compass, we wandered a great deal out of the direct way; and much of the time traveled considerable distances without making any advancement.

The direct distance across the island is about forty or fifty miles, which we could have traveled with ease in two days; but, from the cautious manner we proceeded and the irregular course we pursued, we were nearly five days in accomplishing our under-

[13] Maroons were slaves who escaped to the hills when their Spanish masters surrendered Jamaica to the British in 1655. The word "Maroon" meant "hog hunters" because they lived on wild boar. Around 1730 a maroon named Cudjoe led them in a fairly successful revolt, but they accepted British peace proposals in 1738, and were known as "Cudjoe men" after that.

taking. Considering our ignorance of the interior parts of the island, it has ever since been a matter of surprise to me that we succeeded in getting across the island; and that we did not perish in the woods.

Had we traveled upon either of the before named roads, instead of threading our way through the woods, we should have been overtaken by the parties of soldiers, who were sent in pursuit of us. I received information several years after our escape, of the exertions that were used to overtake us and carry us back to Kingston.

A young man, by the name of Hunt, was carried into Kingston, as a prisoner, taken by a British vessel, the day after our escape. Previous to his sailing from Boston, he had heard that I was in Kingston; and, when made a prisoner, he hoped to obtain some assistance from me in his captivity, as we had been formerly acquainted. He made inquiries of the sergeant of the guard, placed over him, respecting me. The sergeant replied, that "Fox was fool enough to run off last night, with five others: he had no military duty to perform; all he had to do was to shave and dress the officers, and he spent most of the time in walking about the streets. I suppose they think they will show us a Yankee trick; but they will find themselves mistaken, for there are three parties out after them, one on each road, and they had orders to bring them back before night, dead or alive."

It seems by this account that we must have been

taken, had we not pursued our journey in the woods instead of the road.

To return to my narrative: We lay down in the woods, languid and exhausted, after the excitement and fatigue from our contest with the negroes, and slept soundly for some time, when I suddenly awoke, and saw at a little distance from me the head of a monstrous serpent, raised several feet from the ground, and gazing earnestly upon us, with his mouth frightfully distended. I was so much alarmed that, at first, I imagined it to be the "old serpent" himself, and immediately awakened my companions. But I believe the serpent was more alarmed than we were, for he darted off among the bushes with so much rapidity that I could not ascertain his length, but was satisfied that the circumference of his body was of the size of a man's.

As it was now nearly dark, we thought we would venture again upon our journey. Having loaded our musket, the spoils of our victory, we entered the road, and, having looked around with great caution, and finding no obstacles in the way to excite any apprehension, we started forward. We knew not for a certainty where we were; but were satisfied, from the time we had consumed in our journey, that we could not be at a great distance from the northern side of the island.

XII

WE TRAVELED all night, occasionally stopping to rest, and refresh ourselves with some of the hard biscuit, which we had found in the pockets of the negroes, and a draught of water from the springs by the road-side.

As daylight approached, we found ourselves on the summit of a hill, and in sight of the ocean. I doubt whether Columbus and his crew experienced more heart-felt joy when they saw the new world, than our little party did when we discovered the sea. We could hardly refrain from uttering a loud exclamation of joy. Here was an end to our wanderings, our fatigue, and sufferings. We gazed upon the watery expanse with feelings of unutterable delight, upon whose surface we were to be wafted from the shores of captivity.

After we had remained as long as we thought prudent upon the eminence, we retired to the woods, for concealment during the day. We needed rest, and slept the greater part of the day.

We ventured out several times in the course of the day to take a peep abroad, but with great care that we should not be seen. We saw a number of negroes moving about in various directions, but were not discovered by any of them.

Our plan of operations for the future was the subject of much discussion; but we arrived at no definite conclusion, excepting to avail ourselves of any opportunity that should be offered to leave the island.

We had supposed, although perhaps we had no good reason for it, that we might find some merchant vessel on the coast, in which we might be received as sailors; as it was difficult to obtain men, and their wages were high.

Before sun-set, we left our hiding place, after eating the remainder of our bread, and proceeded cautiously towards the shore, keeping ourselves concealed as much as possible behind the bushes.

We saw a number of huts, scattered along the shore, mostly separate, some in small clusters. Part of the time during the day, a fog had prevailed, which now cleared away, and our prospect was uninterrupted.

The island of Cuba could just be seen in the horizon, at the distance of thirty leagues; between that and us lay the ocean smooth and unruffled, and not a sail to whiten its surface.

Dejected and melancholy, we again sought our place of concealment, to reflect upon our situation, and form some determination respecting future operations. To remain where we were long, without starving or being detected, was impossible; but how to get away was the problem to be solved. Undetermined what to do, we left our retreat again, and the first object that met our view upon the water was a sail-boat directing her course to the shore near where we were.

Here was a means of escape that Providence had thrown in our way. Our previous despair was now changed into hope, and, with our spirits suddenly elated, we retreated to the bushes to come to some immediate decision.

We resolved ourselves into a committee, appointed a moderator, and proceeded to business. The question to be discussed was, whether we should attempt to make a prize of the boat, and escape to Cuba.

Without spending much time, as we had none to spare, to discuss the question, or to hear speeches for, much less against it, we put it to vote, and carried it unanimously.

The wind was blowing from the shore, and the boat was consequently beating in against the wind. This was a favorable circumstance for us, if we could get possession of the boat. The undertaking was fraught with difficulty and danger, but it was our only chance for escape.

We left our council place, and crept cautiously down to the shore, keeping concealed as much as possible behind the bushes, till we arrived near to the point, at which we thought the boat was steering. As she was beating against the wind, we concluded, if the man at the helm could be brought down, the boat would luff, which would bring her near the shore, when we were immediately to spring on board. Jones, being the best marksman, took the musket, and seeing that it was well loaded and primed, crept as close to the edge of the shore as he could without being discovered by the crew, and lay down, to wait for a good opportunity to fire at the man at the helm. The rest of us kept as near to him as possible.

Every circumstance seemed to favor our design. The negroes were all in their huts, and every thing around was quiet and still.

The boat soon approached near enough for Jones to take a sure aim; and we scarcely breathed as we lay extended on the ground, waiting for him to perform the duty assigned him.

In a few moments, bang went the gun, and down went the negro from the helm into the bottom of the boat; and, as we had anticipated, the helm being abandoned, the boat luffed up in the wind and was brought close to the shore, which was bold, and the water deep enough to float her. The instant the gun was fired, we were upon our feet, and in the next moment up to our waists in the water alongside the boat.

No time was lost in shoving her about, and getting her bows from the land. There was a fresh breeze from the shore; the sails filled; and the boat was soon under a brisk head way. I remained in the water the last, and, as I attempted to get on board, my hands slipped from my hold on the gunwale, and I fell into the water. I heard an exclamation, "Good God! Fox is lost!" from one of our party; but, as the boat swept by me, I caught with my middle finger in the noose of a rope that hung over the stern, and was seized by the cape of my jacket and drawn into the boat by the powerful arm of Jones, who was managing the helm. All that I have described was apparently the work of a moment. Never did men use greater exertions than we did at this time.

The report of Jones's gun alarmed the negroes, and brought them from their huts in all directions down to the shore, armed with muskets and clubs, and full of rage and fury. They waded out after us, up to their chins in the water; and fired volley after volley, as fast as they could load. The bullets fell thickly around us, but fortunately none of us were injured. Our progress was so rapid, that we were soon out of reach of their shot; but, as soon as we could find time, we loaded our gun and gave one parting salute.

Our attention was next directed to the disposal of the crew of the boat we had captured, consisting of three men and a boy. As soon as we sprang into the boat, they fled with terror and amazement into a sort of cabin in the bow, where they still remained.

It was no wonder that they were frightened, attacked so suddenly by an enemy, who, as it seemed to them, had arisen all at once from the bowels of the earth or the depths of the ocean.

Whether the head of the negro at the helm was bullet-proof, or whether the ball approached so near to it as to frighten him into insensibility, we never knew; but we found him prostrate in the bottom of the boat, when we entered it, apparently dead; but, to our gratification, we soon found that he was alive, and not a curl of his wool discomposed.

He was soon upon his knees, supplicating mercy, in which attitude and tone he was followed by the rest of the crew as we called them from their hiding place.

Had we been disposed to do any unjust action, we had an opportunity of realizing a considerable sum of money, by carrying them to Cuba and selling them for slaves.

The temptation was great to men destitute of funds as we were; but our moral sense overcame the temptation, and we gave them their choice to proceed with us on our voyage, or expose themselves to the hazard of drowning by attempting to swim ashore. They accepted the latter proposition with much gratitude, and were soon swimming lustily for the shore, from which we were at the distance of more than a mile, where we saw them all safely arrive.

We felt some anxiety respecting the ability of the boy to swim so far; but, as he was desirous of going with them, two of our men took him by his arms and legs, and gave him a regular yo-hoi-ho heave; and we had the satisfaction of seeing the little fellow shaking the water from his curly pate upon the shore, before his companions had landed.

The negroes collected around them in great numbers after they landed, probably to hear their account of the transaction; and to obtain information concerning our intentions and destination.

We felt animated by our success. We found the boat in good order; and, with a fresh breeze, we made rapid progress. We found a plenty of provisions in the boat, with which, for the first time for five days, we abundantly satisfied our hunger.

It was now nearly dark, and we had got a considerable distance from the shore; but we continued to watch the movements of the negroes with anxiety, lest they should pursue us. After the negroes had held a short consultation together, we saw them all start off with great rapidity towards a point of land, under which we thought we could see something lying, that had the appearance of a vessel. As the negroes ran in that direction, we had no doubt that they had some plan in contemplation in relation to our capture. Our fears and conjectures were soon reduced to a matter of fact; for we had proceeded but a little distance farther, when we came in plain sight of a schooner at anchor. We could see the negroes rush on board of her, and could just discern, or our fears caused us to imagine it, the uplifted axe, which cut away the cable and liberated her from her moorings.

The schooner was soon under weigh, and sailing in a direction to cut us off; but we trusted that the approaching darkness would in a short time conceal us from the sight of our pursuers. As the schooner was a large object, compared with our little boat, we could see her long after we were invisible to them. After being satisfied of the course the schooner was taking, we thought the best way to avoid her would be to put about directly for Jamaica.

We sailed in this direction till we supposed that our enemy had got considerably past the course for us to pursue, when we again put about, and steered as directly as we were able for Cuba. The sails of our boat consisted of a small jib, and a sort of a square sail; and, the breeze being quite fresh, they were well filled, and our progress was rapid.

In the morning, when from the hill we discovered what we supposed to be Cuba, we ascertained its bearing from Jamaica, by our little compass; and now directed our course to the point, where we should find a place of safety.

Once, during the night, we were alarmed by a noise like the sound of voices, and thought that the schooner was near us. We saw her, or imagined so; but could not determine with certainty whether it was a reality or the result of our excited imaginations.

We sailed without interruption through the night, and, from the rapidity with which we had passed through the water, we concluded we could not be a great distance from the land. As soon as daylight approached, we espied the shore, and lost no time in making for it. Shortly after, we saw, at a considerable distance, the schooner, apparently steering for Jamaica. They discovered us, and altered their course directly for us. Their approach, however, excited no alarm in our minds now, for we were sure that we could run our boat on shore before they could come up with us. Their kind intentions were manifested in the compliment of a few salutes from a swivel,[14] which proved as harmless as the courtesy we endeavored to show them by a half of a dozen salutes from the musket, which had previously done us more faithful service. The schooner soon gave up the chase, "and left us alone in our glory."

As we approached the shore, we saw six or eight men running down towards us, and making signs for us to keep off, and to go round a point of land to the leeward. We were satisfied that their motive was friendly, as, at that part of the shore, a heavy surf was running, which would have made it very dangerous for us to have attempted to land.

After we had passed round the point, we lay to, till we were boarded by four or five Spaniards, who came off in a small boat. We knew as little of their language as they of ours; but, by a variety of gesticulations, and often repeating the words, America, Jamaica, Kingston, &c. we made them comprehend in some degree our circumstances.

[14] A swivel gun was a small cannon mounted upon a yoke fastened to the rail of a ship. Customarily they were one-pounders, although some were two-pounders.

They saw that we were in distress, and probably were not unwilling to appropriate our boat to their use.

It was easy for them to perceive by our looks that we had suffered much from fatigue and hunger; the last two days we had endured as much as human nature was capable of sustaining, and the effects were visible in our appearance. They took us on shore, carried us to a hut, where they placed before us a plentiful supply of pork and pease, together with a large bowl of beans. This was the first comfortable meal we had enjoyed since we left Kingston, and we enjoyed it in peace, without any fear of interruption.

We eat to our stomachs' content, and then were left alone to obtain some sleep, of which we were in great need, having been nearly as destitute of that, as we had been of food, for the last six days. We slept soundly till past noon.

I think I have never since enjoyed a more satisfactory meal or more refreshing sleep, than I did that day. No care for the future crossed our minds. Our dangers were passed, our object was accomplished. We felt ourselves free men. When we reflected upon the events of the last six days; the hazard, to which we had been exposed; the desperate encounters we had maintained; our hair-breadth escapes; our hearts were filled with gratitude to Him, who over-rules all things, and by whose goodness we had been preserved.

Enlisting in the British service I had never ceased to regret, from the moment I left the old *Jersey* prison-ship. There was something revolting to the mind of an American in the reflection of being subject to the authority of the oppressors of his country. It was a thraldom, from which I was determined to be liberated. My mind was occupied with this intention: danger and death were minor considerations, compared with the accomplishment of this object. It was accomplished; we awoke, and rejoiced that we were free. But much remained to be done; and although we were safe from pursuit, we were strangers in a strange land, far from our native soil, and ignorant of what means were in our power to return to our own country.

The people around appeared to be friendly, but still they looked upon us with suspicion; and, though they did not treat us like prisoners, they watched our motions with some degree of vigilance. When we went out of the hut, where we had been so hospitably entertained, we found a large collection of Spaniards, who, by the language common to man, questioned us respecting whence we came, who we were, and whither we wished to go. To all of these questions we replied as well as we were able, by gestures and grimaces, making ourselves as intelligible to them as they did to us.

It was evident to us, that our friends were desirous of our departure, and were willing to offer us every facility to favor their wishes. We reciprocated their good feelings, and were as anxious to leave them as they were to bid us farewell.

Pork, pease, and beans, were again set before us, upon which we made a sumptuous repast, and felt ourselves surprisingly recruited. Our friends then directed our attention to a small vessel, lying up a creek, close under the land, which was ready to sail for St. Domingo, now called Hayti. They engaged a passage for us in this vessel, which was of about fifty tons' burden, and rigged like a lugger.

We weighed anchor about sun-set, but, as it was foggy, our progress was at first rather slow. After a sail of three days, we approached the island of St. Domingo in the night, and lay off till the next day, when, the wind proving favorable, we run into port, and dropped anchor in the harbor of Cape François, now Cape Henri.

During this short voyage, we received much kind treatment from the captain and crew, being plentifully supplied with provisions, and permitted to enjoy as much rest as we desired.

With recovered strength and spirits, we prepared to leave the vessel; and, with gratitude to the captain for his kindness, and to God for his mercies, we went on board of the American frigate *Flora*, of thirty-two guns, commanded by Henry Johnson, esq. of Boston.

XIII

IN THE YEAR 1778, Count d'Estaing, with his fleet,
approached Newport, R. I. with the intention of
attacking the British, who were in possession of that
place.[15] The British destroyed their frigates in the
harbor, to prevent their falling into the hands of the
enemy. The *Orpheus*, *Lark*, *Juno*, and *Cerberus* frigates, they burned; the *Flora* and the *Falcon* they
sunk. The Americans afterwards raised the *Flora*,
and fitted her up for service against her former masters. This frigate I found anchored in the harbor of
Cape Henri.

The sight of the thirteen stripes and stars, floating over an American frigate, gave animation to our
thoughts and actions. We felt sure of safety and protection. With much exultation and satisfaction, we
stepped upon the deck of the *Flora*. We could
hardly realize that we were the same men, who, a
few days before, were fleeing through the woods of
Jamaica, like beasts of night, avoiding the light of
day, and afraid of the sight of a negro. When we
compared our present condition with what it had
been during the greater part of the past year; in

[15] In August, 1778, there was a Franco-American attempt
to drive the English out of Newport. The American land
forces were under the command of Major General John
Sullivan, while the French fleet was commanded by Comte
d'Estaing. When a British fleet appeared d'Estaing put
out to sea. The attack failed and d'Estaing was subject to
much criticism.

confinement on board of that "floating hell," the "*Old Jersey;*" in garrison, serving the enemy of our country, with feelings of disgust and despondency; fugitives from that enemy, under circumstances that rendered our escape almost hopeless, with the certainty of death in case of detection; when we thought of all this, and found ourselves standing erect, among our own countrymen, upon the deck of an American frigate, we almost doubted our personal identity: our feelings may be more easily imagined than described.

Captain Johnson received us kindly, and was willing to employ us for the voyage at a compensation of ten dollars per month; but, when my comrades were informed that the vessel was not going directly to Boston; that she would visit France first, and might stay there some time, they declined engaging in her service. Two of them belonged to Connecticut, one to Rhode-Island, and the other was an Irishman. They succeeded in finding a vessel that was bound to some port near home, and whose voyage would be less circuitous than that of the *Flora.* I was the only one of our little party, who had suffered so much together, who entered into the service of Captain Johnson. I was as anxious to get home as my companions; but there was a degree of safety on board of the *Flora*, which I could not expect on board of a merchant ship.

I likewise felt some desire of visiting France; and I entertained some hope that we might make some captures in the course of the voyage; for I had not yet rested long enough after my sufferings to cultivate the Christian spirit of "forgiveness to my enemies." I felt willing to encounter the hazard of an engagement, for an opportunity to pay off some old scores, which I fancied were then their due.

I received from our noble captain two months' wages in advance, and, being destitute of every thing necessary for the voyage, excepting the miserable clothes which I wore, I was permitted to go on shore to make the purchases that I thought requisite.

As my companions had determined not to engage in the service of the *Flora*, but to seek for a berth on board of some other vessel, I knew that I must experience the painful task of separation from those who were endeared to me as fellow-sufferers in afflictions and dangers. The ties of friendship, which united us, were too strong to be easily broken. The circumstances, which had engaged us in common cause, had created fraternal feeling in our breasts too deep to be soon obliterated. We concluded to grace our parting with a farewell supper. We adjourned to a public house, and gave directions for a sumptuous repast; and, while it was preparing, we regaled ourselves upon a few bottles of claret, in order to elevate our spirits to a proper degree, that the gloomy thoughts of our separation might not allow our supper to be a melancholy one. By the time the feast was prepared, our spirits were raised to a proper state for enjoyment; and a happier or more jolly set of fellows never assembled around a table, than we were that night.

The sufferings we had endured, and the dangers we had passed, were fruitful subjects for conversation. We eat and drank till a late hour, when we arose from the table, and, grasping each other by the hand and with feelings that touched our hearts, we said to each other, "God bless you—farewell." To me this was a final farewell to my companions; from that time to the present I have never seen one of them, nor have I ever heard what became of them.

As they were all older than myself, it is not probable that any of them are now among the living. If they are, I repeat the farewell wish, which I gave fifty-six years ago—"God bless you!"

The next day, after I had purchased what articles of clothing I thought necessary for the voyage, I went on board of the *Flora*, and reported myself ready for duty.

This ship, as I have observed, was formerly a British frigate, but, after she was raised by the Americans, she was fitted out as a letter-of-marque, and sent by her owners on the present voyage.

With mingled feelings of happiness, gratitude, and pride, I entered into the service of my country once more, and stepped with much satisfaction upon the deck of this fine ship. Captain Johnson was an excellent officer; very affable and courteous in his manners; and much beloved by his officers and crew. . . .

There were lying in the port of Cape-François, while we were there, several Spanish and French ships of war, in want of men, waiting till they could obtain their complement, with the intention of sailing in quest of the British fleet.

The Sunday previous to our sailing, I with several of the crew obtained permission to go on shore. It was customary then in foreign ports to allow the sailors to make use of Sunday as a day of recreation. While we were enjoying ourselves over a bottle of good wine in a public house, a large press-gang of Frenchmen suddenly entered, and, seizing upon all of us, hurried us off into their boat; and notwithstanding our protestations against this outrage upon Americans, conveyed us on board of a French seventy-four. We immediately made known to the captain that we belonged to the *Flora*, and demanded to be released. But he showed no disposition to comply with our demands, saying that he was in want of hands and that we should receive as good pay and treatment on board of his ship as in our own.

This was poor consolation for us. It was provoking as well as distressing to be thus imprisoned as it were, in sight of our own ship; but, having no communication with her, we could not give any information of our situation. We were aware that the combined fleet was to sail in days; and although we had no objections to fighting our old enemy the

British, we yet had some choice as it respected the company we fought in, and had but little desire to obey the orders of French officers, or to mingle our blood with that of their crew.

My desire to get away from this ship was as great as it had formerly been to escape from the British at Kingston; and the difficulty of effecting it appeared about as formidable. It was vain to regret, that I did not spend the sabbath on board of the *Flora*, instead of carousing at a public house on shore. My regret was sincere; and I resolved never to be guilty of such imprudence again, were I once more safe on board of our good ship.

Of our impressed party, consisting of four or five, not one could swim except myself. We conferred together, and came to the conclusion that the only chance we had for escape consisted in my attempting to swim in the night to the *Flora*, which lay about a quarter of a mile from the seventy-four. I had no fear of not being able to swim that distance; the only danger I apprehended was from the sharks, which were very abundant in those waters.

I agreed with my companions, that this appeared to be the only practicable method of escape; and, after some urging on their part, and some flattery of the honor I should gain by the achievement, I concluded to undertake it that night.

Late at night I went on deck, accompanied by one of my friends, and, finding the sentinel asleep, we went forward, and divesting myself of my jacket, but keeping on my hat, shirt, and trousers, I slid down by the cable quietly into the water, and struck out for the *Flora*.

Of all the dangers, to which I had been exposed in the course of my adventures, I consider this the greatest. The horror of mind I experienced, whilst swimming, is indescribable. My agitation was so great, that I wonder that I did not sink through fear of being devoured. I imagined a shark at my feet every time I threw them out. I exerted myself with so much vigor, that in a very short time I was alongside of the *Flora*, but in so exhausted a state, that I could hardly raise myself over the side of the boat, which floated alongside of the ship. I threw myself into the bottom, from which I was scarely able to move for some time.

After I had recovered a sufficient degree of strength, I ascended the side of the ship, and, finding no one on deck, I lay down in my wet clothes, and putting my hat under my head, slept soundly all night.

When I awoke in the morning, I found that I was unable to move in consequence of my clothes adhering to the pitch, which the heat of the climate caused to ooze from the seams in the deck. By using considerable exertion, and rolling one way and the other, I at length liberated myself from my confinement, and stood erect once more on the deck of an American ship.

I immediately communicated to Captain Johnson

the cause of my absence and the situation of my companions, and their great desire to be again on board of his ship, and the hazardous undertaking I had accomplished to give him information of the circumstances.

Captain Johnson immediately sent an officer with his boat, and demanded the release of his men. The captain of the French seventy-four gave them up and made many apologies, in the polite manner of a Frenchman, for "the mistake that was made in impressing his friends the Americans." Thus I had the satisfaction of being the instrument in restoring my countrymen to their ship, and of finding myself safe in the protection of our excellent commander.

Having taken in our loading of sugar, and every thing being ready for sea, we hoisted anchor, and set sail about the middle of May, 1782. The first few days after leaving the Cape, we had but little wind; afterwards we made good progress, and continued on our course without interruption for about a fortnight; when we fell in with a British brig from Liverpool, bound to New-York. We took possession of her, and, putting an officer and prize crew on board, ordered her for Boston, where she arrived. I afterwards received thirty dollars as my share of the prize-money.

We continued on our voyage, and, in eight days after, captured a large ship bound to Quebec, loaded with munitions of war and clothing for soldiers, a very valuable prize. She was ordered for Boston, but, unluckily for us, never arrived there, being afterwards recaptured, by a British ship of war, off the Banks of Newfoundland. Had she arrived safely at Boston, my share of the prize-money would have amounted to a considerable sum.

It was nearly three weeks after, when we arrived off the coast of France, and, having taken a pilot on board, our ship was carried up the Garonne to the city of Bordeaux, where, on account of the rapidity of the current, she was moored both head and stern.

Our ship was soon unloaded, and stripped of her sails and rigging, as preparatory to her being laid up till orders could be received from Boston. Part of the crew were paid off and discharged; the remainder, that chose, were permitted to remain on board upon small wages. Captain Johnson hired a house in the city, where he lived with his servants in a style becoming the dignity of the commander of a fine American ship.

As *Flora* was a fast-sailing vessel, our captain was in expectation of receiving orders from home to fit her out as a cruiser. In the hope of having another cruise, and anticipating an abundance of captures with the natural consequence resulting,—an enormous amount of prize-money,—I was willing to remain in the ship, with the expectation of being one of her favored crew. We remained at Bordeaux about nine months, and begun to grow impatient at not receiving any directions from home respecting our future operations. . . .

XIV

WE BEGAN to grow impatient with our long stay in France, and became anxious to return home. An end was soon put to our anxieties upon this subject. Early in the spring of the year 1783, news arrived of the peace, and that Great-Britain, after a contest of seven years, had acknowledged the Independence of the United States. This news ought to have produced as much joy and satisfaction among the Americans in Bordeaux, as it did among their fellow countrymen at home. But this news, so highly prized in the United States, produced much misery and distress among the seamen in foreign ports. A small number of them only were necessary to navigate the ships upon their return; the remainder were of course discharged, and left destitute of means to enable them to return to their own country. He considered himself fortunate, who could obtain a passage home for the labor he might perform, without receiving any other compensation for his services.

Our excellent captain, Johnson, made great exertions to procure passages for those of his crew, whom he did not wish to detain till he received orders respecting the future destination of his ship, and who were anxious to get home.

There happened at this time to be, on a visit at Bordeaux, the captains of two American brigs, lying at Nantes, bound for Boston, who were in want of hands. These gentlemen wished to obtain sixteen or eighteen American seamen, and Captain Johnson kindly offered to recommend me among that number.

We engaged in the service of these captains, and made a bargain with the captain of a French lugger to carry us to Nantes. We immediately repaired on board, and proceeded slowly down the river, as the current is so swift that it is necessary for a vessel to go down the river stern foremost, dragging an anchor all the time from her bows to retard her too rapid progress.

We were nearly three days in getting down the river, and about as much longer in our passage to Nantes.

Nantes, which held the second rank, after Bordeaux, as a commercial city, is on the right bank of the Loire. It is admired for the regularity of its streets, the elegance of its public buildings, and the magnificence of its quays.

The verdant banks of the river, and the many islands scattered in different directions, give Nantes a picturesque and beautiful appearance.

After our arrival at Nantes, we took lodgings at a boarding-house for a few days, until every thing was arranged for our reception on board of the brigs.

In a few days the vessels were loaded, and ready to sail. We weighed anchor, and set sail in April, 1783.

We were two days in getting down the river, and

anchored for a few days at Paimbœuf, a town situated on the left bank of the Loire, about thirty miles below Nantes.

We then weighed anchor, for the last time, with a joyful "Yeo-a-hoi," and set sail for our native land;—a land of freedom, where I anticipated, with emotions that cannot be described, the pleasure of meeting with relations and friends, from whom I had been so long absent, and where I hoped to enjoy the sweets of liberty without any thing "to molest or make me afraid." I had endured much hardship; encountered many dangers, on the ocean and upon the land; and I trust that I felt grateful for the support and protection I had experienced.

After all my wanderings, I found that I coveted rest, in my dear native land, more than all other things. In the morning of life, as I then was, full of health and strength and buoyant spirits, the idea of once more seeing home gave so much animation to my feelings, that I was enabled to perform my duties with a degree of alacrity scarcely equalled by any of the crew. Every little service I could perform was a pleasure to me, as I was conscious that it helped to forward my onward course to the object of all my wishes—*HOME*. . . .

Our voyage was a pleasant one, and nothing uncommon occurred, till we arrived on the American coast, when we fell in with six or eight British ships, bound to England.

Their decks were covered with the well-known

"red coats," who had survived the attempt to conquer our country.

As our flag of stripes and stars was conspicuously displayed, they knew that we were "Yankees," with whom they showed no desire to continue an acquaintance.

Our captain hailed them, to know "whence they were from, and whither bound?" but no answer was returned. Again he repeated his question; but his Yankee curiosity was not gratified. He once more put his trumpet to his mouth, and roared with a voice like thunder, "Go and be ——, we neither love nor fear you."

Our course was directed to Boston, and, shortly after our captain's friendly salutation, we anchored in Nantasket roads, and in a few days arrived in Boston.

I stepped ashore on Long-wharf, in the latter part of May, 1783, after an absence of about three years.

As soon as I could get released from the vessel, I visited my brother James, at Mr. Tuckerman's, where he had lived during my absence, to obtain information respecting my good mother and my brothers and sisters.

From him I received the pleasing intelligence, that the family were all in good health; but that my mother had given up all hope of ever seeing me again on earth. While walking over Boston Neck to Roxbury, where my mother still resided, my brother and I arranged a plan to introduce me to my mother as a sailor, who had just arrived from a foreign port, where he had seen her son Eben, and had some interesting information to communicate concerning him.

We soon arrived at the house, and I was formally introduced in the manner proposed. Time, hardship, and exposure to various climates, produced such an alteration in my personal appearance, that it is no wonder that the eye of maternal love could not recognize me. The good old lady received me very kindly, and manifested all the interest, which it is natural for a mother to feel towards one who has seen and conversed with a long-absent son.

After having conversed with her for some time, and endeavored to answer a multitude of questions, which soon grew too minute for my ingenuity to invent answers satisfactory to her, I could no longer conceal my impatience to make myself known, and exclaimed, as I arose to embrace her, "Mother, don't you know your son?"

Her joy may be more easily imagined, than described. I was at home. The alternate hopes and fears, that had so long agitated her mind, were now all over. She saw me alive and well. It was sufficient; she was satisfied and happy.

She shed tears of gratitude and joy, and we both blessed God that we were permitted to be united in a family circle once more. My four brothers and three sisters, as well as my mother, were all anxious

to hear me relate my adventures, with which I gratified their curiosity as soon as I was able, and which
produced many exclamations of fear, of horror, of
amazement, and joy. . . .

I returned to the service of Mr. Bosson,* and remained with him till I was twenty-one years of age,
when I established myself in business in my native
place, where I have remained to this day. I commenced business in the practice of the trade I had
learned; but, after a few years, I relinquished it, and
opened a store for the sale of crockery, glass, and
hard ware, in which business I continued till the
year 1837, when, finding my infirmities, especially
my deafness, increasing, I thought it time to quit all
active employment; and to ride at anchor the remainder of my days.

* My share of prize-money was eighty dollars; all of which
Mr. Bosson took. As I was his apprentice, and not free, he
had a legal right to it; but, as I remembered his agreement
was to give me one half of the prize-money and wages I was
to receive, and as he retained the whole, I thought I would
make an off-set by keeping about thirty dollars, my share of
the proceeds of a prize, taken while I was on board of the
Flora, and what wages I had not expended in France. This
money I loaned to a friend, who never found it convenient to
repay it. Such was the pecuniary result of my three years'
suffering. In justice to the memory of Mr. Bosson, it is proper for me to state, that he said that the prize-money he received became of no value in his hands, as he took it in the
paper currency of the times.

2

Albigence Waldo's Diary

*

A Surgeon at Valley Forge
1777–1778

Albigence Waldo's Diary

In a war when emotions fluctuated from the depths of despair to the heights of jubilation, Valley Forge became a synonym for the nadir of despondency. Among those who froze, starved, and cried bitter tears of frustration was a young military surgeon who bore the rather whimsical name of Albigence Waldo, a wit, amateur musician and artist, orator, and dedicated diarist.

Being born February 27, 1750, at Pomfret, Connecticut, Waldo studied medicine under the tutelage and personal supervision of Doctor John Spaulding of Canterbury. Young Waldo began his military career as a clerk in Captain Samuel McClelland's company from Woodstock. On July 6, 1775, he was commissioned as a surgeon's mate in Colonel Jedediah Huntington's Eighth Connecticut Regiment, a Continental, or unit in the regular army. The following September he was discharged because of ill health.

As soon as Waldo regained his strength the Connecticut Committee of War, on December 14, 1776, commissioned him as chief surgeon aboard the armed ship "Oliver Cromwell." Apparently the prospect of life at sea did not appeal to the doctor, for just a little over two weeks later, on

January 1, 1777, he accepted a commission as surgeon in the First Connecticut Infantry Regiment, commanded by Colonel Josiah Starr and Lieutenant Colonel Samuel Prentice. This regiment, raised largely in New London County, Connecticut, took the field on active service during that spring at Peekskill, New York.

The First Connecticut was ordered to join Washington in Pennsylvania in September, 1777. Waldo was able to practice his profession in treating the wounded of the regiment after the battle of Brandywine. That winter these troops were among those who suffered in the drafty log huts at a place called Valley Forge.

His chronic bad health once again forced Waldo's resignation from the army October 1, 1779. He died January 29, 1794. Waldo's diary has been published earlier in the old "Historical Magazine" in 1867 and again in the "Pennsylvania Magazine of History and Biography" in 1897.

After the British occupied Philadelphia in 1777, Washington sought a winter quarters that would allow him to keep an eye on the enemy. He selected Valley Forge, a tiny village at the junction of Valley Creek and the Schuylkill River. It was not a particularly good place for a winter quarters. In September, British foraging parties had stripped the area clean and had burned the forge that gave it its name. The long sloping hill on which the soldiers built their crude huts was bleak and windswept. The only local resource was an abundance of timber that could be used in the construction of shelters.

Johann Kalb, the Bavarian giant who had crossed the Atlantic to fight with the American rebels, was disgusted with the choice, declaring that "The idea of wintering in this desert can only have been put into the head of the commanding general by an interested speculator or a disaffected man." In his general orders to his troops, Washington explained that Valley Forge was "such a position as will enable us to most effectually prevent distress and to give the most extensive security. . . ." Despite its barrenness, the site was so naturally strong that an enemy could be defied and was so located as to provide a measure of control over the surrounding countryside.

But not even Washington suspected that Valley Forge would become a classic in the annals of human anguish. It remained for a twenty-seven-year-old surgeon to capture on paper the wretchedness of that winter. Albigence Waldo was a man of delicate sensibilities, responsive to the sufferings of his fellow man. Seldom has human misery been expressed in such eloquent terms. And *no historian can capture the sickness of heart and spirit as did Waldo when he allowed his pen to follow the musings of his mind.*

A Surgeon at Valley Forge

1777

November 10—Captain Lee,[1] of the Light Dragoons brought in Capt. Nichols of the English Packet whom he took prisoner at New Castle. I heard Capt. Nichols observe that one hour before he was taken he had the following reflections:—"His Majesty has made me commander of a fine ship—a packet too; I need not ever fight. I have nothing to do but transport gentlemen and ladies of the first rank. I have a fine stock of provisions aboard, hens, turkeys, geese, pigs, ducks, wine and cider. I have a good interest at home, and what is above all, an agreeable family. I am not troubled in my mind. In short, I've nothing to make me uneasy, and believe I am the happiest man in the world."

Capt. Nichols was now the unhappiest man in the world. His reflections were turned upon the vicissitudes of life, the sudden changes of fortune and the variety of events that may happen to a man in the course of a few hours. If we would set our reasons to work and believe what is undeniably true that there is no dependence to be put on the wiffling wind of

---

[1] Henry Lee (1756–1818), who won fame as the cavalry leader known as "Light Horse Harry." After the war he served in Congress and as governor of Virginia. He was the father of Robert E. Lee.

fortune, we could bear disappointments without anxiety. A man of the least observation will find every state changeable, and while he considers this mutability of time and things, he will be better prepared to undergo the misfortunes of life and the disappointments inseparable from it. When a disappointment overtakes us unguarded by such reflections, it often throws us into a fit of anger which vents itself on those connected with us in opprobrious words against the Providence of God.

An incessant cannonading at or near Red Bank this day. No salt to eat dinner with.

November 11, 12, 13 & 14—Nothing material happened.

November 15—An attack was made on Fort Mifflin[2] by 4 ships, 4 Batteries, & 1 Gally. Our People fired from Fort Mifflin 1 Battery, 12 Gallies & two Shearbacks or small ships. The firing was incessant all Day. Our people defended themselves with unparallel'd bravery amidst a continual storm of Balls 'till at length when Capt. Lee's[3] company of Artillery were almost all cut off, and a reinforcement had stood at the Guns till 9 o'clock in the evening the Garrison evacuated the fort, after having spiked up the Cannon. Capt. Stephen Brown was killed by

[2] Fort Mifflin, on Port Island on the Pennsylvania side of the Delaware River, covered one end of the line of obstructions denying passage of the stream to British men of war and supply vessels. The garrison had been subjected to an attack by British naval vessels since October 10.

[3] James Lee of Philadelphia, an artillery captain.

a shot from the round-top of a Ship that had hauled up in pistol shot of the Fort.

Mem.—Fort Mifflin was a Burlesque upon the art of Fortification.

November 19—The Boston and Hampshire Regiments began to join the Grand Army. This Day Huntington's Brigade consisting of Prentice's, Bradley's, & Swift's, march'd for Red Bank, which the Garrison Evacuated before we arrived. Greene's Division next day march'd for the same place, who, with Huntington's Brigade & the Garrison consisting of Varnum's Brigade[4] met at Mount Holly 5 miles east of Burlington, where we Encamped till the Evening of the 25th. Mount Holly—so call'd from a little Mount nigh the town—is a Compact & Pleasant Village, having a great proportion of handsome women therein. Near this Town in a Wood, a Hermit has dwelt these 27 years, living on Bread and water. His bed is a hole dug in the ground about one foot and a half below the surface, and

[4] The brigade of Brigadier General Jedediah Huntington consisted of the First, Fifth, and Seventh Connecticut regiments of the Continental line, commanded by Lieutenant Colonel Samuel Prentiss, Colonel Philip Burr Bradley, and Colonel Herman Swift. The brigade of Brigadier General James Mitchell Varnum was made up of the Rhode Island Continentals. The division was commanded by Major General Nathanael Greene of Rhode Island. The Americans had erected Fort Mercer at Red Bank, New Jersey, opposite Fort Mifflin. Fort Mercer was defended by a garrison under Colonel Christopher Greene. They had driven off an attack by 2,000 Hessians under Colonel von Donop on October 22, 1777. The fall of Fort Mifflin made Fort Mercer untenable.

cover'd at pleasure with a board—over this is built a small bark hut hardly big enough for a man to sit up in. When he goes to bed he crawls into his hut and at the further end slips into his hole which he calls his grave, drawing over the Board and goes to sleep. He crawls night and morning on his hands and knees about two rods to a particular tree to pray. He says he was warned of God in a remarkable Dream when he first came to America to take this course of Life. He has many Latin and other Books in his lonely Cell, and is said to write considerably. He kisses every man's hand that visits him and thankfully accepts of what is gave him, except Money, which he refuses. His Beard is done up in a loose club under his chin, he is small of stature and speaks very fast, he talks but little English—chiefly German or Latin. He says he shall come out purified & live like other folks if he continues in this State till he is eighty. He says he often wishes for Death, being frequently afflicted with pains of Body by this method of life. He never goes near a fire in the coldest time. Much is said about the reasons of his doing pennance in this manner, but chiefly that he murdered his own sister, and that he killed a Gentleman in a Duel while an officer in the French Service. He was also in the German Service among his countrymen the Germans.

November 25—In the Evening we march for Haddonfield (not far from Red Bank) where we arrived in the morning of

November 26—Lay in the Forest of Haddonfield, cold and uncomfortable. Two Hessian deserters came in who declar'd our little parties had kill'd a number of the Enemy—15 prisoners were bro't in, 2 women.

November 27—Return'd to Mount Holly. Same Day Greene's Division and Glover's Brigade (who had arriv'd from the Northward 2 Days before) march to Burlington. Morgan with his Riflemen[5] were left with the militia to harrass the Enemy as they were Recrossing the River from Red Bank to the City.

November 28—The remainder of us marched to Burlington. P.M. the rear of the army crossed over to Bristol.

A Storm prevented the Baggage going over this Night, which prevented Dr. L. & myself also crossing with our horses.

November 29—Storm increas'd. About one p.m. An alarm was made by a report that the enemy were within 15 minutes march of the Town to take the Baggage. Those of us who had horses rode up to Burdentown. The Baggage and the Sick were all hurried out of Town the same way, but had not got 2 miles before they were turn'd back on its being a false Alarm.

[5]Brigadier General John Glover (1732–1797) of Marblehead, Massachusetts. The Morgan mentioned is Daniel Morgan (1736–1802), who had just returned from the northern army. He and his riflemen had played a significant role in the victory at Saratoga.

For the sake of good living however Dr. L.,[6] Parson E.[7] & myself went to Burdentown up the River, liv'd well & cross'd over to Winsor next Day, and arrived at Bristol in the Evening when I had my Shoes and Silver Buckles stole. Dr. L. had a valuable Great Coat stole the Day before at Burlington.

December 1—We marched on to Head Quarters [Whitemarsh] and our Division (McDougals) encamped on the Left of the Second Line. Our former Station was in the Centre of the Front Line. Here Huts of sticks & leaves shelter'd us from the inclementcy of the Weather and we lay pretty Quiet until

December 5—At 3 o'clock a.m. the Alarm Guns were fired and Troops immediately paraded at their several Alarm posts. The Enemy were approaching with their Whole Strength to give us Battle. Nothing further remarkable ensued this Day—at Night our Troops lay on their Arms, the Baggage being all sent away except what a man might run or fight with.

December 6—The Enemy forming a Line from towards our right to the extremity of our left upon an opposite long height to ours in a Wood. Our men were under Arms all Day and this Night also, as our Wise General was determined not to be attack'd Napping.

December 7—Alarm given. Troops on their several posts. Towards Noon Col. Ch. Webb's Reg[t] were

[6] Probably Surgeon Samuel Lee of the Connecticut line.
[7] Chaplain John Ellis of the Connecticut line.

partly surrounded and Attack' on the Right of the Army. They being overpower'd by Numbers, retreated with loss—the brave Capt. Walbridge was wounded in the head—Lieut. Harrris kill'd.

A scattering fire through to the left soon began & continued a few minutes, till our Piquets ran in. The firing soon ceased on the Right & continued on the Left, as tho' a General Attack was meant to begin there. On this supposition the Left were Reinforced. But a scattering fire was kept up by Morgan's Battalion, at Intervals all Day, and concluded with a little skirmish at Sun Set. Our Troops lay on their Arms this night also. Some firing among the Piquets in the night.[8]

December 8—All at our Several Posts. Provisions & Whiskey very scarce. Were Soldiers to have plenty of Food & Rum, I believe they would Storm Tophet. Our Lines were on a long high hill extending about three Miles—all Man'd. An Abettes[9] in front from Right to Left—another in the rear of the Left, with a Cross Abettee near the Extremety.

Five men from each Reg^t in Varnum's & Huntington's Brigades as Volunteers join'd Morgan's

[8] Having learned Washington planned to leave Whitemarsh, General William Howe led a sortie out of Philadelphia to hit the Americans on the move. After several days of scuffling, Howe decided that Washington's position was too strong and fell back to Philadelphia.

[9] An abatis is a line of felled trees, the branches towards the enemy sharpened. Its purpose was to discourage infantry and cavalry charges, much like barbed wire in modern warfare.

Rifle Men to Harrass the Enemy, and excite an Attack. Some Reg^t were ordered to march out if an Attack should begin in earnest. This Afternoon a small Skirmish happen'd near the Enemies lines against our left. Towards Night the Enemy fired some Cannon against our Right & 2 against our left. Their horse appear'd to be busily moving. In the Evening there were but two spots of fires in the Enemies Camp. One against our Park (or main center); the other against the extremity of our Left, when the evening before they extended from almost our Right to our Left. At 12 o'clock at Night our Reg^t, with Sixteen more were Ordered to parade immediately before his Excellencies Quarters under Command of Sullivan & Wayne.[10] We were there by One, when Intelligence came that the Enemy had made a precipitate retreat and was safely got into the City. We were all Chagrin'd at this, as we were more willing to Chase them in Rear, than meet such Sulkey Dogs in Front. We were now remanded back with several draughts of Rum in our frozen bellies, which made us so glad we all fell asleep in our open huts, nor experienced the coldness of the Night 'till we found ourselves much stiffened by it in the Morning.

December 9—We came from within the breastworks, Where we had been coop'd up four tedious Days, with Cloaths & Boots on Night and Day, and resumed our old Hutts East of the Breastwork. The

[10] Major Generals John Sullivan and Anthony Wayne.

rest of the Army Chiefly had their huts within the Lines. We are insensible what we are capable of enduring till we are put to the test. To endure hardships with a good grace we must allways think of the following Maxim: "Pain succeeds Pleasure, & Pleasure succeeds Pain."

December 10—Lay still.

December 11—At four o'clock the Whole Army were Order'd to March to Swedes Ford on the River Schuylkill, about 9 miles N. W. of Chestnut Hill, and 6 from White Marsh our present Encampment. At sun an hour high the whole were mov'd from the Lines and on their march with baggage. This Night encamped in a Semi circle nigh the Ford. The enemy had march'd up the West side of Schuylkill—Potter's[11] Brigade of Pennsylvania Militia were already there, & had several skirmishes with them with some loss on his side and considerable on the Enemies. An English Serj. deserted to us this Day, and inform'd that Webb's Reg^t kill'd many of their men on 7th, that he himself took Webb's Serj. Major who was a former Deserter from them, and was to be hanged this day.

I am prodigious Sick & cannot get any thing comfortable—what in the name of Providence am I to do with a fit of Sickness in this place where nothing appears pleasing to the Sicken'd Eye & nausiating Stomach. But I doubt not Providence will find out a way for my relief. But I cannot eat Beef if I

[11] Brigadier General James Potter.

starve, for my stomach positively refuses to entertain such Company, and how can I help that?

December 12—A Bridge of Waggons made across the Schuylkill last Night consisting of 36 waggons, with a bridge of Rails between each. Some skirmishing over the River. Militia and dragoons brought into Camp several Prisoners. Sun Set—We were order'd to march over the River—It snows—I'm Sick. Eat nothing—No Whiskey—No Forage—Lord—Lord—Lord. The Army were 'till Sun Rise crossing the River—some at the Waggon Bridge & some at the Raft Bridge below. Cold & uncomfortable.

December 13—The Army march'd three miles from the West side the River and encamp'd near a place call'd the Gulph[12] and not an improper name neither, for this Gulph seems well adapted by its situation to keep us from the pleasures & enjoyments of this World, or being conversant with any body in it. It is an excellent place to raise the Ideas of a Philosopher beyond the glutted thoughts and Reflexions of an Epicurian. His Reflexions will be as different from the Common Reflexions of Mankind as if he were unconnected with the world, and only conversant with immaterial beings. It cannot be that our Superiors are about to hold consultations with Spirits infinitely beneath their Order, by bringing us into these utmost regions of the Terr-

[12]The Gulph on Gulf Creek was so-called "on account of a remarkable chasm in the hills." Now West Coshocken, Pennsylvania.

aqueous Sphere. No, it is, upon consideration for many good purposes since we are to Winter here— 1st There is plenty of Wood & Water. 2dly There are but few families for the soldiery to Steal from— tho' far be it from a Soldier to Steal. 4ly There are warm sides of Hills to erect huts on. 5ly They will be heavenly Minded like Jonah when in the Belly of a Great Fish. 6ly They will not become home Sick as is sometimes the Case when Men live in the Open World—since the reflections which will naturally arise from their present habitation, will lead them to the more noble thoughts of employing their leisure hours in filling their knapsacks with such materials as may be necessary on the Journey to another Home.

December 14—Prisoners & Deserters are continually coming in. The Army which has been surprisingly healthy hitherto, now begins to grow sickly from the continued fatigues they have suffered this Campaign. Yet they still show a spirit of Alacrity & Contentment not to be expected from so young Troops. I am Sick—discontented—and out of humour. Poor food—hard lodging—Cold Weather—fatigue—Nasty Cloaths—nasty Cookery—Vomit half my time—smoak'd out of my senses—the Devil's in't—I can't Endure it—Why are we sent here to starve and Freeze—What sweet Felicities have I left at home; A charming Wife—pretty children—Good Beds—good food—good Cookery—all agreeable— all harmonious. Here all Confusion—smoke &

Cold—hunger & filthyness—A pox on my bad luck. There comes a bowl of beef soup—full of burnt leaves and dirt, sickish enough to make a Hector spue—away with it Boys—I'll live like the Chameleon upon Air. Poh! Poh! crys Patience within me— you talk like a fool. Your being sick Covers your mind with a Melanchollic Gloom, which makes everything about you appear gloomy. See the poor Soldier, when in health—with what cheerfulness he meets his foes and encounters every hardship—if barefoot, he labours thro' the Mud & Cold with a Song in his mouth extolling War & Washington—if his food be bad, he eats it notwithstanding with seeming content—blesses God for a good Stomach and Whistles it into digestion.

But harkee Patience, a moment—There comes a Soldier, his bare feet are seen thro' his worn out Shoes, his legs nearly naked from the tatter'd remains of an only pair of stockings, his Breeches not sufficient to cover his nakedness, his Shirt hanging in Strings, his hair dishevell'd, his face meagre; his whole appearance pictures a person forsaken & discouraged. He comes, and crys with an air of wretchedness & despair, I am Sick, my feet lame, my legs are sore, my body cover'd with this tormenting Itch—my Cloaths are worn out, my Constitution is broken, my former Activity is exhausted by fatigue, hunger & Cold, I fail fast I shall soon be no more! and all the reward I shall get will be—"Poor Will is dead." People who live at home in Luxury and

Ease, quietly possessing their habitations, Enjoying their Wives & families in peace, have but a very faint Idea of the unpleasing sensations, and continual Anxiety the Man endures who is in a Camp, and is the husband and parent of an agreeable family. These same People are willing we should suffer every thing for their Benefit & advantage, and yet are the first to Condemn us for not doing more!

December 15—Quiet. Eat Pessimmens, found myself better for their Lenient Opperation. Went to a house, poor & small, but good food within—eat too much from being so long Abstemious, thro' want of palatables. Mankind are never truly thankfull for the Benefits of life, until they have experienc'd the want of them.

The Man who has seen misery knows best how to enjoy good. He who is always at ease & has enough of the Blessings of common life is an Impotent Judge of the feelings of the unfortunate. . . .

December 16—Cold Rainy Day, Baggage ordered over the Gulph of our Division, which were to march at Ten, but the baggage was order'd back and for the first time since we have been here the Tents were pitch'd, to keep the men more comfortable. Good morning Brother Soldier (says one to another) how are you? All wet I thank'e, hope you are so (says the other).

The Enemy have been at Chestnut Hill Opposite to us near our last encampment the other side Schuylkill, made some Ravages, kill'd two of our

Horsemen, taken some prisoners. We have done the like by them. . . .

December 18—Universal Thanksgiving—a Roasted pig at Night. God be thanked for my health which I have pretty well recovered. How much better should I feel, were I assured my family were in health. But the same good Being who graciously preserves me, is able to preserve them & bring me to the ardently wish'd for enjoyment of them again.

NOTE: Rank & Precedence make a good deal of disturbance & confusion in the American Army. The Army are poorly supplied with Provision, occasioned it is said by the Neglect of the Commissary of Purchases. Much talk about discharges among Officers. Money has become of too little consequence. Congress have not made Commissions valuable Enough. Heaven avert the bad consequences of these things!![13]

*　　*　　*　　*　　*　　*　　*　　*

up the Bristol Road & so got out unnoticed. He inform'd that Cornwallis was embark'd for England, and that some High-landers had gone to N. York for Winter Quarters.

There is nothing to hinder Parties of the like kind above mention'd, continually coming out between Delaware and Schuylkill, and plundering and destroying the Inhabitants.

Our brethren who are unfortunately Prisoners in Philadelphia meet with the most savage and inhu-

[13] Here part of the original manuscript was missing.

mane treatments that Barbarians are Capable of inflicting. Our Enemies do not knock them in the head or burn them with torches to death, or flay them alive, or gradually dismember them till they die, which is customary among Savages & Barbarians. No, they are worse by far. They suffer them to starve, to linger out their lives in extreem hunger. One of these poor unhappy men, drove to the last extreem by the rage of hunger, eat his own fingers up to the first joint from the hand, before he died. Others eat the Clay, the Lime, the Stones of the Prison Walls. Several who died in the Yard had pieces of Bark, Wood, Clay & Stones in their mouths, which the ravings of hunger had caused them to take in for food in the last Agonies of Life! "These are thy *mercies*, O Britain!"

December 21—[Valley Forge.] Preparations made for hutts. Provisions Scarce. Mr. Ellis went homeward—sent a Letter to my Wife. Heartily wish myself at home, my Skin & eyes are almost spoil'd with continual smoke. A general cry thro' the Camp this Evening among the Soldiers, "No Meat! No Meat!"—the Distant vales Echo'd back the melancholly sound—"No Meat! No Meat!" Immitating the noise of Crows & Owls, also, made a part of the confused Musick.

What have you for your Dinners Boys? "Nothing but Fire Cake[14] & Water, Sir." At night, "Gentle-

[14] Fire cakes were thin cakes of flour and water baked on hot stones.

men the Supper is ready." What is your Supper Lads? "Fire Cake & Water, Sir." Very poor beef has been drawn in our Camp the greater part of this season. A Butcher bringing a Quarter of this kind of Beef into Camp one day who had white Buttons on the knees of his breeches, a Soldier cries out— "There, there Tom is some more of your fat Beef, by my soul I can see the Butcher's breeches buttons through it."

December 22—Lay excessive Cold & uncomfortable last Night—my eyes are started out from their Orbits like a Rabbit's eyes, occasion'd by a great Cold & Smoke.

What have you got for Breakfast, Lads? "Fire Cake & Water, Sir." The Lord send that our Commissary of Purchases may live [on] Fire Cake & Water, 'till their glutted Gutts are turned to Pasteboard.

Our Division are under Marching Orders this morning. I am ashamed to say it, but I am tempted to steal Fowls if I could find them, or even a whole Hog, for I feel as if I could eat one. But the Impoverish'd Country about us, affords but little matter to employ a Thief, or keep a Clever Fellow in good humour. But why do I talk of hunger & hard usage, when so many in the World have not even fire Cake & Water to eat.

The human mind is always poreing upon the gloomy side of Fortune, and while it inhabits this lump of Clay, will always be in an uneasy and fluc-

VALLEY FORGE, *a Nineteenth-century Impression*

From James Thacher's, *Military Journal of the American Revolution*, 1862

tuating State, produced by a thousand Incidents in common Life, which are deemed misfortunes, while the mind is taken off from the nobler pursuit of matters in Futurity. The sufferings of the Body naturally gain the Attention of the Mind, and this Attention is more or less strong, in greater or lesser souls, altho' I believe that Ambition & a high Opinion of Fame, makes many People endure hardships and pains with that fortitude we after times Observe them to do. On the other hand, a despicable opinion of the enjoyments of this Life, by a continued series of Misfortunes, and a long acquaintance with Grief, induces others to bear afflictions with becoming serenity and Calmness.

It is not in the power of Philosophy however, to convince a man he may be happy and Contented if he will, with a *Hungry Belly*. Give me Food, Cloaths, Wife & Children, kind Heaven! and I'll be as contented as my Nature will permit me to be.

This Evening a Party with two field pieces were order'd out. At 12 of the Clock at Night, Providence sent us a little Mutton, with which we immediately had some Broth made, & a fine Stomach for same. Ye who Eat Pumkin Pie and Roast Turkies, and yet Curse fortune for using you ill, Curse her no more, least she reduce your Allowance of her favours to a bit of Fire Cake, & a draught of Cold Water, & in Cold Weather too.

December 23—The Party that went out last night not Return'd to Day. This evening an excellent

Player on the Violin in that soft kind of Musick,
which is so finely adapted to stirr up the tender
Passions, while he was playing in the next Tent to
mine, these kind of soft Airs it immediately called
up in remembrance all the endearing expressions,
the Tender Sentiments, the sympathetic friendship
that has given so much satisfaction and sensible
pleasure to me from the first time I gained the heart
& affections of the tenderest of the Fair. A thousand agreeable little incidents which have Occurr'd
since our happy connection, and which would have
pass'd totally unnoticed by such who are strangers
to the soft & sincere passion of Love, were now
recall'd to my mind, and filled me with these tender
emotions, and Agreeable Reflections, which cannot
be described, and which in spite of my Philosophy
forced out the sympathetic tear. I wish'd to have the
Musick Cease, and yet dreaded its ceasing, least I
should loose sight of these dear Ideas, which gave
me pain and pleasure at the same instant. Ah Heav-
en why is it that our harder fate so often deprives us
of the enjoyment of what we most wish to enjoy this
side of thy brighter realms. There is something in
this strong passion of Love far more agreeable than
what we can derive from any of the other Passions
and which Duller Souls & Cheerless minds are insensible of, & laugh at—let such fools laugh at me.

December 24—Party of the 22d not returned.
Hutts go on Slowly—Cold & Smoke make us fret.
But mankind are always fretting, even if they have

more than their proportion of the Blessings of Life. We are never Easy, allways repining at the Providence of an Allwise & Benevolent Being, Blaming Our Country or faulting our Friends. But I don't know of any thing that vexes a man's Soul more than hot smoke continually blowing into his Eyes, & when he attempts to avoid it, is met by a cold and piercing Wind.

December 25, Christmas—We are still in Tents—when we ought to be in huts—the poor Sick, suffer much in Tents this cold Weather. But we now treat them differently from what they used to be at home, under the inspection of Old Women and Doct. Bolus Linctus. We give them Mutton & Grogg and a Capital Medicine once in a While, to start the Disease from its foundation at once. We avoid Piddling Pills, Powders, Bolus's Linctus's Cordials and all such insignificant matters whose powers are Only render'd important by causing the Patient to vomit up his money instead of his disease. But very few of the sick Men Die.

December 26—Party of the 22d not Return'd. The Enemy have been some Days the west Schuylkill from Opposite the City to Derby. Their intentions not yet known. The City is at present pretty Clear of them. Why don't his Excellency rush in & retake the City, in which he will doubtless find much Plunder? Because he knows better than to leave his Post and be catch'd like a d——d fool cooped up in the City. He has always acted wisely hitherto. His conduct when closely scrutinised is uncensurable. Were his Inferior Generals as skillfull as himself, we should have the grandest Choir of Officers ever God made. Many Country Gentlemen in the interior parts of the States who get wrong information of the Affairs & state of our Camp, are very much Surprized at G Washington's delay to drive off the Enemy, being falsely inform'd that his Army consists of double the Number of the Enemy's[15]—such wrong information serves not to keep up the spirit of the People, as they must be by and by undeceiv'd to their no small disappointment;—it brings blame on his Excellency, who is deserving of the greatest encomiums; it brings disgrace on the Continental Troops, who have never evidenced the least backwardness in doing their duty, but on the contrary, have cheerfully endur'd a long and very fatigueing Campaign. 'Tis true they have fought but little this Campaign; which is not owing to any Unwillingness in Officers or Soldiers, but for want of convenient Opportunities, which have not offer'd themselves this Season; tho' this may be contradicted by many; but Impartial Truth in future History will clear up these points, and reflect lasting honour on the Wisdom & prudence of G^{enl} Washington. The greatest Number of Continental Troops that have been with his Excell^y this Campaign, never consisted of more than Eleven thousand; and the greatest Number of Militia in the field at Once were not more than

[15] At this time, 2,898 men were reported as unfit for duty.

2000. Yet these accounts are exaggerated to 50 or 60,000. Howe, by the best, and most authentic Accounts has never had less than 10,000. If then, Gen Washington, by Opposing little more than an equal Number of young Troops, to Old Veterans has kept his Ground in general, Cooped them up in the City, prevented their making any considerable inroads upon him, Killed and wounded a very considerable number of them in different Skirmishes, and made many proselytes to the Shrine of Liberty by these little successes, and by the prudence, calmness, sedateness & wisdom with which he facilitates all his Opperations. This being the case, and his not having wantonly thrown away the lives of his Soldiers, but reserved them for another Campaign (if another should Open in the Spring) which is of the utmost consequence This then cannot be called an Inglorious Campaign. If he had risk'd a General Battle, and should have proved unsuccessfull, what in the name of Heaven would have been our case this Day. Troops are raised with great difficulty in the Southern States, many Regiments from these States do not consist of one hundred men. What then was the grand Southern Army before the N. England Troops joined them and if this Army is Cut off where should we get another as good. General Washington has doubtless considered these matters & his conduct this Campaign has certainly demonstrated his prudence & Wisdom.

This Evening, cross'd the Schuylkill with D^r

Col[16]—eat plenty of Pessimmens which is the most lenient, Sub Acid & Subastringent fruit, I believe that grows.

December 27—My horse shod. A Snow. Lodg'd at a Welchman's this Night, return'd to Camp in the morning of 28th. Snow'd last Night.

December 28—Yesterday upwards of fifty Officers in Gen Greene's Division resigned their Commissions—Six or Seven of our Regiment are doing the like to-day. All this is occasion'd by Officers Families being so much neglected at home on account of Provisions. Their Wages will not by considerable, purchase a few trifling Comfortables here in Camp, & maintain their families at home, while such extravagant prices are demanded for the common necessaries of Life—What then have they to purchase Cloaths and other necessaries with? It is a Melancholly reflection that what is of the most universal importance, is most universally neglected—I mean keeping up the Credit of Money.

The present Circumstances of the Soldier is better by far than the officers—for the family of the Soldier is provided for at the public expence if the Articles they want are above the common price— but the Officer's family, are obliged not only to beg in the most humble manner for the necessaries of Life,—but also to pay for them afterwards at the most exorbitant rates—and even in this manner,

[16] Probably Surgeon Noah Coleman of the Connecticut line.

many of them who depend entirely on their Money, cannot procure half the material comforts that are wanted in a family—this produces continual letters of complaint from home. When the Officer has been fatiguing thro' wet & cold and returns to his tent where he finds a letter directed to him from his Wife, fill'd with the most heart aching tender Complaints, a Woman is capable of writing—Acquainting him with the incredible difficulty with which she procures a little Bread for herself & Children—and finally concluding with expressions bordering on dispair, of procuring a sufficiency of food to keep soul & Body together through the Winter—that her money is of very little consequence to her—that she begs of him to consider that Charity begins at home—and not suffer his family to perish with want, in the midst of plenty. When such, I say—is the tidings they constantly hear from their families—What man is there—who has the least regard for his family—whose soul would not shrink within him? Who would not be disheartened from persevering in the best of Causes—the Cause of his Country,—when such discouragements as these ly in his way, which his Country might remedy if they would?

December 28—Building our Hutts.

December 29—Continued the Work. Snow'd all day pretty briskly—The party of the 22d return'd—lost 18 men, who were taken prisoners by being decoyed by the Enemies Light Horse who brought up the Rear, as they Repass'd the Schuylkill to the City. Our party took 13 or 14 of their Horsemen. The Enemy came out to plunder—& have strip'd the Town of Derby of even all its Household furniture. Our party were several times mixed with the Enemy's horse—not knowing them from our Connecticut Light Horse—their Cloaks being alike.

So much talk about discharges among the Officers—& so many are discharged—his Excellency lately expressed his fears of being left Alone with the Soldiers only. Strange that our Country will not exert themselves for his support, and save so good— so great a Man from entertaining the least anxious doubt of their Virtue and perseverance in supporting a Cause of such unparallel'd importance!!

All Hell couldn't prevail against us, If Heaven continues no more than its former blessings—and if we keep up the Credit of our Money which has now become of the last consequence. If its Credit sinks but a few degrees more, we shall then repent when 'tis too late—& cry out for help when no one will appear to deliver. We who are in Camp, and depend on our Money entirely to procure the comforts of life—feel the Importance of this matter—He who is hording it up in his Chest, thinks little more of it than how he shall procure more.

December 30—Eleven Deserters came in to-day— some Hessians & some English—one of the Hes took an Ax in his hand & cut away the Ice of the Schuylkill which was $1\frac{1}{2}$ inches thick & 40 Rod wide and waded through to our Camp—he was ½ an hour in the Water. They had a promise when they engag'd that the war would be ended in one year—they were now tired of the Service.

Sir Wm Askins commanded the 8000 who were out over the Schuylkill the Other Day—but part of two Brigades were left in the City. Cold Weather. Hutts go on moderately—very cold lying in Tents—beyond what one can think.

December 31—Adjutant Selden learn'd me how to Darn Stockings—to make them look like knit work.

Valley Forge, Dec. 31st, 1777.
Doct. Waldo Surgeon of Col. Prentices Reg^t,
is recommended for a Furlow.
J. HUNTINGTON, B. General.

Apply'd with the above for a furlow, to Doct. Cochran,[17] who reply'd, "I'm willing to oblige every Gentleman of the Faculty, but some of the Boston Surgeons have by taking an underhand method of getting furlows, occasion'd a Complaint to be log'd with his Excellency, who has positively forbid my giving any furlows at present. We shall soon have regimental Hospitals erected—and general Ones to receive the superabundant Sick from them;—if you will tarry till such regulations are made—you will have an honourable furlow, and even now—I will, if you desire it—recommend you to his Excellency for

[17] Dr. John Cochran (1730–1807) at this time was Physician and Surgeon General of the Middle Department. In 1780 he became Chief Physician and Surgeon of the Army.

one—but desire you would stay a little while longer—and in the mean time, recommend to me some
young Surgeon for a Regiment, and I will immediately appoint him to a chief Surgeoncy from your
recommendation—I shall remember the rascals who
have us'd me ill."

I concluded to stay—& immediately set about
fixing accommodations for the Sick &c. &c.

We got some Spirits and finish'd the Year with a
good Drink & thankfull hearts in our new Hutt,
which stands on an Eminence that overlooks the
Brigade, & in sight of the Front Line. The Major
and Commissary Little are to live with us which
makes our Hutt Head Quarters.

In the Evening I joyfully received a Letter from
my good and loving Wife. The pleasure and satisfaction a man enjoys upon hearing of the health &
peace of a Friend, and more especially of a Wife, on
whose affections & peace his own happiness depends, is a greater pleasure than . . .

1778

January 1, New Year—I am alive. I am well. Hutts go on briskly, and our Camp begins to appear like a spacious City.

A party of our Army at Wilmington took a Ship in the Delaware from New York tother day, in which were a Number of Officers Wifes and about 70 or 80 men.

His Excellency Issued an Order this day that No one in the Army should have a new Coat made without first obtaining a pattern. . . .

Nothing tends to the establishment of the firmest Friendship like Mutual Sufferings which produces mutual Intentions and endeavours for mutual Relief which in such cases are equally shar'd with pleasure and satisfaction—in the course of this, each heart is laid open to full view—the similar passions in each, approximate themselves by a certain impulsive sympathy, which terminates in lasting esteem.

Bought an embroidered Jacket.

How much we affect to appear of consequence by a superfluous Dress,—and yet Custom—(that law which none may fight against) has rendered this absolutely necessary & commendable. An Officer frequently fails of being duly noticed, merely from the want of a genteel Dress;—and if joined to this, he has a bungling Address,—his situation is render'd very disagreeable. Neatness of Dress, void of unnecessary superfluities is very becoming—and discovers a man at least to have some Ambition—without which he will never make any figure in life. A man Appears to much greater advantage, especially among strangers, with a genteel Dress, which will naturally prepossess the Company in his favour, before they hear him speak. In this way,—even the fool may pass for a man of consequence—A man ought always to dress according to his business let his Abilities be what they will;—for if his Business is not sufficient to support a Credible appearance in the world, let him discontinue it and undertake some other branch.

But these are trifles not to be compared with Virtue and good Sense: by these is the road to true fame & Glory,—by these we walk thro' the world with the least hazzard—and obtain that peace of mind; that variety of agreeable Reflection—and that esteem among the Virtuous & Amiable, which the Vicious Fool is a stranger to.

January 3—Our Hutt, or rather our Hermits Cell, goes on briskly, having a short allowance of Bread this morning we divided it with great precision, eat our Breakfast with thankful hearts for the little we had, took care of the Sick, according to our dayly practice, and went to Work on our little humble Cottage. Now ye poets give me my Wife & Children, with your daisies, your Roses, your Tuleps and your other insignificant poetical materials, & I believe I should be pretty contented in this humble Cottage which the muses have so often described.

Another Ship was taken from the Enemy this Week, the lading taken out & the Ship burnt. The other Ship mention'd New Years day, was loaded with Officers Baggage and Medicines, with other valuable matters, & Cloathing for 2000 men Compleat. . . .

Fresh Beef and Flour make me perfectly Sick, especially as we have no Spirits to drink with it;—but others stand it, so must I.

To day his Excellency in Orders acquainted the Troops of the Congress's high approbation of their spirited perseverance and good Conduct this Campaign, that Rations should be raised monthly in proportion to the rise of the Articles of life, that the Congress were exerting themselves to supply the Commissary, and Cloathiers Departments, with a greater quantity of better Stores, than hitherto, that the Troops may be Supply'd with a greater quantity of Provision than they have been of late; and that a Month's Wages extraordinary shall be given to every Officer & Soldier who shall live in Hutts this Winter.

Good encouragement this, and we think ourselves deserving of it, for the hunger, Thirst, Cold & fatigue we have suffer'd this Campaign, altho' we have not fought much, yet the oldest Soldiers among us have called the Campaign a very severe & hard one. . . .

January 4, Sunday—Properly accouter'd I went to work at Masonry, None of my Mess were to dictate me, and before Night (being found with Mortar & Stone) I almost compleated a genteel Chimney to my Magnificent Hutt, however, as we had short allowance of food & no Grogg, my back ached before Night.

I was call'd to relieve a Soldier tho't to be dying—he expir'd before I reach'd the Hutt. He was an Indian—an excellent Soldier—and an obedient good natur'd fellow. He engaged for money doubtless as others do;—but he has serv'd his country faithfully—he has fought for those very people who disinherited his forefathers—having finished his pilgrimage, he was discharged from the War of Life & Death. His memory ought to be respected, more than those rich ones who supply the world with nothing better than Money and Vice. There the poor fellow lies not Superior now to a clod of earth—his Mouth wide open—his Eyes staring. Was he affrighted at the scene of Death—or the consequences of it?—doubtless both;—but he has doubtless acted agreeable to the dictates of Nature in the course of his whole life—why should he then be afraid of the consequences of Death. Where then is his immaterial part taken its flight—undoubtedly the scene Changes, and admits him into another State,—and there fixes him forever,—but what is that state—is it happy or miserable. He has been an honest fellow—has done his duty to his Maker and his fellow creatures as far as his Inclinations and Abilities would permit of,—therefore we'll suppose him happier now than ever.

What a frail—dying creature is Man. We are Certainly not made for this world—daily evidences demonstrate the contrary. . . .

The Marquis De la Fayette, a Volunteer in Our Army—& he who gave three Ships to Congress, is very agreeable in his person and great in his Character; being made a Major General—Brigadier Conway,[18] an Irish Colonel from France, took umbrage thereat, and resigned—but is now made Inspector General of the Army—he is a great Character—he wore a Commission in the French Service when he was but ten years old. Major General Lord Stirling,[19] is a man of a very noble presence,—and the most martial Appearance of any General in the Service—he much resembles the Marquis of Granby—by his bald head—& the make of his face—and figure of his Body—He is mild in his private Con-

[18] Thomas Conway (1733-1800), an Irish Catholic serving in the French Army who volunteered to fight for the Americans. Involved in the famous "Conway Cabal," supposedly a plot to replace Washington with Horatio Gates. Waldo was wrong here, for Conway did not enter the French Army until he was fourteen years of age.

[19] William Alexander (1726-1783) of New York and New Jersey, major general in the American Army. He was called Lord Stirling despite his unsuccessful claim to the Earldom of Stirling. His contemporaries always referred to him by that title and his wife was called Lady Stirling, while his daughter was referred to as the Lady Kitty.

versation, and vociferous in the Field;—but he has allways been unfortunate in Actions.

Count Pulaski[20]—General of the Horse is a Man of hardly middling Stature—sharp Countenance—and lively air;—He contended a long time with his Uncle the present king of Poland for the Crown—but being overcome he fled to France—and has now joined the American Army, where he is greatly respected & admired for his Martial Skill, Courage & Intrepidity. Gen Greene[21] & Gen¹ Sullivan are greatly esteemed. Baron De Kalb,[22] a Major General is another very remarkable Character, and a Gentleman much esteemed.

January 5—Apply'd for a Furlow, Surg Gen not at home—come back mumping & Sulkey.

January 6—Apply'd again—was deny'd by reason of Inoculations being set on foot—& because the Boston Surgeons had too many of them gone—

[20]Casimir Pulaski (c. 1748–1779), Polish nobleman who came to America in 1777. He served as chief of cavalry until March, 1778. Disliked taking orders from superiors. Received a mortal wound at the siege of Savannah, October 9, 1779, while leading a foolhardy charge against the enemy.

[21]Nathanael Greene (1742–1786), major general from Rhode Island who was to become quartermaster general. A fine quartermaster, he won even greater fame against the British in 1780–1783 as commanding general of the Southern Department.

[22]Johann Kalb (1721–1780), German soldier of fortune and major general in the American Army. Although he was the son of a peasant, he was often called "Baron de Kalb." He received mortal wounds in the battle of Camden, South Carolina, August 16, 1780.

one of whom is to be broke for his lying & deceiving in order to get a furlow—and I wish his cursed tongue was pull'd out, for thus giving an example of scandal to the New England Surgeons, tho' the Connect Ones are well enough respected at present. Came home sulkey and Cross—storm'd at the boys—and swore round like a piper and a fool till most Night—when I bought me a Bear Skin—dress'd with the Hair on:—This will answer me to ly on—Set on. . . .[23]

Case;—it serves to keep off those melancholly Ideas which often attend such a person, and who loves his family and wishes to be with them. If I should happen to lose this little Journal, any fool may laugh that finds it,—since I know that there is nothing in it but the natural flowings & reflections of my own heart, which is human as well as other Peoples—and if there is a great deal of folly in it—there is no intended Ill nature—and am sure there is much Sincerity, especially when I mention my family, whom I cannot help saying and am not asham'd to say that I Love. But I begin to grow Sober, I shall be home sick again.—Muses attend!—File off to the right grim melancholly! Seek no more an asylum in thine Enemy's breast!—Waft me hence ye Muses to the brow of Mount Parnassus! for to the summit, I dare not, will not presume to climb— . . .

We have got our Hutts to be very comfortable, and feel ourselves happy in them—I only want my

[23] Here another part of the original manuscript is missing.

family and I should be as happy here as any where, except in the Article of food, which is sometimes pretty scanty.

The Brigg taken from the Enemy (& mention'd New Year's Day) is the greatest prize ever taken from them—There is Scarlet—Blue—& Buff Cloth, sufficient to Cloath all the Officers of the Army—& Hats—Shirts—Stockings—Shoes—Boots—Spurs— &c. to finish compleat Suits for all. A petition is sent to his Excellency, that this Cloathing may be dealt out to the Regimental Officers only—at a moderate price—Excluding Commissaries—Bull Drivers &c.—there are 4 or 5000 Apelets of Gold & Silver—Many Chests of private Officers Baggage—& General Howe's Silver Plate—& Kitchen furniture, &c. This Cargo was sent to Cloathe all the Officers of the British Army.

January 8—Unexpectedly got a Furlow. Set out for home. The very worst of Riding—Mud & Mire.

We had gone through Inoculation before this furlow.

3

Chevalier de Pontgibaud

*

*A French Volunteer
in the War of Independence*

Chevalier de Pontgibaud

The exigencies of war sometimes make strange bedfellows. A case in point is that of France during the American Revolution. Since the late seventeenth century France had been the continuing enemy of Britain and that nation's American colonists. The many wars had culminated in the Seven Years, or French and Indian War. France had been brought to her knees, losing Canada in the Treaty of Paris in 1763. It was felt at the time that the French were but biding their time and recouping their strength for the resumption of the war with England. The colonists were not fond of the French; Protestant New England held little affection for Catholic France, while along the frontier there were the memories of bloody raids by French-led Indians. But France was the natural enemy of England and yearning for "revanche," and so it was to that country that the rebellious colonies turned when the war broke out.

Yet France could not seek open alliance with the colonies of another nation until she was sure they were seeking independence and demonstrated the capacity to win that freedom. On the side of France, it was hoped that England would wear herself down in a transatlantic war and would so weaken herself that she could be easily conquered.

In July, 1776, Arthur Lee, Silas Deane, and Benjamin Franklin were sent as envoys representing the Continental Congress to Paris seeking assistance from that nation. In May, 1776, Comte Charles Garvier Vergennes, French Foreign Minister, gave the task of secretly aiding the American rebels to a literary man, Pierre Augustin Caron, who had assumed the pseudonym Beaumarchais in 1756, and who was to write two famous comedies, "The Barber of Seville" and "The Marriage of Figaro." Beaumarchais had but recently completed a secret mission to London and seemed to thrive on the excitement of intrigue. He proposed that the French government subsidize the Americans to the extent of a million livres (about $200,000) and supply them with war materials through a fictitious firm he called Rodrique et Cie. By September, 1777, Rodrique et Cie. had sent supplies valued at five million livres to America, and between 1776 and 1783, when the company was dissolved, there was a total of forty-two million livres involved. Additional aid for the American cause came in the shape of European military volunteers, the most famous being a twenty year old French army captain by the name of Marie Joseph Paul Yves Roch Gilbert

du Motier, Marquis de Lafayette. In company
with another volunteer, Johann Kalb, Lafayette
landed at Georgetown, South Carolina, on June
13, 1777. Six weeks later his reception by the Continental Congress was cool, but after the young
Frenchman offered to serve without pay, they
commissioned him a major general without command.

Lafayette became a great favorite of Washington and was to distinguish himself on the battlefield. More important, he became something of a
living symbol of French aid to America.

By this time the French had become impressed
with the staying power of the Americans, and after the victory over John Burgoyne by Horatio
Gates at Saratoga on October 17, 1777, French
authorities reported to the American envoys in
Paris that France had decided to recognize American independence. On January 8, 1778, Vergennes reported that France was ready to draw up
an alliance. On May 4, 1778, the Continental
Congress ratified two treaties, a treaty of amity
and commerce (recognizing independence), and a
treaty of alliance, to become effective in the event
of a war between France and England. The war
between the two nations broke out on June 17,
when the British Admiral Keppel, leading twenty ships on a cruise out of Portsmouth, England,

fell in with two French frigates and fired his guns to make them heave to.

Although the French Navy under Admiral d'Estaing was involved in several abortive Franco-American adventures at Newport in Rhode Island and Savannah in Georgia, the most effective French aid came in the form of an expeditionary force of 5,500 soldiers who landed at Newport July 11, 1780. This army was under the command of Jean Baptiste Donatien de Vimeur, Comte de Rochambeau, sometimes affectionately called "Papa" by his men.

The arrival of Rochambeau and his men marked the beginning of a new and decisive phase of Franco-American cooperation which was to result in the ultimate victory over Cornwallis at Yorktown.

Among those French volunteers who came over in the earlier days of the war was Charles-Albert de Moré, Chevalier de Pontgibaud. He was born April 21, 1758, in the chateau of his father, the Comte de Pontgibaud, in the village of Pontgibaud. His mother, the former Marie Charlotte de Salaberry, died when he was quite young. His father, the count, held a number of feudal rights and, as Pontgibaud put it, "No one in the district knew anything about the rights of man, but all did know, and practice, the duties of grati-

tude and respect." Yet young Pontgibaud was something of a rebel.

At age sixteen Pontgibaud was sent to Paris to further his education. He stayed with an uncle, identified in the story as "Baron d'A-------."

After the death of his first wife, the Baron had married "Madame P------," who had managed to marry off her daughter to Pontgibaud's older brother. His aunt held the idea that if the younger brother was out of the way her son-in-law would inherit the entire estate of his father. This, in turn, would mean much to her daughter if her husband died.

The aunt saw her opportunity in the current rumor that young sons were attempting to poison their fathers. She managed to cast suspicion on Pontgibaud and his father brought together a family council who conducted a trial of sorts and secured a royal "lettre de cachet" condemning him to prison. The royal letter read, "The Chevalier de Pontgibaud, being of a fierce and violent character, and refusing to do work of any kind, is to be taken to Saint Lazare, at the expense of his father."

On February 19, 1777, Pontgibaud was locked up in the castle of Pierre-en-Cize, a country house of the Archbishop of Lyon. After eighteen months imprisonment he managed a daring escape by tunneling through a ten foot wall and fighting off the guard.

He made his way home where his father agreed that he should go to America to fight with the rebels. To make sure he would be able to make ends meet his father granted him an allowance.

After his American adventures, Pontgibaud was stationed in Paris with his regiment, spending some time studying mathematics. He took a wife in 1789. He became aware that a revolution was developing in France, and when the revolution did break out he became an emigré, fleeing the country.

He returned to France with the King of Prussia in 1792, but that army retired from the country in confusion. Pontgibaud went to Switzerland with his brother, the latter becoming a successful banker and merchant.

When he heard that the United States Congress would finally pay back salary to foreign military officers who had served in the Revolution, with interest, Pontgibaud sailed for the new nation. After visiting many old haunts and friends, he slipped into France, but travelled on to Trieste where his brother was now in business. He returned to Paris in 1814, where he lived until his death in 1830, just a few months after his wife died.

He completed writing his memoirs in 1814. They were published in 1828 as the "Mémoires du Comte de M----," as Pontgibaud was then known as the Comte de Moré. The book became a collector's item, not for its content, but because of its publisher. This was Honoré de Balzac who had a brief career in publishing before he returned to making his living with his pen. It was later published in Paris in 1896, translated and edited by Robert D. Douglas. The following portion of the memoir is from the second edition of 1898.

CHEVALIER DE PONTGIBAUD

From Robert B. Douglas's,
A French Volunteer of the War of Independence, 1898

The Journal of
A French Volunteer

I

OUR VOYAGE, which was a very bad one, lasted
sixty-seven days. We met with a heavy storm
off the Bermudas, and were often chased by British
cruisers. At last we came in sight of Capes Charles
and Henry at the entrance to Chesapeake Bay.

As it was then almost night-fall the captain
tacked about, intending to enter the Bay next
morning. We then had a good wind behind us, and
we hoped, but in vain, for a pilot to come off and
take us in. The fear of being captured, however,
made the captain determine to enter the Bay, which
is very large. The destination of the vessel was Baltimore, but we were obliged to run into James River. The morning was very foggy, and we could not
see more than a hundred yards or so. A few minutes
later the fog lifted, the sun came out, and we found
ourselves within a couple of cannon shot of the *Isis,*
a British war vessel of 64 guns, which was moored at
the entrance to the river. We might have run ashore
on the coast, and the *Isis* could not have come near
us as the wind was against her, but our captain lost
his head and gave no orders, so we drifted within
range of the *Isis,* and then went aground near the

shore. The British being now convinced we were enemies, began to fire on us.

All the shore pirates of the district at once embarked to pillage us, and a scene of terrible disorder ensued. These sea wolves, nearly all negroes or mulattos, and numbering, as near as I could guess, about sixty, came on board under the pretext of saving the vessel, but they cared more for pillage than salvage, for they staved in casks of wine and brandy, and the greater part of them were soon very drunk. I noticed that their boats were secured to the ship by thin cords, so I quickly engaged a boy and one of our sailors to help me to bring up from the cabin my trunk which contained my goods,—alas! all my fortune,—and my other effects. We threw these into a boat belonging to one of the Lestrigons, whilst the owner was engaged in drinking and stealing, then we jumped in ourselves, cut the rope, and in a very few minutes were on shore.

The bullets whistled over our heads but we were safe, and I had, moreover (as I thought), preserved all my property. Seated on my trunk, with my feet on the shore of America, I watched the total destruction of our ship, which was accomplished in a very few hours. We did not know what to do, or where to go, for we could not tell in which direction any houses lay. We could not speak the language, and we could not see any of the inhabitants of the country. At last several of the boats belonging to the robbers arrived, loaded with booty taken from the ship. Some of our sailors were in the boats. The leader of the pirates sent to the neighbouring town of Hampton for wagons, and when they came packed in them all which had been brought to shore, including my trunk and all that belonged to the passengers. I heard, however, the words, "Public Magazine," and that reassured me a little, for I imagined that when all the passengers were assembled, each would be allowed to claim and take away his own property.

In two or three days the crew got together, except two killed, and one or two drowned, and the doors of the Public Magazine were opened for us. My eyes filled with joy at again beholding the trunk which contained all my riches. The key was in my pocket; I approached my trunk, but, alas! found that the padlock had been broken off, the lock forced, and, instead of the fine Dutch linen upon which I expected to make such a profit, I found only sail covers, stones, and a few rags of sails.

You may imagine my distress. I was thousands of miles from home, with no property except the clothes on my back, and no money except the nine or ten louis I chanced to have in my pocket.[1]

Being weak and fatigued by the long voyage and its exciting incidents, I rested for a day or two, but not wishing to expend all my slender stock of

[1] A louis was a French gold coin first struck in 1640 and issued up until the French Revolution. After the revolution it became the French twenty franc piece.

money in an inn at Hampton, I set off to join the army, and, in order to get information, I first directed my steps towards Williamsburg, the capital of Virginia, about twenty or twenty-five miles distant from my starting point.

I was sure that, when once I had joined the army, I should run no risk by dying of hunger at all events; but it was a long way to the camp, and I did not know within a trifling matter of a hundred miles or so, where the head-quarters then were. Besides there were forests to pass through, and I was not sure whether I might not meet with bears, panthers, or rattlesnakes[2]—at least that was what I had to expect if I believed all the books of travel I had read whilst I was in prison. I foresaw that I should often have to sleep under the stars, which, in the month of November, is neither safe nor pleasant in any country remote from the equator, and I was also doubtful as to whether I should find a dinner every day. With thoughts like these, but with no anxiety as to my baggage, I started off on the road—which was only a worn path—to Williamsburg.

There I found some Frenchmen, for they are to be met with everywhere. They provided me with a map of the country and I planned out my route. I learned that the army was camped at Valley Forges, three leagues from Philadelphia, and that there I

[2]Most European travellers were fascinated by the rattlesnake. Nearly all travel accounts during this period describe the serpent in great detail.

should find the Marquis de la Fayette. It was a long journey to make on foot. I related the story of my shipwreck on the coast of Chesapeake Bay, and, as advice costs nothing, everybody was ready to give it, and all recommended me to complain to Mr. Jefferson,[3] then governor of Virginia, of the robbery of my effects.

After my experience in the Old World, and more recent vicissitudes in the New, I was not inclined to be too hopeful, but, to ease my mind, I called on the governor, accompanied by an interpreter. I found that Mr. Jefferson had been informed of our misfortunes. He expressed his regret that in such troublous times as we were then in, it was impossible for him to pay me the compensation to which I was entitled. In my presence he ordered his secretary to give me a certificate. This curious document was in English, which I could neither speak nor read, but later on I was able to peruse the document. The governor terminated his passport by recommending me to the charity of all with whom I might meet!

What freaks fortune had played with me. At nineteen years of age I had escaped from Pierre-en-Cize,—two months later had been shipwrecked a

[3]Thomas Jefferson was governor of Virginia from June 1, 1779 to June 12, 1780. Pontgibaud's memory failed him here as Patrick Henry was governor at this time. Although Pontgibaud gives no dates, the sequence of events would suggest that he was in Williamsburg in late 1777 or early 1778.

thousand leagues from home,—had been robbed of all I possessed, on a friendly shore, by the very persons I had come to help to regain their liberty,— and now I was trudging on foot to the head-quarters of the army, the bearer of a licence to beg on the road. Fortunately the little money I had sufficed, and I was not obliged to take advantage of the charitable verb "to assist", slipped in for my special benefit at the foot of the passport.

From Williamsburg to the camp at Valley Forges, near Philadelphia, is not less than 200 miles, and it must not be supposed that it required any superhuman effort to accomplish that. There was plenty of mud to be found—but that I expected; the weather was not always fine, for it rained often—in the months of November and December it rains even in France.

In the midst of all these discomforts, which I foresaw would have an end, the knowledge that I was free sustained me, and comforted me. Moreover, I was young, and had health and strength. It is not astonishing therefore that I found at every step something fresh to drive away sad thoughts.

Birds unknown in France enlivened my view, and made me admire the richness and variety of their plumage, and in the almost continuous forest through which I had to pass, I was never tired of watching the thousands of little squirrels which leaped from bough to bough and tree to tree round me.

My baggage consisted of a single shirt. I had in my pocket a flask which I filled with gin (whenever I could get it) and in another pocket a hunk of bad maize bread.[4] I had also five louis in my purse and a passport, signed "Jefferson."

Sand and forest, forest and sand, formed the whole way from Williamsburg to the camp at Valley Forges. I do not remember how many days I took to accomplish this difficult journey. Being badly fed, as a natural consequence I walked badly, and passed at least six nights under the trees through not meeting with any habitation.

Not knowing the language, I often strayed from the right road, which was so much time and labour lost. At last, early in November, I arrived at Valley Forges.[5]

The American army was then encamped three or four leagues from Philadelphia, which city was then occupied by the British, who were rapidly fulfilling the prophecy of Dr. Franklin.[6]

That celebrated man—a noted ambassador who

[4] Corn bread.

[5] Here again Pontgibaud's memory failed him. The American army was encamped at Valley Forge from December 19, 1777, until June 18, 1778. He probably arrived at Valley Forge around February, 1778.

[6] Benjamin Franklin was often referred to as "Dr. Franklin" after the University of Edinburgh conferred an LL.D. upon him in 1759. Oxford University gave him a doctorate of civil law in 1762.

These and other honorary degrees bestowed upon him were because of his scientific achievements.

amused himself with science, which he adroitly made to assist him in his diplomatic work—said, when some friends came to Passy to condole with him on the fall of Philadelphia, "You are mistaken; it is not the British army that has taken Philadelphia, but Philadelphia that has taken the British army." The cunning old diplomatist was right. The capital of Pennsylvania had already done for the British what Capua also did in a few months for the soldiers of Hannibal.

The Americans,—the "insurgents" as they were called,—camped at Valley Forges; the British officers, who were in the city, gave themselves up to pleasure, there were continual balls and other amusements; the troops were idle and enervated by inaction, and the generals undertook nothing all the winter.

Soon I came in sight of the camp. My imagination had pictured an army with uniforms, the glitter of arms, standards, etc., in short, military pomp of all sorts. Instead of the imposing spectacle I expected, I saw, grouped together or standing alone, a few militia men,[7] poorly clad, and for the most part without shoes;—many of them badly armed, but all well supplied with provisions, and I noticed that tea and sugar formed part of their rations. I did not then

[7] There were few militia, or citizen soldiers, at Valley Forge. The majority of men camped there were Continentals, or soldiers of the regular army. One suspects that Pontgibaud got the impression that they were militia because of the lack of uniforms.

know that this was not unusual, and I laughed, for it made me think of the recruiting sergeants on the Quai de la Ferraille at Paris, who say to the yokels, "You will want for nothing when you are in the regiment, but if bread should run short you must not mind eating cakes." Here the soldiers had tea and sugar. In passing through the camp I also noticed soldiers wearing cotton night-caps under their hats, and some having for cloaks or great-coats, coarse woollen blankets, exactly like those provided for the patients in our French hospitals. I learned afterwards that these were the officers and generals.

Such, in strict truth, was,—at the time I came amongst them,—the appearance of this armed mob, the leader of whom was the man who has rendered the name of Washington famous; such were the colonists,—unskilled warriors who learned in a few years how to conquer the finest troops that England could send against them. Such also,—at the beginning of the War of Independence,—was the state of want in the insurgent army, and such was the scarcity of money, and the poverty of that government, now so rich, powerful, and prosperous, that its notes, called Continental Paper Money, were nearly valueless, like our own assignats in 1795.[8]

---

[8] In January, 1778, Continental currency was down seventy-five per cent below face value. A year later it was ninety per cent. This depreciation gave rise to the term, "Not worth a Continental."

Impressed by these sights, which had quite destroyed my illusions, I made my way through this singular army to the quarters of the Marquis de la Fayette.

This young general was then, I believe, not more than 20 or 21 years of age. I presented myself to him, and told him frankly my whole story. He listened to my history with attention and kindness, and at my request enrolled me as a volunteer. He also wrote to France and before long received a reply confirming the truth of my statements; he then appointed me one of his *aides-de-camp*, with the rank of Major, and from that moment never ceased to load me with benefits and marks of confidence. The Marquis de la Fayette presented me as his *aide-de-camp* to the commander-in-chief. Washington was intended by nature for a great position,—his appearance alone gave confidence to the timid, and imposed respect on the bold. He possessed also those external advantages which a man born to command should have; tall stature, a noble face, gentleness in his glance, amenity in his language, simplicity in his gestures and expressions. A calm, firm bearing harmonized perfectly with these attributes. This general, who has since become so celebrated for his talents and successes, was just beginning to play that important part in history that he has since so gloriously sustained, in every capacity, military, civil, and political. But I intend here only to speak of the general.

He was surrounded by his officers, who for the most part were, like me, on their first campaign. Many of them had been far from imagining, a short time before, that they were intended for a military career. I saw, standing near the Commander in Chief, Gates,[9] the victor at Saratoga, a small man, about fifty years of age: two years before that he was merely a rich farmer, yet quiet and simple as he looked he had made himself a name in history. This agriculturist turned soldier, who was wearing on his head a woollen cap surmounted by a farmer's hat, had just received the sword of General Burgoyne, who, dressed in full uniform, and with his breast covered with all the orders England could give, came to him to surrender.[10]

Near Gates was Arnold, as brave as he was treacherous; he was lamed for life by a bullet he had received at Saratoga whilst sharing the dangers and glories of General Gates. A few months before he was a distinguished officer in the army, General

[9] Horatio Gates (1728–1806). As a British officer Gates had participated in the French and Indian War. Retired as a major in 1772, he had settled in Virginia. When the Continental Congress created a Continental army, Gates was made adjutant general with the rank of brigadier general. On May 16, 1777, he was promoted to major general. His victory over Burgoyne at Saratoga on October 17, 1777, played a role in France's decision to make an alliance with the United States.

[10] John Burgoyne (1722–1792), military hero, minor playwright, and member of the British Parliament since 1761 ended his military career with his surrender at Saratoga.

Arnold was nothing more than a horse-dealer.[11] General Lee, however, was a soldier before the War of Independence.[12] General Sullivan was a lawyer, and when peace was declared he returned, not to his plough but to his office.[13] Colonel Hamilton,[14] the friend of Washington, when the war was over,

[11] Benedict Arnold (1741–1801) was a daring, and sometimes reckless, battlefield leader. He suffered two wounds in combat, at Quebec and at Saratoga. After his treasonable act in attempting to turn over West Point to the British he became a brigadier general in the British army. Before the war he had been a fairly successful merchant, engaging in horse-trading among other things, leading some to refer to him scornfully as a "horse-jockey."

[12] Charles Lee (1731–1782) was a soldier of fortune. He had served as an English officer in the French and Indian war and under Burgoyne in Portugal. He had also been a major general in the Polish army. He had come to Virginia in 1773. Congress had appointed him a major general in June, 1775. His behavior was both arrogant and eccentric. He was suspended from the army because of his conduct during the battle of Monmouth in June, 1778.

[13] John Sullivan (1740–1795), lawyer of New Hampshire. A delegate to the Second Continental Congress, he was commissioned a brigadier general in June, 1775, and promoted to major general in August, 1776. His military career was spotty. After the war he was a member of the New Hampshire legislature and later attorney general and governor of that state. He later became a federal judge.

[14] Alexander Hamilton (1757–1804), began the war as an artillery officer, but served most of the revolution as secretary and aide to General Washington. He was instrumental in securing the adoption of the Federal Constitution. Hamilton became the first Secretary of the Treasury of the United States. In 1798 he was commissioned a major general with the post of Inspector General. On July 11, 1804, he was killed in a duel with Aaron Burr.

also became a lawyer, and pleaded at Philadelphia. General Stark was the proprietor of a large and well-managed estate.[15] Brave General Knox, who commanded the artillery, had, before the war, kept a book-store.[16] Under him served Duplessis-Mauduit, a brave young officer, only twenty-six years old, and of whom I shall often have occasion to speak in these pages;—he afterwards perished at Saint-Domingo, vilely murdered by his own soldiers.[17]

I also saw arrive at the mill which served our commander as his head-quarters, Colonel Armand, then commanding a troop of light horse. The life of this young Frenchman, who was then twenty-four, had been like mine, adventurous from the beginning. He was the nephew of the Marquis de la Beliniese, and had been an officer in the Gardes

[15] John Stark (1728–1822), had served with Rogers' Rangers during the French and Indian war. Began his revolutionary career as a colonel of the First New Hampshire Regiment. He achieved spectacular success as commanding officer at the Battle of Bennington, August 16, 1777. After the war he retired to his farm. He lived to be ninety-three years old.

[16] Henry Knox (1750–1806). On November 17, 1775, he was appointed Colonel of the Continental Regiment of Artillery. Promoted to brigadier general December 27, 1776, and to major general March 22, 1782. Served as Washington's chief of artillery. After the war he served as the first Secretary of War of the United States.

[17] Chevalier de Mauduit was another French volunteer, landing at Boston on March 20, 1777. He had been recommended to the Congress by Benjamin Franklin. He became Henry Knox's brigade adjutant.

Françaises. Having fallen madly in love with Mlle
Beaumesnil, of the Opera, and been refused by her,
he retired to the Monastery of La Trappe, which he
left to seek danger by the side of General Washington. He had earned some glory and distinction
under the name of Colonel Armand, and was to
become more celebrated under the name of the
Marquis de la Rouarie.[18]

Lastly I saw there, for the first time, Monsieur de
P——, who commanded the Engineers, and who
was afterwards Minister of War to Louis XVI, at the
beginning of the Revolution.[19]

Amongst all these officers of different nationalities and habits I noticed more particularly the striking figure of the man before whom all bowed, as
much from admiration and respect as from duty.
General Washington appeared to be about forty.

[18] Marquis de La Rouerie Tuffin (1750–1793). After
wounding a cousin of the king in a duel, and being forced to
break off an affair with an opera singer, he sailed for America in 1776. He adopted the surname of Armand as more in
keeping with his republican principles. He was active as a
leader of mounted troops. He returned to France after the
war and was a royalist during the French Revolution.

[19] Louis Le Begue de Presle Duportail (1734–1802). Duportail was one of the four officers chosen by the French
court in response to Franklin's request for trained military
engineers. He became Chief of Engineers for the American
army. At the time Pontgibaud saw him he was a brigadier
general and was promoted to major general November 16,
1781. He became Minister and Secretary of State for War for
France in 1790. Later became a lieutenant general in the
French army. When his politics became suspect he fled to
America and died at sea while returning to France in 1802.

He had served in the British army, and as Major Washington commanded in 175– Fort Necessity, when M. de Jumonville, a French officer bearing a flag of truce, was shot by a private soldier, who did not see the white flag, and who fired without orders.[20] According to all reports it is certain that the commander of the fort never gave any order to fire, and the most irrefutable proof of this is the gentleness, magnanimity, and goodness of General Washington,—a character which he never once belied amidst all the chances of war, and all the trials of good or bad fortune. M. Thomas[21] has deemed it proper and patriotic to paint this unfortunate occurrence in the worst light, and severely blame the British officer. Had the name of Major Washington remained obscure, it would have been stained with an undeserved blot which no one would have thought it worth while to remove, but, as it is, any attempt to answer the charge would be an insult to one of the most beautiful and noble characters in history, and all suspicions fall to the ground before the name, the virtues, and the glory of General Washington. The assassin of De Jumonville could never have become a great man.

When the war broke out, General Washington

[20] The correct date is 1755. Washington did not build Fort Necessity until after Jumonville was killed in ambush, while Half King, an Indian chief, boasted that he had killed the Frenchman.

[21] Antoine Leonard Thomas, French poet. There is no mention of Washington in his poem, "Jumonville."

was the proprietor of a splendid estate in Virginia, and he brought with him when he joined the army, a number of fine horses. He dressed in the most simple manner, without any of the marks distinctive of a commanding officer, and he gave away large sums to the soldiers, by whom he was adored. But all that he gave was from his own purse, for he had refused to receive any emoluments from the Government.[22]

I ought to mention to the praise of the Marquis de la Fayette, that he followed the example of the commander-in-chief, and incurred great expense, purchasing with his own money all that was necessary to clothe, equip, and arm his men. The war cost him immense sums, and certainly no one will suspect him of any other motive than the noble one of glory, for the chances of reimbursement were not very probable. His motives were perfectly pure, and the enormous sacrifices he made can only be accounted for by the love of liberty, and the chivalric spirit which will always exist in France;—enthusiasm, love of danger, and a little glory were his sole rewards. The pleasure of commanding, fighting, and distinguishing himself were of some weight in the scale, it is reasonable to conclude, but honour and merit were the principal motives. The war in America only offered a chance of danger, priva-

[22] When Washington was appointed commander-in-chief he offered to serve without pay, although he did expect to be reimbursed for expenses.

tions, fatigues, and difficulties; the Marquis de la Fayette was the only one of all the young lords of the Court of France who had the courage and determination to leave the pleasures of the palace, and travel eighteen hundred leagues to obtain glory without profit.

Moreover, there was not an opportunity every day of acquiring even this much, under General Washington. It did not enter into his plans to readily engage with the enemy on every opportunity. He watched his time and chance before he struck a blow; the principle of "armed temporization" was his daily study, and, as events have proved, he well deserved the title which has been claimed for him of the American Fabius.

The British, occupied in the pleasures which they found in Philadelphia, allowed us to pass the winter in tranquillity; they never spoke of the camp at Valley Forges except to joke about it, and we for our part might almost have forgotten that we were in the presence of an enemy if we had not received a chance visitor. We were at table at the headquarters,—that is to say in the mill, which was comfortable enough,—one day, when a fine sporting dog, which was evidently lost, came to ask for some dinner. On its collar were the words, *General Howe.* He was the British commander's dog.[23] It was sent back under a flag of truce, and General Howe replied with a very warm letter of thanks to this act

[23] General William Howe, British commander-in-chief.

of courtesy on the part of his enemy, our general.

When I arrived at the camp I was in a pitiable condition, but the Marquis de la Fayette had the extreme kindness to furnish me with the means of procuring horses and a suitable equipment.

A plan was proposed to effect a diversion by attacking Canada, where, we were informed, we should find few troops to oppose us, and towards the middle of January, the Marquis de la Fayette went to take command of the troops in the district round Albany.

We made the journey on sledges on the North River,[24] and travelled with great speed, but the weather was "wickedly cold." One of our companions was the brave Duplessis-Mauduit, who was to command our artillery. But before undertaking any measures we thought it prudent to make a treaty with the savage races who live on the borders of Canada and New England.

After resting some days in the town of Albany, we went up Mohawk River to the house of Mr. Johnston whose residence was close to the huts of the various tribes known under the names of Tuscaroros, Oneidas, etc.[25]

[24] The Hudson River was sometimes also called the North River.

[25] Sir William Johnson (1715-1774). Johnson had been Superintendent of Indian Affairs north of the Ohio River. He had been knighted for his exploits during the French and Indian war, especially for keeping the Iroquois on the British side.

We were prepared with the usual presents required to conciliate them, and in this case it might be said that little presents cement great friendships. Our gifts, which they thought magnificent, consisted of woollen blankets, little mirrors, and, above all, plenty of paint, which the savages esteem highly and use to paint their faces. There was also some gunpowder, lead, and bullets, and some silver crowns of six francs bearing the effigy of the King of France, who is known to these savages, by tradition, as the "Great Father."

About two thousand Indians, men and women, came to the appointed rendezvous, and thanks to our presents and the "fire water" which we distributed, the treaty was easily concluded. I was very anxious to observe the manners and customs of these people, who were a great novelty to me, but at the end of a few days I had seen quite enough, for the European beggar is far less disgusting than the American savage. Their numbers are diminishing rapidly from various causes.

We found amongst them an old soldier who had belonged to the Marquis de Montcalm's army.[26] This man had become a savage; he had almost entirely forgotten French, and lived like the Indians, except that he had not let them cut his ears, which is the sign of a warrior. We left these tribes equally

[26] The Marquis de Montcalm had been killed in the French and Indian War while defending Quebec against the British force under General James Wolfe.

satisfied on both sides. The projected attack on Canada was postponed, for some reason of which I am ignorant, and we returned to the Camp at Valley Forges.[27]

I remarked, however, that even in treating with these children of nature, there was a reciprocal distrust and an impression that caution was the mother of safety, for we brought with us fifty of the young warriors as a guarantee that the treaty should be duly executed, and one of our men remained with the Indians as a hostage—it was not I.

A little later some of these Indians joined our army, and I will here note two singular incidents concerning them. One day we were at dinner at head-quarters; an Indian entered the room, walked round the table, and then stretching forth his long tattooed arm seized a large joint of hot roast beef in his thumb and fingers, took it to the door, and began to eat it. We were all much surprised, but General Washington gave orders that he was not to be interfered with, saying laughingly, that it was apparently the dinner hour of this Mutius Scaevola of the New World.

On another occasion a chief came into the room where our generals were holding a council of war. Washington, who was tall and very strong, rose,

[27] The expedition was postponed because Lafayette discovered that few preparations had been made as to supplies, only about half of the troops showed up, and he learned that the enemy had strengthened their defensive positions.

coolly took the Indian by the shoulders, and put him outside the door. The son of the forest did not protest; he concluded probably that his ejectment was a way of expressing by signs that his company was not wanted.

At another time a meeting was appointed with the chiefs and warriors belonging to several tribes, which resided at great distances from each other in different directions. They had to pass through vast and thick forests where there were no paths. Though without neither watch nor compass they found their road, by means known to themselves alone. The meeting was to be on a plain, and it is a fact that on the day appointed we heard their songs and cries, and saw the various bodies of Indians arrive from all sides almost simultaneously.

I was astonished, on my return, to find what peculiar ideas our hosts, the Americans of New England, had of the French.

One day I dismounted from my horse at the house of a farmer upon whom I had been billeted. I had hardly entered the good man's house when he said to me, "I am very glad to have a Frenchman in the house."

I politely enquired the reason of the preference.

"Well," he said, "you see the barber lives a long way off, so you will be able to shave me."

"But I cannot even shave myself," I replied. "My servant shaves me, and he will shave you also if you like."

"That's very odd," said he. "I was told that all Frenchmen were barbers and fiddlers."

I think I never laughed so heartily. A few minutes later my rations arrived, and my host seeing a large piece of beef amongst them, said, "You are lucky to be able to come over to America and get some beef to eat."

I assured him that we had beef in France, and excellent beef too.

"That is quite impossible," he replied, "or you wouldn't be so thin."

Such was,—when Liberty was dawning over the land,—the ignorance shown by the inhabitants of the United States Republic in regard to the French. This lack of knowledge was caused by the difficulty of intercourse with Europe. Their communications were almost entirely cut off, and even Boston[28] and Philadelphia were in the hands of the English; nor were the people on the sea-coast in a more advanced state of civilization than those of the interior. More than a century of progress has been made in less than twenty years. I shall hardly be believed now when I state that, about this time, one of our men having left a pair of jack-boots[29] behind him, the Americans were so astonished at them, that they placed them, as a curiosity, in the New York Museum, where the man who had forgotten them afterwards found them ticketed *French Boots.*

[28] The British had evacuated Boston in March, 1776.
[29] A heavy leather military boot extending above the knee.

We returned to the camp at Valley Forges about the 15th March. The enemy was still quiet in Philadelphia, dancing and drinking in true English style, and deeming themselves perfectly safe. We were not sufficiently strong to attempt to dislodge them, and were obliged to wait till 15th April, when our recruits and reinforcements were to arrive. We remained inactive till then. The weather was still very cold. A peculiarity of the climate of this country is that often there is no spring, and owing to the absence of one of the most pleasant seasons of the year you pass straight from a long and hard winter to weather of insupportable heat, which has followed, without any intermediate gradations, a severe frost. The autumns, on the other hand, are long and very fine.

By 15th April our reinforcements had arrived, and we were preparing to open the campaign when we learned, with as much surprise as pleasure, that the British army had received orders to evacuate Philadelphia and fall back on New York. Their army was composed of veteran soldiers, was superior to us in numbers, and, moreover, protected by entrenchments. We imagined that the Cabinet at London had probably heard of the expected arrival of the squadron under Comte d'Estaing.[30] But,—

[30] Sir Henry Clinton, who had replaced Sir William Howe as commanding general, had received orders from home. Because France had now entered the war, a two-front offensive threatened England, but England also now had an excuse to seize the rich French West Indian islands. Clinton had been

whatever was the cause,—the British prepared to leave Philadelphia and retire on New York, which was also in their hands at that time. They had to make a march of thirty leagues, and cross two rivers,—the Delaware at Philadelphia, and North River,—before arriving at New York. We, on our side, prepared to harass their rear-guard.

General Washington—partly out of friendship, and partly from policy—was anxious to afford the Marquis de la Fayette every opportunity to distinguish himself, and ordered him to take a strong body of troops and cross the Schuylkill, at a spot on the left of the British position, and cut off their rear-guard, if the opportunity should occur. La Fayette had already brilliantly distinguished himself at the Battle of Brandywine, where he had received a ball in the leg.

We left about midnight, silently crossed the Schuylkill, and took up a position in a wood very close to Philadelphia, in order to be able to reconnoitre the enemy at daybreak, and attack if we had the chance. The main body of our army was ready to support us in less than two hours if we signalled for help.

The British, who had spies amongst our men, were soon informed of our plans. The greater part ordered to detach something like 8,000 men to the West Indies and Florida. With this decline in strength, it was felt that the British army could not hold both New York and Philadelphia, and the British considered New York to be the more important.

of their army was still in Philadelphia; they made a sortie, carried the weak post we had established on the banks of the Schuylkill to secure our retreat, and then marched in our rear, hoping to catch us between two fires. Our little army, ignorant of the danger of the position, was about to be caught in a trap.

It happened otherwise, however. We had bivouacked and were resting, and waiting for daybreak.

Fortunately, a surgeon had heard,—I do not know how,—of this night march of the garrison of Philadelphia to cut off our retreat and take us in the rear. In the interests of his own safety, most probably, he had searched along the banks of the river and had found a ford where there was only three or four feet of water. I was lying on the ground, near our general, when the Esculapius[31] came up and whispered the information he had found out, and the discovery of the ford, of which we did not suspect the existence. La Fayette, awakened by the sound of our voices, asked what was the matter, and made the surgeon repeat what he had already told me. Our general was admirably cool, and showed that presence of mind so valuable in a commander in a time of danger. He quietly told the surgeon to return to his post, and as soon as he had left, ordered me to mount my horse, and see for myself if the information was true. I did not go very far before I ascertained that Esculapius was quite correct.

[31] Aesculapius, the Greek god of healing.

I saw the head of a moving column, so I returned at full speed.

The next moment the order to march was given, and our retreat was effected quietly and promptly, and our little army crossed the Schuylkill in good order, by the ford which the surgeon had discovered. We were drawn up in order on the right bank, and made the signals previously agreed upon. Our soldiers believed that the march and counter-march formed part of a strategic movement. The enemy did not dare to show himself, being afraid of being caught in a snare.

Our expedition, which had served to puzzle the enemy, and our cleverly executed retreat, brought a good deal of praise to our general, which, to say truth, he deserved, but thanks were also due to the cautious and watchful surgeon who found the ford so opportunely;—nothing was said about *him*, however.

A few days later the British army had completely evacuated Philadelphia. We followed it almost within sight, and at Rareton Rivers,[32] General Lee attacked the enemy's rear-guard, in the morning. This was composed of 7,000 men, the flower of the army, and comprised the regiment of Foot Guards. I was present at this affair, where the Marquis de la Fayette was under Lee's orders.

We were thoroughly beaten, our soldiers fled in the greatest disorder, and we could not succeed in

[32] Raritan River.

rallying them, or even in getting thirty men to keep together. As usually happens, the general who commanded was accused of treason.[33] This was my first battle.

The stragglers re-formed behind our main army, which they met with in their flight, whilst the British, proud of their victory, though it was but a partial one, had the imprudence to pursue us with the reinforcements which they had drawn from the advance guard. General Washington waited for them in a strong position, with all his army drawn up in battle order.

The English had a deep ravine to cross before they could reach us: their brave infantry did not hesitate an instant, but charged us with the bayonet, and was crushed by our artillery. The fine regiment of the guards lost half its men, and its colonel was fatally wounded.

This engagement, called the Battle of Monmouth, from the name of a neighbouring village, began at ten o'clock in the morning: the heat was so excessive that we found soldiers dead without having received a wound. I did not see much of my first battle as we had not remained masters of the field; but that of Monmouth gave me some painful thoughts, even in the midst of the pride and plea-

[33] For his erratic behavior during the battle of Monmouth, a court-martial convicted Charles Lee of disobedience of orders, misbehavior before the enemy, and disrespect to the Commander-in-Chief. He was suspended from the army for a year.

sure of victory, and I cannot reproach myself with the callous heartlessness of the man who, on the field of Eylau, amidst the bodies of 24,000 of the victors and vanquished, said, "What a fine slaughter of men!" We slept on the field of battle amongst the dead, whom we had no time to bury. The day had been so hot, in both senses, that everyone had need of rest.

The British army retreated, about midnight, in silence, and we entered the village at six o'clock in the morning. The enemy had left behind some of his baggage and all his wounded; they were to be found in every house, and in the church. Every possible care was taken of them. I cannot even now think without pity of the young officers of the guards who had lost their limbs. Their colonel, one of the handsomest men I have ever seen, and sixty years of age, died of his wounds after suffering for twenty-four hours.

There was no further fighting until the English reached New York. We arrived before the city at almost the same moment as they entered it, and took up our position.

The siege was conducted under circumstances of great difficulty; a British squadron was anchored in the port; the town was protected on one side by North River, and on the other by East River,—both much larger than the Seine, or even the Loire. We should have needed a hundred thousand men if we had wanted to attack the place, and we had but fifteen thousand. The American army remained therefore "in observation," and contented itself with preventing the enemy from foraging in the country round about.

Whilst we were mutually engaged in watching each other, a plot was brewing which, if it had succeeded,—and it was within a hair's breadth of doing so,—would have been disastrous for our army, and perhaps even affected the fate of the newly-born Republic. I allude to General Arnold's conspiracy to betray the Fort of West Point into the hands of the English.

West Point, some twenty leagues from New York on the right bank of North River, was the chief arsenal of the American government. All the heavy artillery was kept there, and also that captured at the surrender of Saratoga. Congress had taken the precaution to make every approach to the place bristle with fortifications. The heights were surmounted by formidable batteries which could bring a heavy cross fire to bear upon several parts of the river, and the passage of the river was also barred—like the port of Constantinople in the time of the Greek Emperors—by a chain, every link of which weighed more than four hundred weight. The fortifications were erected under the direction of MM. Duportail and de Gouvion, officers sent from France.

Amongst the causes which brought about the liberty and independence of the United States, perhaps these impregnable fortifications should count for something more than has been before indicated.

The British could not hope to capture West Point by main force, for their ships could not approach without running the gauntlet—for fully two miles—of a heavy cross fire from the banks and the neighbouring heights. They resolved to try King Philip's "mule laden with gold."[34]

The possession of the fort of West Point would allow the enemy to cut off all our communications with the Northern States, from whence we derived all our provisions, particularly cattle. The loss of this place would have been the heaviest possible misfortune for us, and the consequences would have been incalculable. General Arnold commanded the fort.

Major André, a young officer of French extraction,[35] and an adjutant in the British army, often had occasion to visit the American camp to make arrangements concerning the exchange of prisoners. By chance or design, he had made the acquaintance of Arnold. This general, a man of rare courage, had often rendered us signal services, but he had not been rewarded as well as he wished. Major André

[34] French writers of the day were fond of quoting Philip of Macedon's remark that "there was no fortress so impregnable that a mule laden with gold could not enter."

[35] John André (1751-1780). He was actually the son of a Swiss merchant who had settled in London. He came to America as a lieutenant in 1774, and by 1780 had been promoted to major and was acting as deputy adjutant general. He had conducted the negotiations with Arnold for the surrender of West Point.

guessed that he was discontented, and could be easily bought over, and a compact was made between
them. Arnold was promised a large sum of money,
and a position of equal rank in the British army
with full pay. On his side he undertook to surrender the fort. The enemy was to make a night attack
by the river, and it was agreed that Arnold was to
allow himself to be surprised.

There were still, no doubt, some minor points to
be arranged, and it was necessary that the major
should meet the general in order to discuss these.
André came disguised, and was met by three of our
militia men who were patrolling outside our lines,
who stopped him and asked the usual questions.
The major, who was dressed as a countryman, and
badly mounted, replied quietly, and with an affecta-
tion of simplicity, that he was a farmer. The three
militia men, who by the way were but badly armed,
for the musket of one of them had no hammer, were
just deciding to let him pass, when he imprudently
complained of the delay they had caused him, and
was stupid enough to offer them money, and this
aroused their suspicions. Thereupon he proposed
that they should conduct him to West Point, where
he said he wished to go, but one of the militia men
remarked that they would have five miles to walk,
whereas by going only a mile or so they would meet
General Washington, who ought then to be crossing
North River on his return from a council of war
held at Hartford. This was agreed, and the three

militia men conducted their prisoner, without
knowing who he was, to Kingsferry, where they
awaited at the inn the arrival of the commander-in-
chief.

Arnold, however, being suspicious, had had the
major followed by a farmer of the district. Being
advised by his messenger that André was captured,
Arnold at once jumped into a boat manned by English sailors in disguise, and which was waiting for
him below the fortifications, and was rowed to the
Vulture, a British corvette lying about two cannon
shot off, and so the unfortunate major was the only
victim of Arnold's treason.[36]

All this passed at very little distance from our
camp. I had gone, out of curiosity, to see the generals arrive, and so was a witness, by accident, of this
great drama. The inn-keeper told me that three militia men had arrested a very suspicious looking person, who had offered them money to let him go
free, and showed me the place where this unknown
personage was temporarily confined. I went to see
him, and spoke to him, but as I did not know Major
André by sight, I imagined the man to be nothing
more than one of the enemy's spies. I was not the
only person astonished a quarter of an hour later.

General Washington arrived with his staff, and

[36]The sailors were not English, as our author indicated.
Other victims were the American soldiers who rowed Arnold out to the *Vulture*. He allowed the British to make
them prisoners of war.

having been told of the arrest, ordered Colonel
Hamilton to go and examine the accused and bring
back a report. I followed the colonel. The low room
was very dark, and as night was falling, a light was
brought. The colonel sprang back in astonishment
and dismay, on recognizing at the first glance the
unfortunate Major André. The prisoner wore no
military insignia—a regimental jacket under his
countryman's coat, might perhaps have saved him.
Deeply pained by the recognition, Colonel Hamilton ordered the militia men not to lose sight of
their prisoner for a moment, and hurried back to
the general. "It is Major André," he cried in a tone
of despair. Washington's first words were, "Take
fifty horse, and bring me Arnold dead or alive."
Then he at once gave orders for all the army to be
under arms. His next care was to have the prisoner
searched; there was found on him a paper containing all the particulars of the plan agreed upon—the
surprise of the fort at West Point, and a simulta-
neous attack on our army. God knows what would
have become of the American cause if the plot had
succeeded.

The major was brought into the camp, under a
strong escort, to be tried and sentenced; the least
indulgence shown to him, would, in the circumstances in which we were placed, have been followed by a mutiny in the army.

Few culprits in modern history have inspired and
deserved more general interest than this unhappy

young man; a distinguished, brave, and active officer, handsome, amiable, and only twenty-six years
of age. We received quite a procession of envoys
who came to treat for his release. The English generals came in person, and offered almost anything
to save his life. There was only one condition we
could accept, and that was that Arnold should be
delivered into our hands. The English were sorrow-
fully obliged to refuse this; they could not accede to
the terms.

Major André was tried and condemned to be
hanged; he did not even obtain the privilege of being shot. I can certify that when they came out after
the court-martial the faces of all our generals
showed marks of the most profound grief: the Marquis de la Fayette had tears in his eyes. The unfortunate young man met his death courageously; he
said loudly that he did not think it dishonourable
to have acted as he did against "rebels."

The inevitable doom of Major André only served
to accentuate the scorn and hatred that Arnold obtained and deserved. The traitor received his promised reward from the British government, but care
was taken not to employ him as a general, the soldiers, both men and officers, being exasperated
against him.[37]

[37] Pontgibaud was here indulging himself in a bit of righ-
teous indignation. The British made Arnold a brigadier general and he led raids into Virginia and against New London,
Connecticut, in 1781.

His wife and children, whom he had left behind, were in our power. He was base enough to suppose that they would be held responsible for his crime, and insolently wrote to General Washington threatening severe reprisals, and the destruction of Washington's beautiful estate in Virginia if any harm happened to his family. The sole reply Washington made was to order Mrs. Arnold and her children to be conducted into the British lines, with every possible attention. It was, I believe, Colonel Hamilton who was charged with this duty, with instructions to spare them every possible inconvenience.

No event of importance happened during the next few weeks, but we learned that the British government was sending Commissioners to New York to arrange the terms of peace. One of the representatives was Lord Carlisle,[38] a very young man. He was the cause of a scandal, the odium and ridicule of which affected him alone. He had inserted in the English papers, which were read at New York, a paragraph to the effect that the Marquis de la Fayette had been very well received at the Court of St. James, but a very short time before his departure for America, and therefore it was base ingratitude on his part to play the Don Quixote, and help the colonists in their rebellion against their sovereign. The

[38] Frederick Howard, Fifth Earl of Carlisle, led an abortive peace commission to America in 1778 and arrived just as the British were evacuating Philadelphia. At this time he was in New York.

Marquis de la Fayette felt personally insulted by this, and deemed himself justified in demanding satisfaction. A messenger was sent with a flag of truce to carry the challenge, but though the noble lord could not have thought this opponent beneath him in rank, he contented himself with replying that he would leave the quarrel to be settled by Admiral Howe[39] and Comte d'Estaing. My lord was well known in the fashionable circles of London, and we therefore caused to be inserted in the papers, that he was nothing more than a young dandy, who wore rouge and patches, and was afraid to fight, and the laugh was on our side.

A little later on, Comte d'Estaing appeared before New York with a fleet of twelve vessels of the line and several frigates.[40]

The American army, encouraged by the presence of the French Fleet, advanced the lines close to the city.

D'Estaing had hoped to be able to attack the British fleet in the port, with the advantage of superior force. Admiral Howe's squadron consisted only of seven or eight vessels of 50 guns. The French ships,

[39] Lord Richard Howe (1726-1799). Elder brother of Sir William Howe and commanding admiral on the American station.

[40] Comte Charles Hector Théodat d'Estaing (1729-1794) began his career as a soldier but switched to the navy. In 1763 he had been promoted to vice admiral. Despite his intense hatred for the English he was singularly unsuccessful against them in North American waters. He was executed during the French Revolution, April 28, 1794.

being much larger, drew too much water, and were afraid of venturing too far in, for fear of running aground. The *Languedoc*, d'Estaing's flag vessel, mounted 110 guns. They were therefore obliged to renounce their original plan, and change tactics.

The Marquis de la Fayette gave me a letter of introduction to Comte d'Estaing, which I presented, though I was a trifle nervous at the idea of an interview with such an important personage.

He received me very well, and asked a good many questions which I was easily able to answer. I was closeted with him fully two hours. I partook of a most excellent dinner on board the Admiral's vessel, and was therefore much surprised to hear Comte d'Estaing complain that he was in need of many of the necessaries of life;—it certainly did not appear so. I announced the speedy arrival of fifty fat oxen;—which caused such universal pleasure that, before I had finished speaking, the good news was being conveyed by speaking trumpet or signals to all the vessels of the fleet.

All the officers surrounded me, and cross-questioned me closely as to our position, forces, etc. I was quite an important personage. Le Bailly de Suffren[41]—then only in command of a 50-gun ship— sent for me on board his vessel. I was obliged, in

[41] Pierre André Suffren de Saint-Tropez (1729–1788). This French admiral was usually called Bailli de Suffren. Some have termed him the best admiral of the French fleet at this time.

order to please him, to drink such a quantity of punch that when I left the ship I was afraid I should fall into the sea.

I was very happy to meet my cousin, the Chevalier de F—, now the Comte de F—, Grand Cross of the Order of St. Louis, and Vice Admiral: he was then a midshipman on board *La Provence*. He had heard of my escape from Pierre-en-Cize, and we now met, eighteen hundred leagues from home, in the midst of a campaign;—the proper place for both of us, however. I was greatly obliged to him for many kindnesses, and more particularly for a small supply of clothes, with which naval officers are always well supplied, and which, as I greatly needed them, I took care not to refuse.

At last I took leave of Comte d'Estaing, who entrusted me with dispatches for the commander-in-chief. I remember that he also gave me some kegs of lemons and pine-apples, which he had found on board a prize he had taken. To regain the camp, I had a voyage of twenty miles to make in a boat. I was so hungry during the night that I devoured several of the pine-apples; and they nearly killed me.

The plan of campaign of 1778 was changed; a combined attack was to be made, the French Fleet was to blockade Newport, Rhode Island, between New York and Boston, whilst a part of the army, under the command of General Sullivan, and comprising the division of the Marquis de la Fayette, was to besiege the place by land as part of the attack.

We effected our landing on this beautiful island in the most orderly manner, and without any difficulties, under the protection of three frigates sent by Comte d'Estaing.

Hardly had the troops disembarked before the militia,—to the number, I believe, of about ten thousand men, horse and foot,—arrived. I have never seen a more laughable spectacle; all the tailors and apothecaries in the country must have been called out, I should think;—one could recognize them by their round wigs. They were mounted on bad nags, and looked like a flock of ducks in crossbelts. The infantry was no better than the cavalry, and appeared to be cut after the same pattern. I guessed that these warriors were more anxious to eat up our supplies than to make a close acquaintance with the enemy, and I was not mistaken,—they soon disappeared.

A few days after we had disembarked, we opened our trenches before the place, and the works were being pushed on with great activity, when the British fleet appeared before Newport.

Comte d'Estaing at once gave orders to sail; there was little wind, but what there was was favourable. Our fleet defiled majestically in front of the enemy's earthworks; each vessel as she passed gave a broadside of half her guns, amongst them many 24- and 36-pounders, to which the forts replied with their 10- and 12-pounders. Our fleet gave chase to the British, who made all sail. Both fleets were soon lost to sight. We awaited the news of a victory, but our fleet was dispersed by a terrible storm, and our admiral's vessel, the *Languedoc*, dismasted by the gale, was very nearly captured by the enemy. The *César*, a vessel of 74 guns, commanded by M. de Raimondis, separated from the rest of the squadron, had a very severe engagement with some of the enemy's vessels. The captain lost his right arm, but managed to save his ship, which we thought had been captured. It was in the midst of this tempest that Admiral Byron's[42] fleet arrived and joined that of Admiral Howe. The enemy then had the advantage in strength.

The siege still went on, but when M. d'Estaing re-appeared before Newport he told us he must withdraw the three frigates he had left to protect us, and we must raise the siege. D'Estaing took all the fleet to Boston for repairs.

General Sullivan, angry at finding himself no longer supported by the French fleet, went so far as to insult our nation, and call the French traitors. Our two generals were almost on the point of fighting a duel. The Marquis de la Fayette complained bitterly, and with good reason, to Washington, of the treatment he had received. The retreat was made in good order; we rejoined the main army.

In this expedition the commanders, both by land

[42] John Byron (1729–1786), British admiral. Grandfather of the poet, Lord Byron. He succeeded Lord Howe as commander of the British navy in American waters.

and sea, were dissatisfied with each other and themselves, but for me the siege had been rather pleasant, and on one occasion I received compliments which were as numerous as they were sincere. The occasion was as follows:

The Chevalier de Preville, who commanded the three frigates intended to protect our communications, wrote to me to ask if he could obtain some supplies for his sailors. I handed his letter to the Marquis de la Fayette, and General Sullivan authorized me to take a detachment and forage between the two camps.

For twenty-four hours I was in chief command, and had to make all the military and gastronomic dispositions required. The space between the enemy's forts and our lines was covered with houses and gardens, the owners of which had deserted them, not caring about living between two fires. My work had to be carried out right under the enemy's nose, and I fully expected there would be some bullets to receive. I had requisitioned all the carts I could find, and filled them with fruit and,—so well does heaven protect good works,—not a shot was fired at us.

The frigates, being informed by signal, of the success of my expedition, sent off a number of boats, and I protected the convoy down to the beach. You should have seen with what gusto the sailors devoured the apples, and with what alacrity they unloaded the carts of potatoes, carrots, and other vegetables. Their gratitude was all the greater as they had been some time without any fresh vegetables. They hailed me as the good fairy of the fleet, and when I went on board I was enthusiastically welcomed.

The French government at last decided to recognize the United States as independent, and sent out M. Gerard[43] as French Ambassador to Congress. It was quite time France took a step of this kind, for the help that she had sent through Caron de Beaumarchais had not given much satisfaction. The letters that he wrote to Congress, for instance, displayed a levity which amounted almost to insolence. I have kept a copy of one of his letters.

> GENTLEMEN,
>
> I beg to inform you that the ship *Amphitrite*, of 400 tons burden, will leave with the first fair wind for whatever port of the United States she may be able to reach. The cargo of the vessel, which is consigned to you, consists of 4,000 muskets, 80 barrels of gunpowder, 8,000 pairs of boots, 3,000 woollen blankets, also some engineer and artillery officers; *item*, a German Baron, formerly aide-de-camp to Prince Henry of Prussia, of whom you can make a general.
>
> I am, Gentlemen,
> Your obedient Servant,
> C. DE BEAUMARCHAIS

The members of Congress were very indignant

[43] Conrad Alexandre Gerard (1729–1790). Gerard was the first French Minister to the United States from July, 1778 to October, 1779.

about this letter, with the contents of which they made all us Frenchmen acquainted, but it was on a par with all that he did, and what might have been expected from such a man.

The German Baron of whom he spoke so slightingly, was Baron Steuben,[44] a great tactician, who was accompanied also by the Chevalier de Ternan,[45] a very distinguished officer. I have already named M. Duportail, M. Duplessis-Mauduit, and M. de la Rouarie. When the last-named presented himself before Congress, he was attended by his valet, a tall, handsome, and very brave man, named Lefevre. M. de la Rouarie at once received his commission as colonel, and, so simple and inexperienced were the members of the Committee, that they offered a similar commission to the valet on the strength of his good looks. He thanked Congress for the proffered honour, but begged leave to refuse it. Congress then consisted of thirteen members, one

[44] Friedrich Wilhelm Augustus von Steuben (1730-1794). Prussian officer. Although he had only reached the rank of captain in the army of Frederick the Great, Beaumarchais's letter of introduction termed Steuben a "Lieutenant General in the King of Prussia's service." First serving in the American army as an unpaid volunteer, he was credited with turning the armed mob at Valley Forge into some semblance of a military machine. Later he was made a major general and Inspector General. After the war he became an American citizen and lived in New York.

[45] Jean de Ternant, a French officer. In April, 1778, he was appointed as a sub-inspector under Steuben. In 1789 he returned as ambassador to the United States from revolutionary France.

from each State of the Union, but men very different from us in their habits and ways.[46] They took their seats in the Congress Hall, as we should enter a reading room in Paris, and the wisdom of their magnanimous resolutions was even surpassed by the simplicity of their manners.

After the siege of Newport was raised, we returned to the camp. General Washington and Congress decided to send La Fayette to France to ask for further supplies of men and money, the American paper money having fallen into utter discredit.

Great haste was made to finish building the frigate *Alliance*, which was to be a fast sailer, armed with thirty-six 12-pounders. The command of the new vessel was given to a Frenchman, Captain Landais of St. Malo, but the ship was under the orders of M. de la Fayette, and the captain was to land him wherever he wished. To complete the crew we, unfortunately, took seventy English prisoners. They were fine sailors, and as they had all taken an oath of fidelity, it was thought they could be trusted.

The winter was very severe, and the ship was not fitted out till the end of January. The port of Boston was then frozen, and we were obliged to cut a passage for the ship through the ice. The wind was extremely violent, though favourable. We put up our mainsail only and that alone took us along at the rate of ten knots an hour. There were many

[46] This was obviously a committee of Congress, for that body had far more than thirteen members.

French officers on board, amongst others M. de Raimondis, the captain of the *César*, who had lost his right arm in the last naval battle.

Off the Bank of Newfoundland we were assailed by a terrible tempest. It lasted so long, and grew so much worse, that first inquietude, then alarm, and at last consternation, seized everybody on board.

M. de la Fayette was invariably very ill at sea: he was down on the sick list. He often sent me to enquire after old Captain Raimondis, who suffered much pain from his amputation,—sufferings which were increased by the heavy rolling of the ship. The old sailor did not take a hopeful view of the situation; he told me that he had never, in all his voyages, met with such a fearful tempest. I carried these remarks back to M. de la Fayette, but to comfort him as well as myself, I told him that I thought the state of health of Captain Raimondis must necessarily influence his mind, and make matters look worse than they really were. M. de la Fayette lay on his back and soliloquized on the emptiness of glory and fame.

"Diable!" he said, philosophically, "I have done well certainly. At my time of life—barely twenty years of age—with my name, rank, and fortune, and after having married Mlle de Noailles,[47] to leave everything and serve as a breakfast for codfish!"

For my own part I was better off; I had nothing to

[47] Lafayette had married Marie Adrienne Françoise de Noailles in 1773 when he was but sixteen years of age.

lose and no one to regret me. I went back to the old sailor. He occupied a cabin on the deck below that where M. de la Fayette was lodged, so that in going from one to the other I met with frequent falls, and had plenty of bruises to show as the result of my messages. It was impossible to keep one's feet, owing to the continual heavy seas which struck the ship. There was some talk of cutting the masts. One of my comrades M. de N——, became so excited that I saw him charge his pistols, so as to shoot himself rather than be drowned. There did not seem to me a pin to choose between either fate, but his last hour had not yet come. This unlucky fellow had a mania for suicide. In 1792, after the 10th August, he was an officer in the Constitutional Guards, and when the "patriots" came to drag him away to the Abbaye, he escaped from their hands by passing his sword through his body. At the end of three days,—which seemed very long, I must admit,—the tempest ceased, and during the rest of the voyage we had favourable weather.

But heaven had yet another trial in store for us. Whilst we were at dinner one day, thinking no more of bad weather, but of France, from which we were now only some five hundred miles distant, one of the crew entered, and asked to speak to M. de la Fayette. He took the Marquis on one side, and told him a good deal in a very few words; namely, that the English sailors had laid a plot to kill us, take possession of the vessel, and turn her head towards

England. This was to be effected at five o'clock in the evening, when the English sailors came off their watch. Our informant added, that many of the men, especially the ringleaders, would be found to have arms concealed in their hammocks. He had only joined in the plot, he said, in order to be able to save us.

There was not a moment to be lost. We numbered in all fourteen officers. We began by securing the man who had warned us, and Duplessis-Mauduit stood over him with a cocked pistol in his hand. Some of us then went to fetch the bravest and trustiest of our sailors, who came quickly and ready armed. Thirty of us went down between decks, and, as the hammock of each of the ringleaders was pointed out to us by the man who had betrayed the conspiracy, the cords were cut with one blow of a hatchet, and the man thrown out, seized, and bound, before he was half awake. The scoundrels were so taken by surprise that they made no resistance. At first they all denied the existence of a plot, but on being questioned separately, the fear of being hanged on the spot made them confess their crime, one of the motives for which, it appeared, was that they had noticed amongst the baggage of M. de la Fayette, some very heavy cases which they supposed contained treasure. The informer was, of course, rewarded as he deserved. None of us went to bed that night; we had to watch over sixty men, bound, and shut up between decks. In the cabin which served as our council-chamber, nothing was to be seen but loaded pistols and drawn swords.

At daybreak we found that a Swedish merchant vessel was close to us. Captain Landais made the master come on board. The poor man's terror at seeing our cabin was ludicrous, the sight of all these deadly weapons made him imagine that his last hour had come. We tried to re-assure him by signs, for he did not know a word of French. For two whole days he was too frightened to either eat or drink, but he ended by finding our dinners very good, and our wine excellent. Captain Landais maintained that the Swede was a legitimate capture, but, when we arrived in France, we were forced to let him go.

We were all anxious to see land, for we were tired out, and we were worried moreover, by the fear of meeting a hostile vessel stronger than ourselves, in which case it was tolerably certain that the men we were guarding below decks would have helped her. We had lost our top masts in the tempest, so flight would have been impossible. We were not yet in sight of land,—though it could have been at no great distance,—when an English cruiser of 16 guns, saw us and gave chase. As we showed no guns she no doubt thought ours was a vessel of the French East India Company, and a rich prize. So sure of this were her crew, that, as she neared us they mounted the rigging and cheered. When she was within half range she fired a shot to make us show our colours. We instantly ran up the American flag, and followed that by giving her a broad side.

She quickly saw her mistake, and lowered her flag. We contented ourselves with sending a boat's crew on board, and throwing all her guns and powder into the sea. We took a lot of Madeira wine, which we found on board, and then let her go in this pitiable condition. In our peculiar situation that was the most we could do.

When we came within sight of the French coast, I noticed that our captain was making towards the English Channel. He would no doubt have been glad to revisit St. Malo, his native town. I told M. de la Fayette, who caused him to put the vessel about and make for Brest, where we disembarked.

II

OUR FIRST CARE was to conduct to the town jail the rascally British sailors we had had so much trouble to guard. Instructions were given that they should be taken back to America, at the first opportunity, and there judged according to the laws of the country.

The naval officers received us well, but we could not make a long stay at Brest. Everyone of us wished to turn his steps toward home. The Marquis de la Fayette, who no longer philosophized now that he was safe on dry land, went to the Hôtel de Noailles. His arrival was the news of the day, both at Paris and Versailles. The Queen of France did him the honour to bring Madame de la Fayette in her own carriage. She was surprised to meet her husband, for she had not been apprised of his return.

As for me, I took the *diligence*[48] and made my way first to Clermont, and then to the paternal mansion, the Château of Pontgibaud. Gratitude took precedence of natural affection, however, for as the places happened to be on my road, I first went to Nantes, and thanked M. de la Ville-Hélis, and then to La Rochelle to thank M. Seigneur for past services. I did not want to surprise my father by arriving unexpectedly, and therefore took care to write and announce my return. Along with my

[48] A stage coach.

own very respectful letter, I enclosed one which the Marquis de la Fayette had been kind enough to write to my father.

In spite of these precautions, I felt a sort of fear as I entered his room, and appeared before him for the first time. We were both equally embarrassed. His clouded brow betokened a storm, not an approaching storm, however, but one that is dying away in the distance. He addressed some reproaches to me, but they were merely a matter of form, intended to keep up the appearance of paternal dignity, and mainly concerned the heavy expenses which my journey from Paris to Pierre-en-Cize, and my imprisonment there had cost him.

I very naturally observed that perhaps if he had given me all that money he would have made a better use of it, and so should I. This very sensible reflection was too much for his gravity; he quite unbent, and it was with difficulty that he could prevent himself from laughing.

At the end of two hours he was no longer the same man, his curiosity had got the better of him, and he wanted me to give a full account of my Odyssey, my escape, voyage across the Atlantic, shipwreck, campaigns, and all. He made me read to him many times M. de la Fayette's letter, which corroborated all my statements. I say advisedly that he made me read it to him, for he had lost one of his eyes, many years before, at the Battle of Dettingen, and old age had enfeebled the sight of the other. I passed a fortnight at home, and by that time every cloud had passed away, and the sky was blue. I was so well restored to my father's affection that when I was leaving him to return to Paris to ask for a position in the army, he made me a present of 200 louis, increased my allowance to 1000 crowns, and gave me the address of a banker whom he had instructed to repay M. de la Fayette all the advances he had made on my account. He even offered to purchase a cavalry company for me if I could obtain one. He gave me besides a letter of thanks to my general. It was with a heart full of gratitude that I left him and started for Paris.

The nine beatitudes awaited me there. Certainly there must be some communication between heaven and earth, for no sooner was I restored to my respected father's good graces than all sorts of good fortune fell upon me.

At Paris I lodged in furnished apartments, not having the least idea where I should find any of my numerous relations, whom I believed to all be at their country houses at that season of the year. My uncle, the President de Salaberry took me to his house, and asked me to consider it as my home. He was a kind, good man, but that did not prevent him from being murdered during the Revolution. . . . He heaped kindnesses upon me with the same serenity of conscience with which, as my father's brother-in-law he had loaded me with abuse in my earlier days; but at that time he had been prejudiced against me by falsehoods and innuendoes which he was now annoyed with himself for having believed.

When he had finished welcoming and embracing me, my kind but over-hasty uncle handed me a letter from my father, dated at Pontgibaud, 19th April, 1779. I shall never forget the date—*albo dies notanda lapillo*. I pressed to my heart this letter, which was addressed to my uncle, and in which I was happy to read these words, which showed me that my father's present kindness was due to his sense of justice.

"Monsieur le Comte," wrote the secretary, for the good old man was obliged to dictate his letters, "desires that the Chevalier shall want for nothing; his intention being to compensate him amply for the misfortunes he has suffered by the injustice which was done him. He has been the victim of a sordid conspiracy which was discovered too late."

I thought no more of the injury that had been done me, except as a pleasing reminiscence, and dated my happiness back to the day of my escape, which after all had been something of a feat.

But I was far from knowing all the favours that fortune had in store for me. After I had been three weeks in Paris, the Marquis de la Fayette informed me that the King had given him a regiment of dragoons, and that His Majesty had granted me a commission as *capitaine de remplacement,* which entitled me to half-pay. The Minister of War confirmed the good news in an official letter, in which he said that by the wish of an important personage who did not wish his name to be known,—though I easily guessed it,—and who had taken me under his protection, the price of the brevet, that is to say 7000 francs, was remitted, and I had nothing to pay for my commission. I had no further happiness to desire, for, since the end of the "Seven Years' War", France had been at peace, and the army swarmed with young officers with aristocratic names. It was more difficult to be a cavalry captain in 1779 than it was to be a colonel twenty or thirty years later.

The French Government was then meditating a descent on England. A large army assembled in Brittany and Normandy, under the command of the Comte de Vaux.

Many transport ships were also collected at Havre and St. Malo. M. de la Fayette sent for me and told me that I was to start for Lorient, in company with the Chevalier de Gimat,[49]—who had been one of his *aides-de-camp* in the American War,— and there wait for orders. There were some hints of a secret expedition. My heart beat with joy. My comrade, who was much older than I, a colonel, and a very experienced officer, was in the secret, but it

[49]Jean-Joseph Sourbader de Gimat (1743-?). Coming to America with Lafayette, Gimat was commissioned a major in the Continental army. He was cited for his bravery at Yorktown. After the war he was promoted to colonel in the French army. From 1789 to 1792 he served as governor of the West Indian island of St. Lucia.

was in vain that I tried to draw it out of him. He confined himself to repeating that I was very lucky, and that I should find that the patronage of the Marquis de la Fayette would be of great service to me. Beyond this he would tell me nothing.

Many armed vessels were awaiting us in the port of Lorient; the *Bon Homme Richard*, a vessel belonging to the India Company mounting 54 guns of various calibres; the frigate *Alliance*, on which we had made the voyage back to France; the *Pallas*, 32 guns, commanded by Captain Cottineau of Nantes, an able officer of the merchant service, etc. These were under the orders of the celebrated American commodore, Paul Jones, who commanded the *Bon Homme Richard*. A number of brigs and corvettes completed the little squadron.

We were to receive, on board these vessels and some transport ships, about 3000 men drafted from different regiments of the French army, and under the command of Marquis de la Fayette. I know now, what I did not know at that time, though I much wished to, that the object of this expedition was to make a descent upon Ireland, whilst the army of Comte de Vaux, protected by the combined fleets of France and Spain, under Comte d'Orvilliers, were to co-operate at the same time in a similar descent on the English coast. For some reason, unknown to me, the execution of this plan was deferred, and finally abandoned by the French Government.

During the six weeks that I spent in idleness at Lorient, I was eye-witness of a most curious, ridiculous, and incredible incident. A man in uniform dashed up the staircase, rushed into the room where I was sitting, and begged me to protect him. He looked scared, and anxious. It was no other than our brave,—indeed more than brave,—Commodore, the famous Paul Jones.

"Shut the door," he cried. "That scoundrel Captain Landais[50] met me in the town and wants to fight me. He is pursuing me from street to street, sword in hand. I do not know how to fence and I do not want to be killed by that rascal."

I closed the door and double-locked it, but the Captain never came. Certainly Paul Jones acted very sensibly, for the match was not equal; Captain Landais with his drawn sword would have made short work of him, and Paul Jones had nothing but blows to gain by the encounter. This adventure does not in the least detract from his reputation. His recent fight with the *Serapis*, that he captured

[50]Pierre Landais (1734–?). French naval officer. After a distinguished naval career he was discharged from the French navy in 1779 and assigned to the American squadron of John Paul Jones. He and Jones disliked each other from the beginning. During Jones's famous engagement with the *Serapis*, Landais, who commanded the *Alliance*, unaccountably fired a broadside into the side of Jones's *Bon Homme Richard*. His naval career was not ended as suggested by Pontgibaud. He remained in American service until 1792, and he became a vice admiral in the French revolutionary navy.

by boarding, placed his courage above all suspicion, and put him on an equality with all the boldest, luckiest, and bravest sailors of ancient or modern times.

His quarrel with Captain Landais, of which this fight was a part, was not for the possession of a Helen, but for the command of the frigate *Alliance*, which had been ordered to sail at once for America, for, owing to some veering of the political compass, everything had been changed.

Six thousand Frenchmen, under the command of Comte de Rochambeau, and including a great number of young noblemen of the Court, anxious to have the privilege of serving as volunteers, were sent to the aid of the Americans, and embarked on a fleet of vessels, commanded by the Chevalier de Ternan, which was to sail from Brest.

M. de la Fayette having sent in his resignation as Colonel of Dragoons, had taken leave of the King in the uniform of a Major General of the United States' army, and was already on board the French frigate *Aigle*, commanded by M. de la Touche Treville. La Fayette was to take the command of a division of Washington's army which was then encamped in Jersey Province, near New York. We received orders to join him, and embarked on the frigate *Alliance*, which was to sail without delay. Captain Landais had secured the command without striking a blow.

The conqueror of the *Serapis* had hardly left my

sheltering roof than he went to Paris to show himself. The Parisians went to their windows to see him pass, and thronged to the Opera the night he went there. Marshal de Biron, who did the honours of the capital to all the great personages, received Paul Jones with every mark of respect, and placed the regiment of Gardes Françaises under arms, in order to show it to the commander of the *Bon Homme Richard*.

But during this time, Captain Landais remained at Lorient, and the American Minister we were to take back, being in haste to depart, took it upon himself not to wait for Paul Jones, and nominated Landais to the command.

We had sailed about a week when Paul Jones returned from Paris, and found himself without a command. We had on board two commissioners from Congress, and we were bound for Boston. It was decreed, apparently, that I should meet with strange adventures during my transatlantic voyages. On this voyage the captain went out of his mind. We had previously noticed some peculiarities in his manner, and we were soon to acquire the certainty that he was insane.

His madness broke out one day at dinner, the cause being a turkey that he was carving. Mr Lee,[51] one of the commissioners, who sat beside him, took the liver, and was about to eat it when Landais rose

[51]Arthur Lee, one of the original American envoys to France. He was recalled by Congress in September, 1779.

in a fury, and threatened to kill him with the carving-knife. Everyone rose, and the two nephews of the American commissioner ran to call some of the crew to prevent their uncle being murdered. Landais shouted out that the best morsel belonged by right to the captain. He said and did all sorts of foolish things. I took up my dinner knife in order to defend myself, for he seemed as though he were coming at me to take vengeance on me because I was roaring with laughter. He was raving mad. A number of the sailors ran up, and the commissioners ordered them to seize and bind the captain, which was done. We drew up an official report of the incident; and the command of the vessel was given to the first officer.

Under the direction of the new captain, we made a good passage, and disembarked at the end of ten or twelve days.

Our course of action (in deposing the captain) was approved by the authorities at Boston. Such was the end of Captain Landais, the rival of Paul Jones—as far as my knowledge of him is concerned, at all events, for I never heard what became of him afterwards.

I hastened to rejoin the American army, which three weeks after my arrival, marched for Virginia.

This was in 1780. The little army of Comte de Rochambeau was blockaded in Rhode Island, where it had disembarked about the middle of the year. It was completely powerless to undertake any

COMTE DE ROCHAMBEAU
Jean Baptiste Donatien de Vimeur
Commander of the French Army in America

From Edwin M. Stone's, *Our French Allies*, 1884

decisive action until the arrival of the French fleet.

It was not till 1781, almost a year after the landing, that the fleet under Comte de Grasse[52] entered Chesapeake Bay. During this long interval, the American army, to which I belonged, performed no action of historical interest. I, for my part, shared with the others the dangers, and took part in the few indecisive skirmishes of the campaign, which we passed in marching and counter-marching, with occasional out-post affairs—in fact it was a war of observation.

The approach of the French fleet favoured a plan of attack which might result in a general and decisive engagement, and Comte de Rochambeau at last left Rhode Island. Washington's army embarked, joined the French forces, and we hemmed in the principal British army which then occupied Virginia and was in position at York Town. Lord Cornwallis, the commander-in-chief, was attacked by us on 6th October. One of the two principal redouts was carried by the Marquis de la Fayette and the Americans a quarter of an hour before the French, headed by the regiment of "Grenadiers de Deux-

[52] Comte François Joseph Paul de Grasse (1722–1788). After a long and distinguished naval career he was promoted to rear admiral in 1781. He played a decisive role in the victory at Yorktown by defeating Admiral Samuel Graves in the naval battle off the Chesapeake Capes, September 5, 1781, thereby cutting off effective aid for Cornwallis in Yorktown. He later suffered disgrace when he was defeated in the battle off Saints Passage, April 9–12, 1782.

Ponts" captured the other. The French and Americans emulated each other in courage and obstinacy, and the English also fought like devils. But British pride was humbled and Marquis Cornwallis was obliged to capitulate.

The young Duc de Lauzun[53] was sent by the two generals to arrange the terms of surrender. He went alone, waving his white handkerchief in his hand, for the chivalric Duc de Lauzun never acted like anyone else would in the same circumstances. The British army did not come out with drums beating, colours flying, and all the honours of war, but was forced to defile between a double row of French and Americans, and lay down their arms, to the shame and confusion of their brave and unfortunate soldiers. Marquis Cornwallis wished to give up his sword to Comte de Rochambeau, but the French general made a sign with his hand to show that the honour of receiving it belonged to Washington as the commander-in-chief.

The English, now shut in New York State, were no longer in a condition to continue the campaign, and there followed a kind of tacitly arranged truce extending over the eighteen months which preceded the declaration of peace. The combined armies of Washington and Comte de Rochambeau were

[53]Armand Louis de Gontaux Biron, Duc de Lauzun (1747–1793). Lauzun was stationed across the York River at Gloucester Point and he was appointed to negotiate with the British force under Banastre Tarleton. It would appear that Pontgibaud was also at Gloucester throughout the siege.

compelled to remain inactive, for the surrender at York Town had settled the question of American Independence, though the French and English continued to fight at sea for a few months longer. Being unacquainted with that kind of diplomacy which leads to nothing more than an exchange of cannon shot between hostile fleets, and finding that not another musket was to be fired in war on the American continent, M. de la Fayette left for France, and I did the same, for we had nothing in common with the little French army which remained in the United States until further orders.

Comte de Rochambeau's officers had nothing better to do, I suppose, than travel about the country. When we think of the false ideas of government and philanthropy which these youths acquired in America, and propagated in France with so much enthusiasm and such deplorable success,—for this mania of imitation powerfully aided the Revolution, though it was not the sole cause of it,—we are bound to confess that it would have been better, both for themselves and us, if these young philosophers in red-heeled shoes had stayed at the Court.

But a truce to these reflections which have nothing to do with my memoirs. In the autumn of 1781, my friend, the Chevalier de Capellis, was about to sail for France in the frigate *Ariel*, which he commanded, and he took me on board. The *Ariel* was a prize captured by Comte d'Estaing's squadron; a fast sailer, she carried only eighteen 9-pounders.

We started with a favourable wind, but a few days later were assailed by a tempest, which are frequent in these seas. My friend swore, as all sailors do, that this should be his last voyage; he was rich and would certainly never expose himself again to any of the dangers of this cursed profession. I did not believe a word of it, and I was quite right. He related to me the history of his brother, who had perished at sea,—this story always occurred to his recollection whenever the weather was bad. To my way of thinking, the storm, however, was not to be compared to that which I had originally encountered on my first return, when I was on the frigate *Alliance*.

After a voyage of fifty-five days, we sighted the coasts of Spain. I must not omit to mention that when fifty leagues from land we had the pleasure of meeting the *Dublin*, armed with twelve 9-pounders. She rightly guessed that our vessel was of English build, and supposed that we were English, but she very soon found out her mistake, greatly to our satisfaction, though not to hers. Both ships having shown their flags, a cannonade ensued which lasted three quarters of an hour, at the end of which time the *Dublin* struck, for we were twice her size. She was loaded with merchandise.

The vessel and cargo belonged to the *Ariel*. I could not help laughing at my friend Capellis. During the fight he was everywhere at once, animating the gunners, swearing, and crying that our fire was not fast enough or heavy enough. When the *Dublin* struck, our gunners between decks, being unable to see on account of the smoke, or to hear on account of the noise, still went on firing.

Capellis then felt that the enemy's vessel was his property, and that every extra bit of damage done her was a loss to him. He quite changed his tone and cried, "Cease firing! cease firing!" but no one heard him. "Upon my word, that fellow has fired again!" he shouted as he saw one of the gunners let fly another shot. His anger was really comic, and I believe he would have killed the man if he had not been restrained.

We entered the port of Corunna in triumph, with our prize, and moored close to the *Argonaut*, a French vessel of 74 guns, commanded by M. de Caqueray. He was about to give a fête on board that day, and we received invitations.

Even before we touched land, I thus enjoyed the honour and pleasure of seeing the ladies of Corunna, who had been invited, so to speak, on purpose to meet us, but before the ball we were regaled with an unexpected sight which much astonished us.

Before we had even cast our anchor, we were surrounded by a host of small boats containing women bringing fruit, and who climbed up the ship's sides as though they had been sailor boys. Many of the women were young and pretty, and did not sell fruit. In spite of orders they stormed our vessel, and, as the sailors favoured them, they were soon all over the ship,—except in the gunroom there were women everywhere; we could not help laughing at this strange invasion.

The fête given by M. de Caqueray was a very grand one, and the ladies appeared to me charming, for it was so long since I had seen any.

I was not quite so enthusiastic about the city of Corunna which these beautiful ladies and damsels inhabited. I had just left the United States, a new country where the towns were all new and where the greatest cleanliness prevailed even in the most humble habitation; where nothing to excite disgust was ever seen, and there were no rags, and no beggers. At Corunna, I found old houses, mendicity at every corner, an atmosphere infected with smoke, and the smell of fried oil, and in fact all the innate dirtiness of people whose natural element is filth. Add to this the clatter of carts with wooden wheels rumbling over the most uneven pavement in the world. . . . we were invited to a ball given specially in our honour. Madame Tenoria, the wife of the naval commissioner, held a faro bank at her house every night. I remember that I once had a mind to play there, and I lost a hundred louis,—one of the clearest of all my recollections of my wanderings.

I saw my pieces of gold disappear without ever uttering an impatient word,—but the devil lost nothing by my silence. Inwardly I was harrowed with grief and rage. My face looked calm, but nevertheless I was just on the point of kicking over the

cursed gaming-table, when I was restrained by a remark of one of the bystanders. I distinctly heard
someone near me say, "What a fine gambler that
young officer is; he loses and never says a word." I
felt I was something of a hero, and that as a soldier I
had to sustain the honour of the cloth. I put my
hand back on the table, but if anyone could have
looked under my coat they would have seen that I
had buried the nails of the other hand in my flesh.
Nevertheless I left behind me at Corunna, not only
all my money, but the reputation of being a first-
rate gambler. The experience served me in good
stead, however, for since then I have never played
again.

An incident of another nature happened to us
whilst we were at Corunna,—one that might have
had serious consequences for us, though we were
not to blame.

We passed our evenings in one or other of the
best houses of the city, returning on board about
ten o'clock, at which time the boat was waiting for
us. One night, when the weather was very bad, we
happened to meet a religious procession in a narrow street; the *viaticum*[54] was being carried to some
great personage, I should imagine by the number of
people who followed the dais; there were a great
many women in the crowd. We three officers stood
on one side respectfully, removed our hats, and as it

[54] The Christian Eucharist given to a person in danger of
death.

was pouring with rain, we received all the water from the gutters on our unprotected heads, and were drenched to the skin. When the procession had passed, and was about thirty yards away, we thought we could with decency put on our hats, but the people tore them off again, crying and shouting something we could not understand, as we did not know Spanish. With that we all three drew our swords, whereupon these exceedingly pious Christians all tumbled over one another to get out of the way, and left us a clear road. We hastened our steps and took the first cross street we could find. The people, not wishing to lose anything of the ceremony, did not pursue us. Not knowing the town well, we probably did not take the shortest road to the boat, but we found it at last, and were very glad to take our seats in it.

I mentally recounted to myself all that had happened to me since Pierre-en-Cize, and I could not prevent saying to myself, all that is needed is to see myself flogged to slow music through this cursed town, and then figure in an *auto-da-fe*[55] with a *benito* on my head. But that would have been too much spite on the part of fortune, to heap so many misfortunes upon a simple individual like me.

Providence watched over us. Our adventure had, however, created some excitement in the town, and the commandant requested us to give him the true account of the matter. When he heard it, he recom-

[55] The burning of a heretic during the Inquisition.

mended us not to set foot on shore for some days, and he promised to come and dine on board with us the following day. He was an Irishman, very kind and very witty, and we agreed together perfectly, but we were disenchanted with Corunna, and a few days later, the wind being favourable, we weighed anchor, and after a good passage of a few days landed at Lorient.

I, and my friend the Chevalier de Capelis at once started for Paris.

4

Baroness von Riedesel

*

Her Revolutionary Journal

Baroness von Riedesel

As early as 1775 the government of George III had begun to seek soldiers who would fight for pay against the American rebels. First, the British turned to Catherine the Great of Russia, for that nation still had 20,000 Cossacks under arms who had not been disbanded after a war against the Turks. But Frederick the Great of Prussia and French envoys to the Russian court worked against the British negotiators and blunted their efforts. Catherine would only express a desire to enjoy the continued good will of the King of England and the hope that the American war might be settled by peaceful means.

Germany at this time was little more than a geographical expression, made up of small principalities, governed by princes who searched for the funds to continue the life style they felt they should maintain. Since George III was Elector of Hanover as well as King of England, it was only natural that he look in the direction of Germany for the manpower that he needed. The result was that almost 30,000 German mercenaries fought for the British during the American Revolution. Of the 29,867 Germans who landed on American shores, nearly 5,000 deserted; another 7,754 found graves in America from disease as well as wounds.

The Duke of Brunswick was the first German ruler to conclude a treaty with the British. It might be interesting to examine the details of the first contract. The British were to provide the German soldiers with the same pay, food, and medical care as they supplied their own troops. The Duke was to receive four pounds, four shillings, and four and one-half pence for each of the 4,300 men he provided, and would receive the same amount for each replacement needed to maintain this original strength. For each wounded Brunswicker the Duke would get half of the original payment, and for each one maimed he would receive one-third of that payment. He was to replace at his own expense those who died of illness or deserted. In addition to these payments for individuals, the British also agreed to annual payments, beginning January 9, 1776, when the treaty was signed, of an additional subsidy of £11,517. 17s. 1-1/2d; they were to pay twice this amount each year for the first two years after these mercenaries returned to Europe. And it should be noted that the Landgrave of Hesse-Cassel received more than twice as much per man, while Hesse-Hanau also held out for more money. These soldiers came from Brunswick,

Hesse-Cassel, Hesse-Hanau, Anspach-Bayreuth, Waldeck, and Anhalt-Zerbst. The total amount of money appropriated to pay for these troops was £4,584,450.

In general, the German soldiers were known as "Hessians," perhaps because Hesse-Cassel sent the greatest number of men, 16,992. Also the three successive commanders in chief of the German troops were Hessian: von Heister, von Knyphausen, and von Loosberg. Baron von Riedesel, who commanded the Germans during the Burgoyne campaign, began his military career as a Hessian officer, but came to America in command of the detachment from Brunswick.

These Hessians played an important role in the campaign against New York in 1777 under "Gentleman Johnny" Burgoyne. This was to be a thrust southward from Canada along a line through Lake Champlain, down the Hudson River to New York. In 1776, Sir Guy Carleton, governor of Canada, had driven down to Fort Ticonderoga on the southern end of Lake Champlain before the onset of cold weather forced him to pull back into winter quarters.

Major General John Burgoyne, member of Parliament, raconteur, man about London, and better than average playwright, had returned to England at the end of the campaign of 1776, his *purpose to further his martial career. To indulge his swelling ambition, by February 1777, he submitted a plan of conquest to the King. Although he suggested that it was original with him, similar ideas had been put forth earlier by Lord Dartmouth, Sir William Howe, and Carleton. The proposal involved a three-pronged movement of troops that was calculated to isolate New England from the remaining colonies. The main force, under Burgoyne, was to sweep almost majestically southward by way of Lake Champlain, Ticonderoga, and Albany. General William Howe was to dispatch troops up the Hudson, while a smaller force under Lieutenant Colonel Barry St. Leger was to strike inland from Fort Oswego on Lake Ontario. The three columns were to converge at Albany.*

On paper, the plan looked good, but paper plans too often fail to take into consideration the foibles of human behavior. The home government had been vague in its instructions to Howe and he had embarked on a strike against Philadelphia, thereby eliminating one arm of the three-pronged strike. Then Barry St. Leger, surging through the Mohawk Valley, had turned back at Fort Stanwix when his Indian allies deserted him.

The army under the command of Burgoyne was in itself something of a handicap, for his

*planning appeared to have been based on a Euro-
pean campaign rather than a trek through the
wilderness. It was a great cumbersome military
machine, numbering nearly 8,000 men, composed
of three British and three German brigades, plus
250 Canadians and 400 Indians. Over 1,500
horses were needed to transport the baggage—
thirty of the two-wheeled carts carried Burgoyne's
own resplendent wardrobe. One hundred and
thirty-eight pieces of artillery dictated the pace of
the march. Not only did Burgoyne bring along
his mistress, but there were a number of women
camp followers, including several gentlewomen
following their husbands off to war. Among the
latter was the dainty and vivacious Baroness von
Riedesel, wife of the general commanding the
German troops.*

*Frederika Charlotte Louise von Massow, the
Baroness von Riedesel, was from a military family. Her father, Hans Jürgen Detloff von Massow,
was a lieutenant general and commissary for
Frederick the Great. Frederika was born July 11,
1746, in Brandenburg-an-der-Havel. Apparently she accompanied her father on his military
travels, for it was during the Seven Years' War
(known as the French and Indian War in the
American colonies) that she met her future husband in 1759. At the time he was a dashing*

*young captain serving as aide-de-camp to the
Duke of Brunswick. Although the marriage in
1762 was arranged by the families concerned, it
was clearly a love match and continued so
throughout their lives.*

*The bridegroom of this sixteen-year-old girl
was twenty-four at the time. Friedrich Adolf
Riedesel had been born at his father's ancestral
castle at Lauterbach in Rhine-Hesse in 1738. Although his mother was the daughter of a Prussian general his father wanted him to study law,
but the martial spirit ran too strong through his
veins. He had joined a Hessian regiment at Mar-
burg. The first two children of this union died,
but by 1774 the baroness had borne her husband
two additional daughters.*

*By 1776 the thirty-eight year old Riedesel had
attained the rank of colonel. The day after the
treaty between the Duke of Brunswick and Great
Britain was signed, January 10, 1776, he was
appointed to command the first detachment destined for America. Despite her two small children
and the fact that she was pregnant once again,
the baroness persuaded her husband that she
should follow him to America. His reluctant
agreement included the proviso that she would
not travel during her pregnancy and that she
must be accompanied by a "lady of quality." And*

so it was that her husband marched off in February without his adoring wife. A few days later the baron was promoted to major general and he proudly wrote his wife, addressing her as "Mrs. General." In early April the general's command sailed from Portsmouth, England, for Canada where they arrived just in time to participate in Carleton's drive down Lake Champlain.

Unbeknownst to the general, the baroness, in March, had given birth to another daughter, even before he had sailed from England. By April mother and daughters were ready to begin their journey. She reached Calais in France June 1, 1776, the same day that her husband landed in Quebec. She experienced a number of frustrations and was forced to spend that winter in England. There were some pleasurable moments when she was presented at court, where she was kissed by George III and invited to informal visits by Queen Charlotte.

Madame Riedesel departed from Portsmouth April 6, 1777, aboard a merchant ship in a large convoy. But she was doomed to disappointment when she landed at Quebec on June 11, for her husband was off up the St. Lawrence making preparations for Burgoyne's campaign against the American rebels. So anxious was she to see her general that the baroness resolved not to spend even one night in Quebec. She did remain long enough to attend a dinner party given by Lady Carleton, but then was rowed up the St. Lawrence in search of her husband. The following journal reports her adventures from the time of her arrival in Quebec.

After their release as prisoners of war the Riedesels returned to Brunswick by way of Canada and England. In 1785 the baroness managed to present her husband with a male heir. And in 1782 the general inherited his father's castle at Lauterbach, although he did not retire to the estate. Instead, when the Duke appointed him a lieutenant general, he and his family settled in Brunswick. The general fought the Duke's wars until 1793 when he retired to Lauterbach, but after the "reign of terror" broke out in France the Duke recalled him as commandant of Brunswick, a post in which the baron served with distinction for the next five years. He died in his sleep on January 6, 1800, at the age of sixty-one.

"Mrs. General" survived her husband by eight years. Her journal was first printed in a limited edition for the family in 1800, but it aroused so much interest that a public edition was published that same year in Berlin. A Dutch edition appeared in 1801, while fragments of the journal were extracted and translated and pub-

lished in various English books. In 1827 the first complete English version was brought out by a New York publishing firm, but great license was taken in the translation. A much better effort, and the account used here, was translated by William L. Stone in 1867, reproduced in facsimile by the Arno Press in 1968. The latest and most modern edition was translated and edited by Marvin L. Brown in 1965 and published by the University of North Carolina Press. This later edition has been most useful in many of the identifications for this edition. I have taken the liberty of breaking the journal into chapters and have added chapter titles.

The baroness wrote with a directness and simplicity that flows through the printed word with grace and charm, and must be considered a reflection of her own personality. And that personality must have reached down through the ranks, for the soldiers referred to her as "Red Hazel," and "Lady Fritz." And during the six years she served in the field with her husband, her love for him moves like a swirling undercurrent throughout the journal. In a sense, this is one of the first on-the-scene accounts of warfare by a woman reporter. And for those reading the baroness's account for the first time, it will be like finding an old lace valentine in a cartridge box.

THE BARONESS RIEDESEL
Frederika von Massow

From her memoirs, edited by William L. Stone, 1867

Her Revolutionary War
Journal

I. THE REUNION

THE SAME Captain Pownel,[1] who, as I have already mentioned, brought my husband to Canada, tendered his services to bring me by water to
Point de Tremble; and a Mrs. Johnson offered, also,
to accompany me. About six o'clock in the evening
of the 11th of June (the same day that I arrived in
Quebec), we embarked on board one of the men-of-
war's boats; and at midnight arrived at a place seven
English miles from Quebec, having had with us all
the way, the most beautiful moonlight, and a splendid band of music. I put my children to bed; and
the rest of us sat up and drank tea together.

On the 12th, at half past two o'clock in the morning, we again set out in three calashes,[2] which are a
kind of light chaise or carry-all, very small and uncomfortable, but very fast. I could not bring my

[1]Philemon Pownell, as captain of the *Blonde*, had escorted
General Riedesel's Brunswickers to Canada in 1776. In
1777 he was captain of the *Apollo*, the ship returning Burgoyne to Canada.
[2]Here the baroness probably meant a calèche, a two-
wheeled vehicle. A calash is a four-wheeled vehicle and
probably would have been unsuited for travelling over wilderness roads.

heart to trust a single one of my children to my women servants; and as our calashes were open and very small, I bound my second daughter, Frederica, fast in one corner; took the youngest, little Caroline, on my lap; while my oldest, Gustava, as the most discreet, sat between my feet on my purse. I knew that if I would reach my husband I had no time to lose, as he was constantly on the march. I therefore promised a reward to the servants if they would drive me fast, and consequently we always went as quickly as the vehicles and horses would allow. The Canadians are everlastingly talking to their horses, and giving them all kinds of names. Thus, when they were not either lashing their horses or singing, they cried, *"Allons mon Prince! Pour mon General!"* Oftener, however, they said, *"Fi, donc, Madame!"* I thought that this last was designed for me, and asked, *"Plait-il?" "Oh,"* replied the driver, *"ce n'est que mon cheval, la petite coquine!"* ("It is only the little jade, my horse!") At every place through which I passed, the peasants greeted me, and cried, *"Voilá la femme de notre cher general!"*—treating me, at the same time, with great affection. Especially was I rejoiced to see my husband so beloved on every hand, and to have them all say to me, *"Oh qu'il sera content! Combien il a parlé de vous! Oh, qu'il vous aime!"* ("Oh, how delighted he will be! How often he has talked about you! Oh, how he loves you!") In the afternoon I came to Berthieux, where I was assured that no calash was to be had, and that I would be obliged to make use of a boat, or rather, a very light canoe, made of the bark of a tree. I begged and implored, and offered money upon money for a calash; for it was horrible weather, and I had to pass the three rivers, which cross each other, and lead to the village of Three Rivers. But it was all of no avail, since they pretended to consider these ferries as a regular post route, and wished to make money out of an ignorant foreigner. There remained, therefore, nothing farther for me to do than to embark. Seated on the bottom of the canoe in one corner, I had my three children upon my lap, while my three servants sat on the other side. We were obliged, at considerable trouble, to preserve our exact equilibrium, the necessity of which, however, I did not learn from our boatman, until we were overtaken by a severe hail storm; whereupon my daughter, little Frederica, became alarmed, screamed, and wanted to jump up. Then it was that the boatman told me that the canoe would be overturned by even the slightest movement. I was obliged, therefore, to hold her very firmly, and not mind her cries; and in this manner, we finally arrived the same evening at Three Rivers in safety, where our officers clapped their hands over their heads for joy; and I, by this manifestation, first learned the danger which I had risked.

Two gentlemen, while engaged in fishing, had been overtaken by a storm which upset their canoe, and they both were drowned. I thanked God that I had accomplished the passage so successfully, and yet it was not pleasing to me to know of my danger, for this very knowledge, ever afterward, rendered me timid in crossing the smallest river, even in the most beautiful weather.

The grand vicar had no sooner heard of my arrival, than he at once called upon me. He had conceived a great affection for my husband, who had spent the entire winter in this town, and he increased still more my eagerness to follow him as soon as possible, by all that he related of his tender love and apprehension for us, and his solicitude on account of our journey. He said that my husband had been sick, which he felt assured, had been caused by his distress at having been obliged to set out without seeing us; especially as he had been thrown into great anguish of mind by constant, though happily, false reports. For example, he had heard that a lady, who had embarked with three children, had gone down with the ship; and again, that I had actually sailed, but had become so frightened as to have repented of my resolution, and caused myself to be set ashore. I was, therefore, more strongly than ever fixed in my determination to hasten my journey in every possible way; and I immediately sent ahead an express to my husband, apprizing him of our coming. As the horrible weather still continued, the grand vicar had the kindness to offer me a covered calash, which I ac-

cepted, and departed in it the following morning at
six o'clock. This vehicle went so rapidly, that I
could scarcely recover my breath, and in addition
to which I was so jolted about (as I was constantly
obliged to hold my children), that I was completely
beaten to pieces. I was, therefore, obliged at every
post station, to stretch out my arms and walk
around a little, to render my joints more limber. In
going to Chambly, where it was possible that my
husband still was, I had to choose one of two roads.
I took the one through Montreal, where I arrived on
the evening of the 13th; passed the night there; and
set out the next morning very early, that I might see
my husband as soon as possible. I reached Chambly
on the 13th, and immediately caught sight of a
group of officers, and our coachman, whom my husband had left there. I at once ran to him and asked
where my husband was? "He has driven over to
Berthieux," he replied, "to meet you" (Berthieux
was fifteen English miles off !) Then I saw that I had
chosen the wrong road, and had consequently
missed him.

Upon this, General Carleton, who was among the
above mentioned party of officers, came up, and
assured me that my husband would be back at the
latest on the following day. He, thereupon, took his
departure and went back to Quebec, after having
delivered over the command of the troops to General Burgoyne. An adjutant of my husband remained
with me, and I awaited the following day—the 15th

of June—with impatience. My children and my faithful Rockel[3] kept a constant watch on the high road, that they might bring me news of my husband's arrival. Finally, a calash was descried having a Canadian in it. I saw from a distance the calash stop still, the Canadian get out, come nearer, and fold the children in his arms. It was my husband!

As he still had the fever, he was clothed (although it was summer) in a sort of cassock of woolen cloth bordered with ribbons, and to which was attached a variegated fringe of blue and red, after the Canadian fashion of the country. My joy was beyond all description, but the sick and feeble appearance of my husband terrified me, and a little disheartened me. I found both my oldest daughters in tears—Gustava for joy at again seeing her father, and little Frederica because she saw him in this plight. For this reason she would not go to him at all, but said, "No, no! this is a nasty papa; my papa is pretty!" This conduct arose from the fact, that I had often shown her the picture of her father, and had, at those times, said that he had handsome clothes. She was, therefore, not prepared for him in this costume. The moment, however, that he threw off his Canadian coat, she tenderly embraced him.

My husband informed me, that as he was on his way to meet us, he had, in order to rest himself a

[3] Rockel had served Madame Riedesel's father as a forester. He came with her to America as her footman and served her faithfully.

little, taken dinner with Colonel Anstruther,[4] and had then learned, that a woman had just arrived from Berthieux. He at once had her brought in, and asked her whether there was any news at that place? "Nothing more," she replied, "than that a German woman with three children had arrived, who, they say, is the wife of a German general." "How many children did you say?" quickly asked my husband. "Three," answered she. After this last answer, he did not desire to know more, particularly as he had been made happy by learning that all of his three children lived, and had arrived; for he had heard nothing from us the whole winter, as our ships were the first ones which had arrived this year.

We remained with each other two happy days. I wished very much to follow my husband, but he would not agree to it. I was therefore forced, to my great sorrow, to go back to Three Rivers, where I suffered yet more upon witnessing the departure of the troops against the enemy, while I, with my children, was obliged, alone and deserted, to return and live in a strange land among unknown people. Sorrowful and very much cast down I traveled back. What a difference between this journey and that which I had made a little while before! This time I did not move so quickly; for at every post station, which removed me further from him I loved, my heart was torn open afresh.

[4] Lieutenant Colonel John Anstruther, commanding the 62nd British Regiment.

As we were passing through a wood, I saw, all at once, something like a cloud rise up before our wagon. We were at first frightened, until we discovered that it was a flock of wild pigeons, which they call here *tourtres* (turtle doves), and which are found in such numbers, that the Canadian lives on them for more than six weeks at a time. He goes to one of these pigeon hunts with a gun loaded with the smallest shot; and when he comes in sight of them he makes a noise. They then fly up, and he fires into the midst of them, generally with considerable luck; for sometimes he wounds two or three hundred, which are afterward beaten to death with sticks. The Canadians sell part of the birds, and eat the rest, making of them either soups or an excellent tasting fricassee, with cream and garlic. At this time of the year one eats them every where, and generally meets with kindness from the inhabitants of the country, who, for the most part, live in good houses having large rooms and nice bed curtains. Every house has a spacious entrance hall, and, at least, three or four apartments. When a Canadian marries off his daughter, he asks his son-in-law whether he intends residing near him; and should his answer be in the affirmative, he builds him a house and stable not far from his own dwelling; while, at the same time, the surrounding land is rendered productive. In this way, both the cultivation and the population of the country are greatly increased. The houses are painted white, giving them a most beautiful look, especially if seen in passing through the St. Lawrence, for then their appearance, in the distance, is even more splendid. Each dwelling has a little fruit garden; and at evening, the herds returning homeward present a most charming sight. Every where throughout this country, the cows, as well as swine, are driven into the woods, and return at a given time to be milked. But they do not neglect to furnish the cattle on their return with plenty of fodder; otherwise they would remain in the woods. It often happens that a sow big with young, and on the point of bringing forth, remains away until her delivery is accomplished, and then returns with all her sucking pigs. If they were confined in pens as in Germany, they would die miserably. They are very quarrelsome, and appear to be a kind of mixture of wild and tame swine.

I came back to Three Rivers very sad and full of anxiety. My invariable society was the grand-vicar, and his so called cousin. As such, at least, she had been introduced to me by my husband. She was good humored and conversed pleasantly. He had the same qualities, and was a man of intellect. I learned afterward, that every one of these gentlemen had the same kind of cousins residing with them, who acted as their housekeepers; but who, in order to avoid scandal, were forced almost every year to absent themselves for a little while, on account of a certain cause.

Besides these acquaintances, I had, also, the convent of Ursilines, or the Sisters of Mercy, whose sole occupation is to nurse the sick; for which purpose there is a hospital adjoining the establishment. Upon visiting it for the first time, as I was passing by the door leading into the Invalids' Hall, a man caught sight of me, and, throwing himself at my feet besought me, exclaiming—"Become my deliverer! Cause me to be killed, that I may return to Germany!" They told me that he was mad. I gave him something, and got away as soon as possible.

I found among the nuns several very lovely persons, with whom I spent many pleasant days. They had loved my husband very much; and I learned that he had often sent them wine and roast meat. Taking the hint from him I did the same, and even more; for I ordered my dinner to be brought into the convent, and eat with them. The company, and perhaps the wine, but more than all, the wish to divert me, often enlivened them so much, that they would dress themselves up and dance a kind of Cossack dance, dressing me up at the same time like the nuns. A young novice, who had conceived an affection especially for me, traced such a likeness between the holy virgin and myself, dressed in nun's apparel, that she besought me to become a nun on the spot. "Right willingly," I replied, "if you will make my husband the prior, so that he can live with us." She was so inexperienced that she believed this was possible. She left us, and shortly afterward we found her kneeling before a crucifix, and thanking God for my conversion. Soon after I had my children brought in. Little Gustava began to weep, as soon as she saw me in this costume, and said, "Dear mama! do not become a nun I beg you!" In order to quiet my children, I was obliged to take off my nun's apparel quickly.

In this convent there was also a seminary for young ladies, who were taught all kinds of work. The nuns sing exquisitely; and as they sing in the choir behind curtains, one might readily imagine it to be the song of angels.

My household occupations consisted chiefly in taking care of my children, some feminine work, and a little book reading. The officers who had been left behind at Three Rivers were not amiable. Among them was an ill-bred paymaster general, whose rude behavior toward me often roused my indignation, and redoubled my uneasiness. As I waited for an opportunity to pay for my passage to Captain Arbuthnot,[5] whom I daily expected from Montreal, I presented the paymaster with an order from my husband to pay me a hundred and fifty pounds sterling. He refused to honor it. I asked him if my husband was in his debt for any amount? "No," said he, "he has, on the contrary, a considera-

[5] Perhaps Marriot Arbuthnot (1711-1794) who, at this time, was lieutenant governor of Nova Scotia and Commissioner of the Navy at Halifax. He was later to succeed Lord Richard Howe as commander of the British Navy on the American station in 1779.

ble balance yet in his favor;" but as my husband was
in danger and might any day be killed, he thought
it advisable to act with deliberation. I was exceedingly provoked at this conduct, and told him that I
was too much vexed ever again to apply to him; but
I knew that if I should have the misfortune to lose
my husband, there would still be coming to me a
quarter of his yearly allowance, which amounted to
considerable more than the sum for which I had
asked him. "Yes, that is so," sneeringly rejoined he,
"but how about the passage back?" "That," replied
I, "Heaven will take care of;" and I never again
allowed myself to speak with him on the subject,
but went to an English paymaster, who gave me not
only the sum asked for, but in addition, offered to
give me in future as much as I wished. I reported
the whole affair to my husband, who thereupon became very angry, wrote him a letter couched in very
strong language, and gave him a most imperative
injunction to pay me just as much as I wanted. He
now became more courteous; and I had the luck to
advance so far into his good graces, that after his
death letters were found among his effects from his
wife, in which she wrote him, "You write me so
many beautiful things about the general's wife, that
you make me quite jealous!" Four years afterward, I
had the satisfaction of sending him, during his last
sickness, all kinds of nice things for his comfort, at
which time he sent for me to beg my forgiveness for
having treated me so badly. The speeches of this

man, and the various alarming reports that came daily, cast me down exceedingly and embittered my life; especially as my husband's letters often miscarried; for although he wrote me continually, yet when they finally reached me, they were old. It is certain that we are more apprehensive of danger befalling those we love, if they are absent, than if they were near us. I therefore wrote and urged and implored my husband to allow me to come to him. I told him I had sufficient health and pluck to undertake it, and that no matter what happened he would never hear me murmur, but, on the contrary, I hoped to make myself very useful to him on many occasions. He answered me that as soon as it was possible for women to follow the army, I should certainly be sent for. A little while after he wrote me that my wish would now soon be fulfilled; and just as I, in full anticipation, had got myself ready for the journey, Captain Willoe[6] came to escort me. One can easily imagine how warmly he was welcomed by me.

Two days after his arrival we set out. A boat which belonged to my husband and another one brought us to Three Rivers. The troops on board of the first boat were commanded by the good sergeant, Bürich, who showed me every possible attention, and who, since this time, has always kept an eye upon our baggage. Night overtook us, and we

[6] Captain Samuel Willoe of the 8th British Regiment, but attached to General Riedesel as an aide.

found ourselves obliged to land upon an island. The other boat, which was more heavily laden, and was not so well manned, had not been able to keep up with us. We had, consequently, neither beds nor candles; and that which was the most distressing was, that we had nothing more to eat, for we had taken with us upon the boat, only enough to last us (as we supposed) during the day. Besides, we found upon this island nothing but the four bare walls of a deserted and unfinished house, which was filled with bushes that served as a couch for the night. I covered them with our cloaks, making use, also, of the cushions of the boats; and in this way we had a right good sleep.

I could not induce Captain Willoe to come into the hut. I saw that he was very much troubled about something, but could not at all make out the cause of it. Meanwhile, I observed a soldier set a pot upon the fire. I asked him what he had in it? "Potatoes, which I have brought with me," he replied. I looked wistfully at them, but he had so few, that I thought it cruel to rob him of them, especially as he seemed so happy in their possession. Finally, however, my intense desire to give some to my children triumphed over my modesty, and I therefore begged, and obtained half, which, at the most, might have been a dozen. At the same time, he handed me out of his pocket, two or three small ends of candles, which gave me great joy, as the children were afraid to remain in the dark. I gave him for the whole, a

thaler,[7] which made him as happy as myself. In the
meantime, I heard Captain Willoe give an order for
a fire to be kindled around our building, and for his
men to go the rounds the whole night. I heard, also,
during the entire night considerable commotion
outside, which hindered me a little from sleeping.
The following morning as I was at breakfast, which
I had spread upon a stone, that served us for a table,
I asked the captain, who was eating with me, and
who, by the way, had slept in the boat, what was the
cause of the noises? He then acknowledged that we
had been in great danger, from the fact that this
island was *L'Isle à Sonnettes* (Rattlesnake Island), so
named on account of many rattlesnakes being
found upon it; that he had not known of it until too
late; and that when he did become aware of it, he
was very much frightened, but still had not dared to
sail further in the night on account of the storm.
There had been, therefore, nothing left for him to
do, but to build a great fire and make considerable
noise, hoping in this way to frighten the snakes and
keep them off. His knowledge of our danger, however, had kept him from sleeping a wink the whole
night. Upon hearing this, I was very much terrified,
and remarked to him, that we had immeasurably
increased our danger by lying down upon the bushes, in which the snakes like to hide. He acknowledged that I was right, and said that if he had
known at the time where we were, he would have

[7] A thaler is a German silver coin equal to three marks.

had all the bushes taken away, or else would have begged us rather to remain in the boat. He had first learned the fact, however, from the people in our other boat, which had overtaken us later in the evening. In the morning we found on every side the skins and slime of these nasty creatures, and accordingly, made haste to finish our breakfast. After our morning meal, we were ferried over lake Champlain, and came at noon to Fort John, where we were received by the commander with kindness and much courtesy. Thus it was everywhere; so much was my husband loved, both by the English and by the inhabitants of the country. Here we again took our boats in order to reach a cutter, upon which we came to Wolf's island, where we remained the entire night on board the ship. During the night we had a thunder-storm, which appeared to us the more terrible, as it seemed as if we were lying in the bottom of a caldron surrounded by mountains and great trees.

The following day we passed Ticonderoga, and about noon arrived at Fort George, where we dined with Colonel Anstruther, an exceedingly good and amiable man, who commanded the 62d regiment. In the afternoon we seated ourselves in a calash, and reached Fort Edward on the same day, which was the 14th of August. My husband had actually left this place the day before with the further advance of the army; but as soon as he heard of our arrival, he returned on the 15th, and remained with us until

GENERAL RIEDESEL

Shortly before his death, about 1800

This is from a photograph of the portrait made by Marta Huth;
the original portrait was possibly destroyed during World War II

the 16th. On that day he was obliged, to my great sorrow, to rejoin the army. But immediately after the unlucky affair at Bennington,[8] I had the joy of seeing him again with us on the 18th, and spending with him three happy weeks in the greatest tranquility. A few days after my arrival, news came that we were cut off from Canada. If, therefore, I had not taken advantage of this fortunate opportunity, I would have been obliged to remain behind in Canada, three long years without my husband. The sole circumstance, which led to this—as it proved for us—fortunate determination, was as follows: Upon the arrival of milady Ackland[9] at the army, General Burgoyne said to my husband, "General, you shall have your wife here also!" Whereupon he immediately dispatched Captain Willoe for me. We led, during these three weeks, a very pleasant life. The surrounding country was magnificent; and we were encircled by the encampments of the English and

[8]Because his line of communications was now some 185 miles long, Burgoyne had dispatched Lieutenant Colonel Friedrich Baum toward Bennington on a massive foraging expedition. Riedesel had opposed the move. No resistance was expected, but Baum was met by John Stark and 2,000 militia at Bennington on August 14, 1777, and two days later Baum not only met defeat but lost his life. A relief force under Lieutenant Colonel Heinrich Breymann met a similar fate. This defeat resulted in an increase of militia under Horatio Gates, a factor in Burgoyne's subsequent defeat at Saratoga.

[9]Lady Christian Henrietta Carolina Acland, customarily called Lady Harriet, was the wife of Major John Dyke Acland.

German troops. We lived in a building called the Red House.[10] I had only one room for my husband, myself and my children, in which my husband also slept, and had besides all his writing materials. My women servants slept in a kind of hall. When it was beautiful weather we took our meals under the trees, but if not, in a barn, upon boards, which were laid upon casks and served as a table. It was at this place that I ate bear's flesh for the first time, and found it of capital flavor. We were often put to it to get any thing to eat; notwithstanding this, however, I was very happy and content, for I was with my children, and beloved by those by whom I was surrounded. There were, if I remember rightly, four or five adjutants staying with us. The evening was spent by the gentlemen in playing cards, and by myself in putting my children to bed.

[10] Burgoyne's headquarters. It had been constructed from the debris of old Fort Edward by Doctor James Smyth who had fled to Canada at the outbreak of the war.

II. THE BATTLE OF SARATOGA

WHEN THE ARMY again moved, on the 11th of September, 1777, it was at first intended to leave me behind; but upon my urgent entreaties, and as other ladies were to follow the army, I received, finally, the same permission. We made only small day's marches, and were very often sick; yet always contented at being allowed to follow. I had still the satisfaction of daily seeing my husband. A great part of my baggage I had sent back, and had kept only a small summer wardrobe. In the beginning all went well. We cherished the sweet hope of a sure victory, and of coming into the "promised land;" and when we passed the Hudson river, and General Burgoyne said, "The English never lose ground,"[11] our spirits were greatly exhilarated. But that which displeased me was, that the wives of all the officers belonging to the expedition, knew beforehand every thing that was to happen; and this seemed the more singular to me, as I had observed, when in the armies of the Duke Ferdinand, during the Seven Years' war, with how much secrecy every thing was conducted. But here, on the contrary, the Americans were apprised beforehand of all our intentions; so that at every place where we came they already awaited us; a circumstance which hurt us exceedingly. On the 19th of September, there was

[11] Burgoyne's general orders read, "This Army must not retreat."

an affair between the two armies, which, it is true, ended to our advantage; although we were, nevertheless, obliged to make a halt at a place called Freeman's farm. I was an eye witness of the whole affair; and as I knew that my husband was in the midst of it, I was full of care and anguish, and shivered at every shot, for I could hear every thing. I saw a great number of wounded, and what was still more harrowing, they even brought three of them into the house where I was. One of these was Major Harnage, husband of a lady of our company; another, a lieutenant, whose wife, also, was of our acquaintance; and the third, a young English officer of the name of Young.[12] Major Harnage, with his wife, lived in a room next to mine. He had received a shot through the lower part of the bowels, from which he suffered exceedingly. A few days after our arrival, I heard plaintive moans in another room near me, and learned that they came from Young, the young English officer just mentioned, who was lying very low.

I was the more interested in him, since a family of that name had shown me much courtesy during my sojourn in England. I tendered him my services, and sent him provisions and refreshments. He expressed a great desire to see his benefactress, as he

[12] Major Henry Harnage of Colonel Anstruther's staff. Perhaps the lieutenant was Lieutenant Thomas Reynell of the 62nd Regiment. Both Reynell and Young died of their wounds. Harnage survived and was promoted to colonel in 1780.

called me. I went to him, and found him lying on a little straw, for he had lost his camp equipage. He was a young man, probably eighteen or nineteen years old; and, actually, the own nephew of the Mr. Young, whom I had known, and the only son of his parents. It was only for this reason that he grieved; on account of his own sufferings he uttered no complaint. He had bled considerably, and they wished to take off his leg, but he could not bring his mind to it, and now mortification had set in. I sent him pillows and coverings, and my women servants a mattress. I redoubled my care of him, and visited him every day, for which I received from the sufferer a thousand blessings. Finally, they attempted the amputation of the limb, but it was too late, and he died a few days afterward. As he occupied an apartment close to mine, and the walls were very thin, I could hear his last groans through the partition of my room.

I lived in a pretty well built house, in which I had a large room. The doors and the wainscot were of solid cedar, a wood that is very common in this vicinity. They burn it frequently, especially when there are many midges around, as these insects cannot stand the odor of it. It is said, however, that its smoke is very injurious to the nerves, so much so, indeed, as to cause women with child to bring forth prematurely. As we were to march farther, I had a large calash made for me, in which I, my children, and both my women servants had seats; and in this manner I followed the army, in the midst of the soldiers, who were merry, singing songs, and burning with a desire for victory. We passed through boundless forests and magnificent tracts of country, which, however, were abandoned by all the inhabitants, who fled before us, and reinforced the army of the American general, Gates. In the sequel this cost us dearly, for every one of them was a soldier by nature, and could shoot very well; besides, the thought of fighting for their fatherland and their freedom, inspired them with still greater courage. During this time, my husband was obliged to encamp with the main body of the army. I remained about an hour's march behind the army, and visited my husband every morning in the camp. Very often I took my noon meal with him, but most of the time he came over to my quarters and eat with me. The army were engaged daily in small skirmishes, but all of them of little consequence. My poor husband, however, during the whole time, could not get a chance either to go to bed or undress. As the season had now become more inclement, a Colonel Williams[13] of the artillery, observing that our mutual visits were very fatiguing, offered to have a house built for me, with a chimney, that should not cost more than five or six guineas, and which I could steadily occupy. I took him up, and the house,[14] which was twenty feet square, and had a good fire-

[13] Probably Major Griffith Williams.
[14] A log cabin with an overhanging top floor.

place, was begun. They called it the block-house. For such a structure, large trees of equal thickness are selected, which are joined together, making it very durable and warm, especially if covered with clay. I was to remove into it the following day, and was the more rejoiced at it, as the nights were already damp and cold, and my husband could live in it with me, as he would then be very near his camp. Suddenly, however, on the 7th of October, my husband, with the whole general staff, decamped. Our misfortunes may be said to date from this moment. I had just sat down with my husband at his quarters to breakfast. General Frazer,[15] and, I believe, Generals Burgoyne and Phillips,[16] also, were to have dined with me on that same day. I observed considerable movement among the troops. My husband thereupon informed me, that there was to be a reconnoissance, which however, did not surprise me, as this often happened. On my way homeward, I met many savages in their war-dress, armed with guns. To my question where they were going, they cried out to me, "War! war!" which meant that they were going to fight.[17]

[15] Probably Brigadier General Simon Fraser (1729–1777), who had defeated the Americans at the Battle of Hubbardtown, July 7, 1777.

[16] Major General William Phillips (1731–1781). Captured at Saratoga, he was later exchanged and while leading a raid into Virginia, died of typhoid fever, May 13, 1781.

[17] Indian allies of the British on this expedition included the Iroquois, Abenakis, Hurons, Nepissings, and Ottawas. Some were attached to General Riedesel's command.

This completely overwhelmed me, and I had scarcely got back to my quarters, when I heard skirmishing, and firing, which by degrees, became constantly heavier, until, finally, the noises became frightful. It was a terrible cannonade, and I was more dead than alive.

About three o'clock in the afternoon, in place of the guests who were to have dined with me, they brought in to me, upon a litter, poor General Frazer (one of my expected guests), mortally wounded. Our dining table, which was already spread, was taken away, and in its place they fixed up a bed for the general. I sat in a corner of the room trembling and quaking. The noises grew continually louder. The thought that they might bring in my husband in the same manner was to me dreadful, and tormented me incessantly.

The general said to the surgeon, "Do not conceal any thing from me. Must I die?" The ball had gone through his bowels, precisely as in the case of Major Harnage. Unfortunately, however, the general had eaten a hearty breakfast, by reason of which the intestines were distended, and the ball, so the surgeon said, had not gone, as in the case of Major Harnage, between the intestines, but through them. I heard him often, amidst his groans, exclaim, "Oh, fatal ambition! Poor General Burgoyne! My poor wife!" Prayers were read to him. He then sent a message to General Burgoyne, begging that he would have him buried the following day at six o'clock in the eve-

ning, on the top of a hill, which was a sort of a
redoubt.[18] I knew no longer which way to turn. The
whole entry and the other rooms were filled with
the sick, who were suffering with the camp-sickness,
a kind of dysentery. Finally, toward evening, I saw
my husband coming, upon which I forgot all my
sufferings, and thanked God that he had spared him
to me. He ate in great haste with me and his adjutant, behind the house. We had been told that we
had gained an advantage over the enemy, but the
sorrowful and down-cast faces which I beheld, bore
witness to the contrary, and before my husband
again went away, he drew me one side and told me
that every thing might go very badly, and that I
must keep myself in constant readiness for departure, but by no means to give any one the least
inkling of what I was doing. I therefore pretended
that I wished to move into my new house the next
morning, and had every thing packed up. My lady
Acland occupied a tent not far from our house. In
this she slept, but during the day was in the camp.
Suddenly one came to tell her that her husband was
mortally wounded, and had been taken prisoner. At
this she became very wretched. We comforted her
by saying that it was only a slight wound, but as no
one could nurse him as well as herself, we coun-

[18] A small, enclosed, temporary outpost, so located as to
defend strategic passes, hilltops, or the approaches to primary works. They were customarily located within musket
shot of the main fortifications.

seled her to go at once to him, to do which she
could certainly obtain permission. She loved him
very much, although he was a plain, rough man, and
was almost daily intoxicated; with this exception,
however, he was an excellent officer. She was the
loveliest of women. I spent the night in this manner—at one time comforting her, and at another
looking after my children, whom I had put to bed.
As for myself, I could not go to sleep, as I had
General Frazer and all the other gentlemen in my
room, and was constantly afraid that my children
would wake up and cry, and thus disturb the poor
dying man, who often sent to beg my pardon for
making me so much trouble. About three o'clock in
the morning, they told me that he could not last
much longer. I had desired to be apprised of the
approach of this moment. I, accordingly, wrapped
up the children in the bed coverings, and went with
them into the entry. Early in the morning, at eight
o'clock, he expired. After they had washed the
corpse, they wrapped it in a sheet, and laid it on a
bedstead. We then again came into the room, and
had this sad sight before us the whole day. At every
instant, also, wounded officers of my acquaintance
arrived, and the cannonade again began. A retreat
was spoken of, but there was not the least movement made toward it. About four o'clock in the
afternoon, I saw the new house which had been
built for me, in flames: the enemy, therefore, were
not far from us. We learned that General Burgoyne

intended to fulfill the last wish of General Frazer, and to have him buried at six o'clock, in the place designated by him. This occasioned an unnecessary delay, to which a part of the misfortunes of the army was owing. Precisely at six o'clock the corpse was brought out, and we saw the entire body of generals with their retinues on the hill assisting at the obsequies. The English chaplain, Mr. Brudenel, performed the funeral services. The cannon balls flew continually around and over the party. The American general, Gates, afterward said, that if he had known that it was a burial he would not have allowed any firing in that direction. Many cannon balls also flew not far from me, but I had my eyes fixed upon the hill, where I distinctly saw my husband in the midst of the enemy's fire, and therefore I could not think of my own danger.

The order had gone forth that the army should break up after the burial, and the horses were already harnessed to our calashes. I did not wish to set out before the troops. The wounded Major Harnage, although he was so ill, dragged himself out of bed, that he might not remain in the hospital, which was left behind protected by a flag of truce. As soon as he observed me in the midst of the danger, he had my children and maid servants put into the calashes, and intimated to me that I must immediately depart. As I still begged to be allowed to remain, he said to me, "well, then your children at least must go, that I may save them from the slightest danger." He understood how to take advantage of my weak side. I gave it up, seated myself inside with them, and we drove off at eight o'clock in the evening.

The greatest silence had been enjoined; fires had been kindled in every direction; and many tents left standing, to make the enemy believe that the camp was still there. We traveled continually the whole night. Little Frederica was afraid, and would often begin to cry. I was, therefore, obliged to hold a pocket handkerchief over her mouth, lest our whereabouts should be discovered.

At six o'clock in the morning a halt was made, at which every one wondered. General Burgoyne had all the cannon ranged and counted, which worried all of us, as a few more good marches would have placed us in security.[19] My husband was completely exhausted, and seated himself during this delay, in my calash, where my maid servants were obliged to make room for him; and where he slept nearly three hours with his head upon my shoulder. In the mean time, Captain Willoe brought me his pocket-book containing bank bills, and Captain Geismar,[20] his beautiful watch, a ring, and a well filled purse, and begged me to keep all these for them. I promised them to do my utmost.

[19] Burgoyne later explained this halt on the grounds that his troops needed rest and he wanted time to allow the boats loaded with provisions to come up with the army.

[20] Captain von Geismar was an adjutant on General Riedesel's staff.

At last, the army again began its march, but scarcely had we proceeded an hour on the way, when a fresh halt was made, in consequence of the enemy being in sight. They were about two hundred men who came to reconnoitre, and who might easily have been taken prisoners by our troops, had not General Burgoyne lost his head.[21] It rained in torrents. My lady Acland had her tent set up. I advised her once more to betake herself to her husband, as she could be so useful to him in his present situation.

Finally, she yielded to my solicitations, and sent a message to General Burgoyne, through his adjutant, my Lord Patterson,[22] begging permission to leave the camp. I told her that she should insist on it; which she did, and finally obtained his consent. The English chaplain, Mr. Brudenel, accompanied her; and, bearing a flag of truce, they went together in a boat over to the enemy. There is a familiar and beautiful engraving of this event in existence. I saw her again afterward in Albany, at which time her husband was almost entirely recovered, and both thanked me heartily for my advice.[23]

[21] Author indicates that he was mentally unbalanced.

[22] Madame Riedesel probably meant Captain Stanhope, Viscount Petersham, an aide to Burgoyne and later a lieutenant general in the British Army.

[23] Receiving permission from General Gates, Lady Acland crossed over into the American lines to nurse her husband back to health. Shortly afterwards he was killed in a duel with a fellow officer.

On the 9th, we spent the whole day in a pouring rain, ready to march at a moment's warning. The savages had lost their courage, and they were seen in all directions going home. The slightest reverse of fortune discouraged them, especially if there was nothing to plunder. My chambermaid did nothing, cursed her situation, and tore out her hair. I entreated her to compose herself, or else she would be taken for a savage. Upon this she became still more frantic, and asked, "whether that would trouble me?" And when I answered "yes," she tore her bonnet off her head, letting her hair hang down over her face, and said, "You talk well! You have your husband! But we have nothing to look forward to, except dying miserably on the one hand, or losing all we possess on the other!"

Respecting this last complaint, I promised, in order to quiet her, that I would make good all the losses of herself and the other maid. The latter, my good Lena, although also very much frightened, said nothing.

Toward evening, we at last came to Saratoga,[24] which was only half an hour's march from the place where we had spent the whole day. I was wet through and through by the frequent rains, and was obliged to remain in this condition the entire night, as I had no place whatever where I could change my linen. I, therefore, seated myself before a good fire, and undressed my children; after which, we laid

[24] Present day Schuylerville, New York.

ourselves down together upon some straw. I asked General Phillips, who came up to where we were, why we did not continue our retreat while there was yet time, as my husband had pledged himself to cover it, and bring the army through? "Poor woman," answered he, "I am amazed at you! completely wet through, have you still the courage to wish to go further in this weather! Would that you were only our commanding general! He halts because he is tired, and intends to spend the night here and give us a supper." In this latter achievement, especially, General Burgoyne was very fond of indulging. He spent half the nights in singing and drinking, and amusing himself with the wife of a commissary, who was his mistress, and who, as well as he, loved champagne.

On the 10th, at seven o'clock in the morning, I drank some tea by way of refreshment; and we now hoped from one moment to another, that at last we would again get under way. General Burgoyne, in order to cover our retreat, caused the beautiful houses and mills at Saratoga, belonging to General Schuyler,[25] to be burned. Then, an English officer brought some excellent broth, which he shared with me, as I was not able to refuse his urgent entreaties. Thereupon we set out upon our march, but only as

[25] Philip John Schuyler (1733–1804), New York landowner, politician, and major general in the American army. In August, 1777, two months before the surrender of Burgoyne, he was replaced by Horatio Gates. To Schuyler's preparation is due much of the credit for the victory at Saratoga.

far as another place not far from where we had started. The greatest misery and the utmost disorder
prevailed in the army. The commissaries had forgotten to distribute provisions among the troops.
There were cattle enough, but not one had been
killed. More than thirty officers came to me, who
could endure hunger no longer. I had coffee and tea
made for them, and divided among them all the
provisions with which my carriage was constantly
filled; for we had a cook who, although an arrant
knave, was fruitful in all expedients, and often in
the night crossed small rivers, in order to steal from
the country people, sheep, poultry and pigs. He
would then charge us a high price for them—a circumstance, however, that we only learned a long
time afterward. At last my provisions were exhausted, and in despair at not being able to be of any
further help, I called to me Adjutant General Patterson, who happened at that moment to be passing
by, and said to him passionately: "Come and see for
yourself these officers, who have been wounded in
the common cause, and who now are in want of
every thing, because they do not receive that which
is due them. It is, therefore, your duty to make a
representation of this to the general." At this he was
deeply moved, and the result was, that, a quarter of
an hour afterward, General Burgoyne came to me
himself and thanked me very pathetically for having
reminded him of his duty. He added, moreover,
that a general was much to be pitied when he was

not properly served nor his commands obeyed. I
replied, that I begged his pardon for having med-
dled with things which, I well knew, a woman had
no business with, but that it was impossible to keep
silent, when I saw so many brave men in want of
every thing, and had nothing more to give them.
Thereupon he thanked me once more (although I
believe that in his heart he has never forgiven me
this lashing), and went from me to the officers, and
said to them, that he was very sorry for what had
happened, but he had now through an order reme-
died every thing, but why had they not come to him
as his cook stood always at their service. They answered that English officers were not accustomed to
visit the kitchen of their general, and that they had
received any morsel from me with pleasure, as they
were convinced I had given it to them directly from
my heart. He then gave the most express orders that
the provisions should be properly distributed. This
only hindered us anew, besides not in the least bet-
tering our situation. The general seated himself at
the table, and the horses were harnessed to our calashes ready for departure. The whole army clam-
ored for a retreat, and my husband promised to
make it possible, provided only that no time was
lost. But General Burgoyne, to whom an order had
been promised if he brought about a junction with
the army of General Howe, could not determine
upon this course, and lost every thing by his loiter-
ing. About two o'clock in the afternoon, the firing

of cannon and small arms was again heard, and all was alarm and confusion. My husband sent me a message telling me to betake myself forthwith into a house which was not far from there. I seated myself in the calash with my children, and had scarcely driven up to the house, when I saw on the opposite side of the Hudson river, five or six men with guns, which were aimed at us. Almost involuntarily I threw the children on the bottom of the calash and myself over them. At the same instant the churls fired, and shattered the arm of a poor English soldier behind us, who was already wounded, and was also on the point of retreating into the house. Immediately after our arrival a frightful cannonade began, principally directed against the house in which we had sought shelter, probably because the enemy believed, from seeing so many people flocking around it, that all the generals made it their headquarters. Alas! it harbored none but wounded soldiers, or women! We were finally obliged to take refuge in a cellar, in which I laid myself down in a corner not far from the door. My children laid down on the earth with their heads upon my lap, and in this manner we passed the entire night. A horrible stench, the cries of the children, and yet more than all this, my own anguish, prevented me from closing my eyes. On the following morning the cannonade again began, but from a different side. I advised all to go out of the cellar for a little while, during which time I would have it cleaned, as otherwise we would all be sick. They followed my suggestion, and I at once set many hands to work, which was in the highest degree necessary; for the women and children being afraid to venture forth, had soiled the whole cellar. After they had all gone out and left me alone, I for the first time surveyed our place of refuge. It consisted of three beautiful cellars, splendidly arched. I proposed that the most dangerously wounded of the officers should be brought into one of them; that the women should remain in another; and that all the rest should stay in the third, which was nearest the entrance. I had just given the cellars a good sweeping, and had fumigated them by sprinkling vinegar on burning coals, and each one had found his place prepared for him—when a fresh and terrible cannonade threw us all once more into alarm. Many persons, who had no right to come in, threw themselves against the door. My children were already under the cellar steps, and we would all have been crushed, if God had not given me strength to place myself before the door, and with extended arms prevent all from coming in; otherwise every one of us would have been severely injured. Eleven cannon balls went through the house, and we could plainly hear them rolling over our heads. One poor soldier, whose leg they were about to amputate, having been laid upon a table for this purpose, had the other leg taken off by another cannon ball, in the very middle of the operation. His comrades all ran off, and when they again came back they found him in one corner of the room, where he had rolled in his anguish, scarcely breathing. I was more dead than alive, though not so much on account of our own danger, as for that which enveloped my husband, who, however, frequently sent to see how I was getting along, and to tell me that he was still safe.

The wife of Major Harnage, a Madame Reynels, the wife of the good lieutenant who the day previous had so kindly shared his broth with me, the wife of the commissary, and myself, were the only ladies who were with the army. We sat together bewailing our fate, when one came in, upon which they all began whispering, looking at the same time exceedingly sad. I noticed this, and also that they cast silent glances toward me. This awakened in my mind the dreadful thought that my husband had been killed. I shrieked aloud, but they assured me that this was not so, at the same time intimating to me by signs, that it was the lieutenant[26]—the husband of our companion—who had met with misfortune. A moment after she was called out. Her husband was not yet dead, but a cannon ball had taken off his arm close to the shoulder. During the whole night we heard his moans, which resounded fearfully through the vaulted cellars. The poor man died toward morning. We spent the remainder of this

[26] Probably George Tobias Fitzgerald of the 62nd Regiment, as he was the only British officer killed on October 7.

night in the same way as the former ones. In the mean time my husband came to visit me, which lightened my anxiety and gave me fresh courage. On the following morning, however, we got things better regulated. Major Harnage, his wife, and Mrs. Reynels, made a little room in a corner, by hanging curtains from the ceiling. They wished to fix up for me another corner in the same manner, but I preferred to remain near the door, so that in case of fire I could rush out from the room. I had some straw brought in and laid my bed upon it, where I slept with my children—my maids sleeping not far from us. Directly opposite us three English officers were quartered—wounded, it is true, but, nevertheless, resolved not to be left behind in case of a retreat. One of these was a Captain Green,[27] aid-de-camp of General Phillips, a very valuable and agreeable man. All three assured me, upon their oaths, that in case of a hasty retreat, they would not leave me, but would each take one of my children upon his horse. For myself, one of my husband's horses constantly stood saddled and in readiness. Often my husband wished to withdraw me from danger by sending me to the Americans; but I remonstrated with him on the ground, that to be with people whom I would be obliged to treat with courtesy, while, perhaps, my husband was being killed by them, would be even yet more painful than all I was now forced to suffer. He promised me, therefore, that I should

[27]Captain Charles Green of the 31st Regiment.

henceforward follow the army. Nevertheless, I was often in the night filled with anxiety lest he should march away. At such times, I have crept out of my cellar to reassure myself, and if I saw the troops lying around the fires (for the nights were already cold), I would return and sleep quietly. The articles which had been intrusted to me caused me much uneasiness. I had fastened them inside of my corsets, as I was in constant terror lest I should lose some of them, and I resolved in future never to undertake such a commission again. On the third day, I found an opportunity for the first time to change my linen, as my companions had the courtesy to give up to me a little corner—the three wounded officers, meanwhile, standing guard not far off. One of these gentlemen could imitate very naturally the bellowing of a cow, and the bleating of a calf; and if my little daughter Frederica, cried during the night, he would mimic these animals, and she would at once become still, at which we all laughed heartily.

Our cook saw to our meals, but we were in want of water; and in order to quench thirst, I was often obliged to drink wine, and give it, also, to the children. It was, moreover, the only thing that my husband could take, which fact so worked upon our faithful Rockel, that he said to me one day, "I fear that the general drinks so much wine, because he dreads falling into captivity, and is therefore weary of life." The continual danger in which my husband was encompassed, was a constant source of anxiety to me. I was the only one of all the women, whose husband had not been killed or wounded, and I often said to myself—especially since my husband was placed in such great danger day and night— "Shall I be the only fortunate one?" He never came into the tent at night; but lay outside by the watch-fires. This alone was sufficient to have caused his death, as the nights were damp and cold.

As the great scarcity of water continued, we at last found a soldier's wife who had the courage to bring water from the river, for no one else would undertake it, as the enemy shot at the head of every man who approached the river. This woman, how-ever, they never molested; and they told us after-ward, that they spared her on account of her sex.

I endeavored to divert my mind from my trou-bles, by constantly busying myself with the wound-ed. I made them tea and coffee, and received in return a thousand benedictions. Often, also, I shared my noonday meal with them. One day a Ca-nadian officer came into our cellar, who could scarcely stand up. We at last got it out of him, that he was almost dead with hunger. I considered my-self very fortunate to have it in my power to offer him my mess. This gave him renewed strength, and gained for me his friendship. Afterward, upon our return to Canada, I learned to know his family. One of our greatest annoyances was the stench of the wounds when they began to suppurate.

One day I undertook the care of Major Plumpfield,[28] adjutant of General Phillips, through both of whose cheeks a small musket ball had passed, shattering his teeth and grazing his tongue. He could hold nothing whatever in his mouth. The matter from the wound almost choked him, and he was unable to take any other nourishment, except a little broth, or something liquid. We had Rhine wine. I gave him a bottle of it, in hopes that the acidity of the wine would cleanse his wound. He kept some continually in his mouth; and that alone acted so beneficially that he became cured, and I again acquired one more friend.

Thus, in the midst of my hours of care and suffering, I derived a joyful satisfaction, which made me very happy.

On one of these sorrowful days, General Phillips, having expressed a desire to visit me, accompanied my husband, who, at the risk of his own life, came once or twice daily to see me. He saw our situation, and heard me earnestly beg my husband not to leave me behind in case of a hasty retreat. Then, as he marked my great reluctance to fall into the hands of the Americans, he spoke in my behalf; and as he was going away he said to my husband, "No! not for ten thousand guineas would I come here

[28] Refers to Captain Charles Bloomfield (1744–1822). After his return to England he became a member of Parliament, a lieutenant general, a baronet, and marshal to the King.

again, for my heart is now entirely, entirely broken!"

Not all of those, however, who were with us deserved our compassion. There were, also, poltroons in our little company, who ought not to have remained in the cellar, and who afterwards, when we became prisoners, took their places in the ranks and could parade perfectly well. In this horrible situation we remained six days.

Finally, they spoke of capitulating, as by temporizing for so long a time, our retreat had been cut off. A cessation of hostilities took place, and my husband, who was thoroughly worn out, was able, for the first time in a long while, to lie down upon a bed.

In order that his rest might not be in the least disturbed, I had a good bed made up for him in a little room; while I, with my children and both my maids, laid down in a little parlor close by. But about one o'clock in the night, some one came and asked to speak to him. It was with the greatest reluctance that I found myself obliged to awaken him. I observed that the message did not please him, as he immediately sent the man back to head-quarters, and laid himself down again considerably out of humor. Soon after this, General Burgoyne requested the presence of all the generals and staff officers at a council-of-war, which was to be held early the next morning; in which he proposed to break the capitulation, already made with the enemy, in consequence of some false information just received. It was, however, finally decided, that this was neither practicable nor advisable; and this was fortunate for us, as the Americans said to us afterwards, that had the capitulation been broken we all would have been massacred; which they could have done the more easily, as we were not over four or five thousand men strong, and had given them time to bring together more than twenty thousand.

On the morning of the 16th of October, my husband was again obliged to go to his post, and I once more into my cellar.

On this day, a large amount of fresh meat was distributed among the officers, who, up to this time, had received only salted provisions, which had exceedingly aggravated the wounds of the men. The good woman who constantly supplied us with water, made us capital soup from the fresh meat. I had lost all appetite, and had the whole time taken nothing but crusts of bread dipped in wine. The wounded officers, my companions in misfortune, cut off the best piece of the beef and presented it to me, with a plate of soup. I said to them that I was not able to eat any thing, but as they saw that it was absolutely necessary I should take some nourishment, they declared that they themselves would not touch a morsel until I had given them the satisfaction of taking some. I could not longer withstand their friendly entreaties, upon which they assured me that it made them very happy to be able to offer and share with me the very first good thing which they themselves had been able to enjoy.

On the 17th of October the capitulation was consummated.[29] The generals waited upon the American general-in-chief, Gates, and the troops laid down their arms, and surrendered themselves prisoners of war. Now the good woman, who had brought us water at the risk of her life, received the reward of her services. Every one threw a whole handful of money into her apron, and she received altogether over twenty guineas. At such a moment, the heart seems to be specially susceptible to feelings of gratitude.

At last, my husband sent to me a groom with a message that I should come to him with our children. I, therefore, again seated myself in my dear calash; and, in the passage through the American camp, I observed, with great satisfaction, that no one cast at us scornful glances. On the contrary, they all greeted me, even showing compassion on their countenances at seeing a mother with her little children in such a situation. I confess that I feared to come into the enemy's camp, as the thing was so

[29] Because Sir Henry Clinton had come up from New York and had broken through defenses down along the Hudson, constituting a threat to the Americans, Burgoyne was able to negotiate a "Convention." This would allow the British and German troops to be sent to Boston where they would be transported to Britain on the condition they would no longer fight in America. The Continental Congress refused to sanction this agreement because they contended that the return of these troops to Europe would free troops stationed there to come to America to fight.

entirely new to me. When I approached the tents, a noble looking man came toward me, took the children out of the wagon, embraced and kissed them, and then with tears in his eyes helped me also to alight. "You tremble," said he to me, "fear nothing." "No," replied I, "for you are so kind, and have been so tender toward my children, that it has inspired me with courage." He then led me to the tent of General Gates, with whom I found Generals Burgoyne and Phillips, who were upon an extremely friendly footing with him. Burgoyne said to me, "You may now dismiss all your apprehensions, for your sufferings are at an end." I answered him, that I should certainly be acting very wrongly to have any more anxiety, when our chief had none, and especially when I saw him on such a friendly footing with General Gates. All the generals remained to dine with General Gates. The man, who had received me so kindly, came up and said to me, "It may be embarrassing to you to dine with all these gentlemen; come now with your children into my tent, where I will give you, it is true, a frugal meal, but one that will be accompanied by the best of wishes." "You are certainly," answered I, "a husband and a father, since you show me so much kindness." I then learned that he was the American General Schuyler. He entertained me with excellent smoked tongue, beef-steaks, potatoes; good butter and bread. Never have I eaten a better meal. I was content. I saw that all around me were so likewise;

but that which rejoiced me more than every thing else was, that my husband was out of all danger. As soon as we had finished dinner, he invited me to take up my residence at his house, which was situated in Albany, and told me that General Burgoyne would, also, be there. I sent and asked my husband what I should do. He sent me word to accept the invitation; and as it was two days' journey from where we were, and already five o'clock in the afternoon, he advised me to set out in advance, and to stay over night at a place distant about three hours' ride. General Schuyler was so obliging as to send with me a French officer, who was a very agreeable man, and commanded those troops who composed the reconnoitering party of which I have before made mention. As soon as he had escorted me to the house where we were to remain, he went back. I found in this house a French physician, and a mortally wounded Brunswick officer, who was under his care, and who died a few days afterward. The wounded man extolled highly the good nursing of the doctor, who may have been a very skillful surgeon, but was a young coxcomb. He rejoiced greatly when he heard that I could speak his language, and began to entertain me with all kinds of sweet speeches and impertinences; among other things, that he could not believe it possible that I was a general's wife, because a woman of such rank would not certainly follow her husband into the camp. I ought, therefore, to stay with him, for it was better to be with the conquerors than the conquered. I was beside myself with his insolence, but dared not let him see the contempt with which he inspired me, because I had no protector. When night came on he offered to share his room with me; but I answered, that I should remain in the apartment of the wounded officers, whereupon he distressed me still more with all kinds of foolish flatteries, until, suddenly, the door opened and my husband and his adjutant entered. "Here, sir, is my husband," said I to him, with a glance meant to annihilate him. Upon this he withdrew looking very sheepish. Yet, afterward, he was so polite as to give up his room to us. The day after this, we arrived at Albany, where we had so often longed to be. But we came not, as we supposed we should, as victors! We were, nevertheless, received in the most friendly manner by the good General Schuyler, and by his wife and daughters, who showed us the most marked courtesy, as, also, General Burgoyne, although he had—without any necessity it was said—caused their magnificently built houses to be burned. But they treated us as people who knew how to forget their own losses in the misfortunes of others. Even General Burgoyne was deeply moved at their magnanimity, and said to General Schuyler, "Is it to *me*, who have done you so much injury, that you show so much kindness!" "That is the fate of war," replied the brave man, "let us say no more about it." We remained three days with them, and they acted as if they were very

reluctant to let us go. Our cook had remained in the
city with the camp equipage of my husband, but the
second night after our arrival, the whole of it was
stolen from us, notwithstanding an American guard
of ten or twenty men had been deputed for its protection.[30] Nothing remained to us except the beds of
myself and children, and a few trifles that I had kept
by me for my own use—and this too, in a land
where one could get nothing for money, and at a
time when we were in want of very many things;
consequently, my husband was obliged to board his
adjutant, quartermaster, etc., and find them in everything. The English officers—friends, as I am justified in calling them, for during the whole of my
sojourn in America they always acted as such—each
gave us something. One gave a pair of spoons, another some plates, all of which we were obliged to
use for a long time, as it was not until three years
afterward, in New York, that we found an opportunity, although at great cost, to replace a few of the
things we had lost.

Fortunately, I had kept by me my little carriage,
which carried my baggage. As it was already very
late in the season, and the weather raw, I had my
calash covered with coarse linen, which in turn was
varnished over with oil; and in this manner we set

[30] One of Madame Riedesel's children caused some embarrassment. After playing around Schuyler's house, the young
girl rushed up to her mother with, "Mother, is this the palace father was to have when he came to America?" She was
quickly shushed by her mother.

out on our journey to Boston, which was very tedious, besides being attended with considerable hardship.

I know not whether it was my carriage that attracted the curiosity of the people to it—for it certainly had the appearance of a wagon in which they carry around rare animals—but often I was obliged to halt, because the people insisted upon seeing the wife of the German general with her children. For fear that they would tear off the linen covering from the wagon in their eagerness to see me, I very often alighted, and by this means got away more quickly. However, I must say that the people were very friendly, and were particularly delighted at my being able to speak English, which was the language of their country.

In the midst of all my trials, however, God so supported me, that I lost neither my frolicksomeness, nor my spirits; but my poor husband, who was gnawed by grief on account of all that had happened, and on account, also, of his captivity, became by these constant stoppages, peevish in the highest degree, and could scarcely endure them. His health had suffered very greatly, especially by the many damp nights that he had spent in the open air; and he was, therefore, often obliged to take medicine.

One day, when he was very sick from the effects of an emetic, he could not sleep on account of the noise that our American guard made, who never left

us, but were continually drinking and carousing before our very door; and when he sent them a message begging them to keep quiet, they redoubled
their noise. I resolved to go out myself; and I said to
them that my husband was sick, and begged that
they would be less noisy. They at once desisted
from their merriment and all became still. A proof
that this nation, also, have respect for our sex.

Some of their generals who accompanied us were
shoemakers; and upon our halting days they made
boots for our officers, and, also, mended nicely the
shoes of our soldiers. They set a great value upon
our money coinage; which, with them was scarce.
One of our officers had worn his boots entirely into
shreds. He saw that an American general had on a
good pair, and said to him jestingly, "I will gladly
give you a guinea for them." Immediately the general alighted from his horse, took the guinea, gave
up his boots, and put on the badly worn ones of the
officer, and again mounted his horse.

III. PRISONERS OF WAR

AT LAST we arrived at Boston; and our troops were quartered in barracks not far from Winter hill.[31] We were billeted at the house of a countryman, where we had only one room under the roof. My women servants slept on the floor, and our men servants in the entry. Some straw, which I placed under our beds, served us for a long time, as I had with me nothing more than my own field bed. Our host allowed us to eat in his room, where the whole family together eat and slept. The man was kind, but the woman, in order to revenge herself for the trouble we brought upon her, cut up the prank, every time we sat down to table, of taking that time to comb out her children's heads, which were full of vermin—which very often entirely took away our appetites. And if we begged her to do this outside, or select another time for this operation, she would answer us, "It is my room, and I like to comb my children's hair at this time!" We were obliged, therefore, to be silent lest she should thrust us out of the house.

One day the gentlemen of our party celebrated, in this filthy place, the birthday, I believe, of the queen of England, and drank on this occasion a great deal of wine.

[31] These old wooden and poorly-built barracks had been built for the American troops besieging Boston in 1775–1776.

My oldest little daughters, Gustava and Frederica, who had noticed that the wine that was left over had been placed under the stairs, thought it would be a fine thing for them in their turn to drink the queen's health. They, accordingly, seated themselves before the door, and toasted so much—that is, drank healths—that their little heads could not bear more. Frederica became sick of a fever, which gave me the more anxiety as she had spasms with it, and I was entirely at a loss to know the cause. When, finally, nature helped herself by vomiting, then I saw that it was the wine, and blamed the little maidens greatly, who, however, replied that they, also, loved the king and queen, and could not, therefore, resist wishing them happiness.

We remained three weeks at this place, until they transferred us to Cambridge, where they lodged us in one of the most beautiful houses of the place, which had formerly been built by the wealth of the royalists.[32] Never had I chanced upon such an agreeable situation. Seven families, who were connected with each other, partly by the ties of relationship and partly by affection, had here farms, gardens and magnificent houses, and not far off plantations of fruit. The owners of these were in the habit of daily meeting each other in the afternoons, now at the house of one, and now at another, and making

[32] This house, 149 Brattle Street, is still standing, although it has since been moved across Riedesel Avenue and has undergone extensive renovation.

themselves merry with music and the dance—living in prosperity, united and happy, until, alas! this ruinous war severed them, and left all their houses desolate except two, the proprietors of which were also soon obliged to flee.

None of our gentlemen were allowed to go into Boston. Curiosity and desire urged me to pay a visit to Madame Carter, the daughter of General Schuyler, and I dined at her house several times. The city, throughout, is pretty, but inhabited by violent patriots, and full of wicked people. The women, especially, were so shameless, that they regarded me with repugnance and even spit at me when I passed by them. Madame Carter was as gentle and good as her parents, but her husband was wicked and treacherous. She came often to visit us, and also dined at our house with the other generals. We sought to show them by every means our gratitude. They seemed, also, to have much friendship for us; and yet, at the same time, this miserable Carter, when the English General Howe had burned many hamlets and small towns, made the horrible proposition to the Americans to chop off the heads of our generals, salt them down in small barrels, and send over to the English one of these barrels for every hamlet or little town burned down; but this barbarous suggestion fortunately was not adopted.

During my sojourn at Bristol, in England, I had made the acquaintance of a Captain Fenton, from Boston, to whom the Americans, upon the breaking out of the war, had sent a summons, but which, true to his king, he would not obey. Upon this, the women of the exasperated rabble seized his wife—a woman deserving of all esteem—and his very beautiful daughter of fifteen years, and without regard to their goodness, beauty or modesty, stripped them naked, besmeared them with tar, rolled them in feathers, and, in this condition, led them through the city as a show. What might not be expected from such people, inspired with the most bitter hatred!

In the same manner, there were two brothers who had loved each other very much, one of whom had espoused the side of the king, and the other that of the republicans. The former, desiring again to see his brother, obtained permission and paid him a visit. His brother received him with great joy, and said to him, "How rejoiced am I to see you return to the good cause!" "No, my brother," answered the royalist, "I remain true to my king, but this shall not hinder me from loving you." At this, the American sprang up in a fury, seized a pistol, and threatened to shoot him if he did not instantly go away. All the representations of the good brother, that their differences of opinion should not alter his love, availed nothing. The other exclaimed, "Only my old love for you hinders me from shooting you this very moment, for every royalist is my enemy." And he would certainly have carried out his threat if his brother had not finally made his escape. Almost every family was disunited; and I saw here that nothing is more terrible than a civil war. With such people we were obliged to live, or see no one whatever! I naturally preferred the latter.

General Phillips was, and remained, ever our kind and sincere friend, and we saw much of him. Our house, also, was constantly full of Englishmen, after we learned that it was considered by them polite usage to invite them to call again. Before we knew this, we observed, to our astonishment, that some courteous people, whom we had received kindly, came not again. After this we adopted the same custom, and found it very convenient, since one could make a selection of those whose company was most agreeable. Still, a few persons favored us with their presence unasked, who were, as the English term it, "barefaced."

While in Cambridge, I saw an entire house carried off upon long logs, to the ends of which they had attached wheels. The house is raised by a screw, the logs shoved underneath it, and the building is then moved readily.

On the 3d of June, 1778, I gave a ball and supper in celebration of the birthday of my husband. I had invited to it all the generals and officers. The Carters, also, were there. General Burgoyne sent an excuse after he had made us wait till eight o'clock in the evening.

He invariably excused himself, on various pretenses, from coming to see us, until his departure for England,[33] when he came and made me a great many apologies, but to which I made no other answer than that I should be extremely sorry if he had gone out of his way on our account. We danced considerably, and our cook prepared us a magnificent supper of more than eighty covers. Moreover, our court-yard and garden were illuminated. As the birthday of the king of England came upon the following day, which was the fourth, it was resolved that we would not separate until his health had been drank; which was done with the most hearty attachment to his person and his interests.

Never, I believe, has "God save the King" been sung with more enthusiasm or more genuine good will. Even both my oldest little daughters were there, having staid up to see the illumination. All eyes were full of tears; and it seemed as if every one present was proud to have the spirit to venture to do this in the midst of our enemies. Even the Carters could not shut their hearts against us. As soon as the company separated, we perceived that the whole house was surrounded by Americans, who, having seen so many people go into the house, and having noticed, also, the illumination, suspected that we were planning a mutiny, and if the slightest disturbance had arisen, it would have cost us dear. The Americans, when they desire to collect their troops together, place burning torches of pitch upon the hill tops, at which signal every one has-

[33] Burgoyne was paroled and allowed to return to England.

tens to the rendezvous. We were once witnesses of this, when General Howe attempted a landing at Boston in order to rescue the captive troops. They learned of this plan, as usual, long beforehand, and opened barrels of pitch, whereupon, for three or four successive days, a large number of people, without shoes and stockings, and with guns on their backs, were seen hastily coming from all directions, by which means so many people came together so soon that it would have been a very difficult thing to effect a landing.[34]

We lived very happily and contented in Cambridge, and were, therefore, well pleased at the idea of remaining there during the captivity of our troops. As winter approached, however, we were ordered to Virginia.[35] Now I was forced to consider how I should safely carry the colors of our German regiments still further, as we had made the Americans at Saratoga believe that they were burnt up—a circumstance which they at first took in bad part, though, afterwards, they tacitly overlooked it. But it was only the staves that had been burned, the colors

[34] This alarm was caused by the arrival of the transports to take off the "Convention Army," because of the rumor that Howe planned to rescue these troops and take them to New York to reinforce his own command rather than return them to England.

[35] As the Convention of Saratoga was never recognized by the Continental Congress, the captured troops were treated as other prisoners of war. They were removed to Virginia because it was less expensive to maintain them there than in Boston.

having been thus far concealed. Now, my husband confided to me this secret, and entrusted me with their still further concealment. I, therefore, shut myself in with a right honorable tailor, who helped me make a mattress in which we sewed every one of them. Captain O'Connell,[36] under pretense of some errand, was sent to New York, and passed the mattress off as his bed. He sent it to Halifax, where we again found it on our passage from New York to Canada, and where—in order to ward off all suspicion in case our ship should be taken—I transferred it into my cabin, and slept, during the whole of the remaining voyage to Canada, upon these honorable badges.

While we were on the point of taking our departure, I discovered that our cook, whose receipts I had luckily received daily, had paid nothing whatever; and they brought to me unpaid bills which amounted to the sum of one thousand reichs thalers. My husband had him arrested. But he slipped off and went into the service of General Gates, who found him too expensive; whereupon he went to General La Fayette, who afterwards told us that "he would answer only for a king!" My husband wished him well on account of his skillfulness in cooking, which was very great. But the scoundrel had conceived a hatred against me, because I watched him. I

[36] Captain Laurentius O'Connell was an engineering officer on Riedesel's staff who had been taken prisoner at Bennington.

have always believed, also, that he had a share in the robbery of my husband's equipage at Albany. We afterwards found him in New York in the greatest poverty. He had seduced and ran away with the wife of an American, and afterwards deserted her, because he was in such an indigent situation that he was not able to support her.

My husband had often a kind of nervous and anxious feeling, by reason of which he was never easy unless he was walking or working in the garden. I, therefore, always took care, whenever we changed our quarters, to have a garden made in a suitable place. This was not difficult, neither did it cost much, as almost all our soldiers understood garden work, and were, besides, glad of an opportunity to earn something. I thanked God now more than ever that he had given me courage to follow my husband. The grief of being in captivity, the unpleasant situation of our troops, and the want of news from his fatherland—all these things threw him into deep despondency. Yet how much more had he suffered when he had no one to divert him, and when he had often been a whole half year and even longer without receiving intelligence from us! How joyful am I, even now, when I think back upon those times, that I resisted all those who would have prevented me from performing my duty and following the inclination with which my tender love had inspired me; and that I faithfully shared all his sorrows and his cares!

It was in the month of November, 1778, that we received the order to go to Virginia. My husband, fortunately, found a pretty English wagon, and bought it for me, so that, as before, I was enabled to travel easily. My little Gustava had entreated one of my husband's adjutants, Captain Edmonston,[37] not to leave us on the way. The confiding manner of the child touched him, and he gave his promise and faithfully kept it. I traveled always with the army, and often over almost impassable roads. The captain, who was very strong and always at hand, sprang from his horse at every dangerous place, and held our wagon. Our old yäger, Rockel, who was with me and was much delighted at this assistance, as he was very much fatigued, often sat quietly on his box and contented himself with crying, "Captain!" Instantly he was down from his horse. I did not like him to use such freedom; but it amused the good captain so much that he begged me not to notice it.

I had always provisions with me, but carried them in a second, small wagon. As this could not go as fast as we, I was often in want of every thing. Once, when we were passing a town called Hertford,[38] where we made a halt, which, by the way,

[37] Captain Edmonstone was an Englishman serving as an aide to General Riedesel. He became a great favorite of the baroness who hoped that he might marry her younger sister. She was greatly disturbed by his early death.

[38] Hartford, Connecticut, but more likely this was the small village called New Hartford.

happened every fourth day, we met General La Fayette, whom my husband invited to dinner, as otherwise he would have been unable to find any thing to eat. This placed me in rather an awkward dilemma, as I knew that he loved a good dinner. Finally, however, I managed to glean from what provisions I had on hand enough to make him a very respectable dinner. He was so polite and agreeable that he pleased us all very much. He had many Americans in his train, who were ready to leap out of their skin for vexation, at hearing us speak constantly in French. Perhaps they feared, on seeing us on such a friendly footing with him, that we would be able to alienate him from their cause, or that he would confide things to us that we ought not to know. He spoke much of England, and of the kindness which the king had shown him in having had all objects of interest shown to him. I could not keep myself from asking him how he could find it in his heart to accept so many marks of kindness from the king, when he was on the point of departing in order to fight against him. Upon this observation of mine he appeared somewhat ashamed, and answered me, "It is true that such a thought passed through my mind one day, when the king offered to show me his fleet. I answered that I hoped to see it some day; and then quietly retired, in order to escape from the embarrassment of being obliged to decline, point blank, the offer, should it be repeated." Some, however, charged him with being a spy in England, upon which he immediately went to America.

One day we came to a pretty little place, but our supply wagon not having been able to follow us, we could not endure our hunger longer. Observing a quantity of butcher's meat in the house in which we put up, I begged the hostess to let me have some. "I have," answered she, "several different kinds. There is beef, veal, and mutton." My mouth already watered at the prospect. "Let me have some," I said, "I will pay you well for it." Snapping her fingers almost under my very nose, she replied, "You shall not have a morsel of it. Why have you come out of your land to kill us, and waste our goods and possessions? Now you are our prisoners; it is, therefore, our turn to torment you." "See," rejoined I, "these poor children, they are almost dead with hunger." She remained inflexible. But when, finally, my three and a half year old little daughter, Caroline, came up to her, seized her by the hand, and said to her in English, "Good woman, I am very hungry!" She could not longer withstand her: she took her in a room and gave her an egg. "No," said the good little child, "I have still two sisters." At this the woman was touched, and gave her three eggs, saying, "I am just as angry as ever, but I cannot withstand the child." She then became more gentle, and offered me bread and milk. I made tea for ourselves. The woman eyed us longingly, for the Americans love it very much; but they had resolved to drink it

no longer, as the famous duty on the tea had occasioned the war. I offered her a cup, and poured out
for her a saucer of tea. This mollified her completely, and she begged me to follow her into the kitch-
en, where I found the husband gnawing at a pig's
tail, while his wife, to my great satisfaction, brought
out of the cellar a basket of potatoes. When she
came back he reached out to her his tit-bit. She ate
some of it, and gave it back to him in a little while,
when he again began to feast upon it. I saw this
singular mutual entertainment with amazement and
disgust; but he believed that hunger made me be-
grudge it him, and he reached out to me the already
thoroughly gnawed tail. What should I do? Throw
it away, and not only injure his feelings, but lose
my loved basket of potatoes! I accordingly took it,
pretended to eat it, and quietly threw it into the
fire. We had now made our entire peace with them.
They gave me my potatoes, and I made a good supper off them, with excellent butter. But besides this,
they moved us into three pretty rooms with good
beds.

The next morning we again set out on our journey, and still, on every hand, drew upon us the
curiosity of the inhabitants. Upon reaching the
bank of the Hudson river,[39] we were quartered at
the house of a boatman, where we were given, as a
special mark of favor, a half-finished room without
windows. We hung our bed clothes before them,

[39] At Fishkill, New York.

and slept upon some straw, as our baggage wagon was broken, and we had, therefore, no beds. In consequence of this accident, we had, unfortunately, neither coffee, nor tea, nor sugar, which had often, upon this journey constituted our only refreshment. Our landlady, a perfect fury, finally allowed us, on the following morning, when our things had arrived, to breakfast in her room, as it was in the month of December, and we could not make a fire in our room. But we were unable to induce her to let us have a table to ourselves; and we were not once permitted to sit down to hers, until she, with her children and servants, had finished breakfast, which consisted of what had been left over from the evening meal, viz: cabbage, ham, and the like, with coffee and coarse sugar. They left us a filthy table, which we were first obliged to clean before we could use it. And yet they insisted that we should put every thing in order, and replace the cups and saucers in a perfectly clean condition! At the least remonstrance they pointed us to the door. She did all this to torment us, for she was an anti-royalist. Unfortunately, a storm, with adverse winds, came up, so that we, as the boatman assured us, could not cross the river without danger. The wicked woman insisted, notwithstanding, that we should go; and it was only after many entreaties, that we obtained permission to remain two days longer. On the third day, the husband, with a perplexed air, came and announced to us that we must go. I entreated him to think of our danger, and at least to accompany us, as I should then have more courage to attempt the passage over. He promised to take us over himself; and we embarked upon a little boat with one sail; but as he shoved it from the land, our man sprang up and out of the boat, and left us only one sailor, who did not understand very well how to guide the tiller. We were, therefore, on account of his unskillfulness, and the contrary winds, driven hither and thither in the river for more than five hours, until, at last after a thousand anxieties, we landed upon the opposite shore. Even then we were still obliged to wade up to the knees through a morass, till we came to the house of Colonel Horborn[40]—a very rich man, where we were to lodge.

In that place, I had a small room, it is true, but a good one, for myself, husband, children, and both my maids; in which, however, the adjutants had to take breakfast, dinner and tea. As I wished to change my stockings on account of my feet being completely soaked, I begged our officers to go out long enough for me to do this. In the meantime they went into the kitchen to warm themselves, and while there, suddenly the host came in, took them by the arms, exclaiming at the same time, "Here, you nasty royalists! is it not enough that I harbor you; can you not sometimes leave me in peace?" He had just come in from the field; and in his coarse cloth garments, his long beard, and his dirty linen,

[40] Osborn.

looked so like a bear, that we trembled before him. His wife, however, was kind. On the following day, which was Sunday, she begged me to drink coffee with her after dinner. Scarcely had I seated myself, when the husband entered looking much more respectable, as he had shaved himself, and put on his Sunday linen. As I could not yet forget the scene of the day before, I got up and wished to leave the room. But he shut the door and asked me, "Are you afraid of me?" "No," answered I, "I am afraid of no one, not even the devil, whom you so resembled yesterday." "But to-day," replied he, "I look much better." "Yes," said I, "nevertheless, I desire to get out of the way of further discourtesies." My demeanor, instead of vexing, pleased him. He took me by the hand, and urged me to sit down again in my chair. "I am not so bad as you think," said he, "you please me, and if I had no wife I would marry you." "But," rejoined I, "how do you know that I would have you?" "That," said he, "we should soon see. I am very rich; the whole landscape, as far as you can see, is mine, my wife is already old; I think therefore, you had better remain here." From this moment, I could have had every thing that the house afforded; for the good wife was delighted to share with me all that she herself was accustomed to have.

We were obliged to remain here eight days in order to give our troops time to cross the river, which, on account of the scarcity of suitable boats, was very tedious. Our third stopping place for the night from this place, was at the house of a German, where we were well lodged and well fed. The old man, it seemed, was the son of a coachman who had been in the service of Count Görtz in Germany. In his twelfth year, his father on one occasion chastised him on account of some roguish prank. Thereupon he resolved to run away; and chance led him to London. Servants were at that time often sent thence to the American colonies, and he was also sent over with one of these companies. As his lucky star would have it he fell into the hands of a kind master, who, taking a fancy to him, had him well educated, and, after some years of service, gave him some land to cultivate, as was customary in this country, after one had served out his apprenticeship. He was very active and industrious, and soon found himself in a position to take a lease of it from his master, who, finally, when he observed how every thing prospered under his hands, gave him his daughter for a wife. The man had nine sons who were also farmers; and the only thing that disturbed his happiness was, the thought of having left his father, to whom, however, he often sent money. As he knew that the Riedesel family were neighbors and friends of Görtz, he took good care of us, and was exceedingly grieved when we again set out on our journey.

At another time we had our quarters for the night at the house of a Colonel Howe, to whom I thought I was paying a compliment by asking him if he was a relation of the English General? "God forbid," answered he, very much affronted, "he is not worthy of it." They said that this colonel was a brave man. When he was not in the field but at home, he plowed his acres himself, and busied himself with his household affairs. He had a daughter fourteen years old, pretty, but of a wicked disposition. As I was once sitting with her before a good chimney fire, she gazed at the glowing coals, and cried out "Oh, if I only had the king of England here, with what satisfaction I could cut his body in pieces, tear out his heart, dissect it, put it upon these coals, and consume it!" I looked at her with horror, and said, "I am almost ashamed to belong to a sex that is capable of taking such pleasure." I have never been able to forget this detestable girl; and I was glad to get away from this house, although, in other respects, we were very well treated.

Before we passed the so-called Blue mountains, we were forced to make a still further halt of eight days, that our troops might have time to collect together again. In the mean time such a great quantity of snow fell, that four of our servants were obliged to go before my wagon on horseback, in order to make a path for it. We passed through a picturesque portion of the country, which, however, by reason of its wildness, inspired us with terror. Often we were in danger of our lives while going along these break-neck roads; and more than all this we suffered from cold, and what was still worse, from a lack of provisions. When we arrived in Virginia, and were only a day's journey from the place of our destination, we had actually nothing more remaining but our tea, and none of us could obtain any thing but bread and butter. A countryman, whom we met on the way, gave me only a hand full of acrid fruits. At noon we came to a dwelling where I begged for something to eat. They refused me with hard words, saying that there was nothing for dogs of Royalists. Seeing some Turkish meal[41] lying around, I begged for a couple of hands full, that I might mix with water and make bread. The woman answered me "No, that is for our negroes, who work for us, but you have wished to kill us." Captain Edmonston offered her from me, two guineas for it, as my children were so hungry. But she said, "Not for a hundred would I give you any; and should you all die of hunger, it will be so much the better." At this reply, the captain became so provoked, that he wished to take it by force. I, however, entreated him, in order to prevent disturbance, to keep quiet, as we, perhaps, would soon come across better disposed people. But alas that did not happen! We did not once meet with even a hut. The roads were horrible, the horses completely tired out, my three children exhausted by hunger, very wan, and I for the first time was thoroughly disheartened. Captain Edmonston, exceedingly touched at this sight, went from man to man to see

[41] Indian meal.

if he could not obtain something to eat. At last he received from one of the drivers of our baggage-wagons, a piece of old bread, a quarter of a pound's weight, which had been considerably gnawed at, since, on account of its hardness, no one could bite off the smallest piece. The instant he brought it to us, joy sparkled in the eyes of the children. I was about to give the first piece to Caroline as the youngest. "No," said the kind child, "my sisters are more hungry than I." Gustava and Frederica also refused to take it, wishing to leave it for their little sister. I therefore divided it and gave it to all three to eat. Tears ran down both my cheeks; and the good Edmonston was so affected, that he was unable longer to endure the sight. If I had at any time refused a piece of bread to the poor, I should have thought that God wished now to punish me for it. The kind driver, who had so willingly given us his last piece of bread, received a guinea from Captain Edmonston, and, on our arrival at the place of our destination, a large stock of bread for his return journey.

The place of our destination was Colle in Virginia, where my husband, who had gone ahead with our troops, awaited us with impatient longing. We arrived here about the middle of February, 1779, having, on our journey, passed through the provinces of Connecticut, New York, New Jersey, Pennsylvania and Maryland, and having traveled in twelve weeks, six hundred and seventy-eight English miles. The house in which we lived, and the entire estate, belonged to an Italian,[42] who, as he was to be absent for some time, gave it up to us. We looked forward longingly to the departure of himself, wife and daughter, for not only was the house small, but more than all, the scarcity of provisions seemed to trouble them—a circumstance which caused the husband to exercise a kind of guardianship over us. Thus, when he had a ram killed, he gave us on the first day, nothing more than the head, the neck, and the giblets, although I represented to him that more than twenty persons were to make a meal off them. He assured me that a right good soup might be made of these articles, and gave us besides, two heads of cabbage, with which, and half of a putrid ham, we were obliged to be satisfied.

The troops had been expected earlier, and accordingly many oxen and swine had been killed for food; and, as salt was very scarce, they cut the meat into quarters, placed it in a vault in the earth, and scattered between the pieces ashes instead of salt which answered equally as well. But as in this part of the country, the sun, even in January, often shines out very warm, all the top layers were spoiled. The meat was brought to us on a wheel-

[42] Philip Mazzei, an Italian horticulturist who had come to Virginia to introduce the culture of grapes, olives, and other Mediterranean products. His land adjoined Monticello, the home of Thomas Jefferson. Governor Patrick Henry appointed him revolutionary agent for the State of Virginia to serve in Europe. He returned to Europe in 1785.

barrow; but we were often obliged to throw the whole of it away, although sometimes we could wash it, in which case we salted and hung it up to smoke. The day of our arrival, when I had scarcely enough for dinner to satisfy us alone, I saw with tears, eight of our officers ride up just before dinner. What could we do but share with them the little we had? The troops were stationed at Charlottesville, two hours ride from us. To reach them we were obliged to go through a very beautiful piece of woods. At first they endured many privations. They occupied block-houses, which, however, were without plaster, and destitute of doors and windows, so that they were very cold inside. They worked, however, with great industry to build themselves better dwellings; and, in a short time, I saw a pretty little town spring up. Behind each barrack, they laid out gardens and constructed pretty little inclosures for poultry. Afterwards, when the old provisions were consumed, they received fresh meat and meal enough to make bread. As this latter was Indian meal, it served them for omelets and dumplings; so that now they were in want of nothing but money. Very little of this latter commodity was sent to them by the English, and it was difficult sometimes to obtain credit—a circumstance which oftentimes gave great inconvenience to the common soldiers.

In the middle of the month of February the fruit trees, which were already in blossom, were all killed by the night-frost. As soon as the tempera-

ture of the air would allow, we had the garden and
the field tilled and planted; and, as our landlord
went off three weeks after, we took possession of
every thing—swine, wild turkeys, etc. Some of the
latter weighed over fifty pounds, and were perfectly
tame; but when spring came, they all flew off to
hatch their eggs, which they had laid in the forests.
We gave them up for lost, but they all came back
and brought with them a great number of young
ones.

We had built for us a large house, with a great
drawing-room in the centre, and upon each side
two rooms which cost my husband one hundred
guineas. It was exceedingly pretty.

Many of the negroes brought us every thing that
we needed, in the shape of poultry and vegetables.
Every week, General Phillips and ourselves killed,
by turns, an ox and two pigs. Very soon we wanted
nothing. But the heat bothered us very much in
summer; and we lived in constant terror of rattlesnakes. The fruits also were eaten into, by three
kinds of ticks. We had, moreover, heavy thunder-
storms, lasting for five or six days at a time, and
accompanied by tempests which tore up by the
roots more than one hundred trees in our vicinity.
The trees stood very loosely, and their roots were
lightly covered, as the strong winds blew away from
them the earth, which was mostly sand. Besides all
this, the negroes and herdsmen often made fires under the trees, for which they cared nothing. By rea-

son of this the trees were more easily blown down. Often whole forests were set on fire, and burned down in order to obtain new land. At night, we were obliged to leave our windows open, that we might be able to draw in fresh air, and sleep. Thereupon, three or four nasty bats would wake us up, and we were obliged to spend half the night in chasing them around the room. On one occasion a person came in the night to my husband, to tell him that the stable, which was a new one, was in danger of being blown down by the wind. Every one ran out to prop it up, except myself, who was left alone with my children, and women servants. The wind continually grew stronger. A great piece of the chimney fell into the room; the whole house rocked; and I remained half the night in the greatest fear of being killed by a fragment. We were often frightened in this manner.

We had no chairs to sit on, only round blocks, which we also used for a table, laying boards upon them. In this manner we lived for three or four months, pretty contentedly; my husband, only, was always sad, and could not at all endure the heat, which stood at one hundred and three degrees, and was exceedingly oppressive. We endeavored to cheer him up as much as possible. As soon as the vegetables began to grow in our garden, he took considerable satisfaction in busying himself in gardening. But as he would wear no hat on his head on account of having much headache and its uncomfortable feeling, he met with an accident, which I will presently relate, that was the beginning of my great sufferings. I was engaged in putting to rights our new house and my husband's room, when I heard a noise out of doors. I ran to the window and saw my husband being carried into the house by some men. His face was blue, his hands white, his eyes fixed, and great drops of sweat stood upon his forehead. He had received a sun-stroke. I was more dead than alive; and the children uttered piercing shrieks. We immediately laid him down, and tore off all his clothing. Fortunately the surgeon of our regiment, who was already with us, happened at the moment to be in, and at once opened a vein.[43] He now recovered his speech and told us that as he was walking through the garden, the sun shone down intensely upon his head; and he had been scarcely able to reach the house when his adjutant arrived; had it not been for this timely aid he would have been killed. My God! what would then have become of me and my little children in the midst of captives, so far from home, and in an enemy's land! Even now my hair stands on end whenever I think of it. As soon as my husband again came to himself, he took me by the hand, and gazed upon me with an affectionate look. One could not but observe that he considered himself very dangerously ill. If I went away even for an instant, he became very uneasy

[43] Taking a quantity of blood from a patient was a favorite treatment for many ills in eighteenth-century medicine.

and followed me with his eyes. The physician, whom we had summoned, came; and after we had used all possible care, God was finally pleased to preserve for me my beloved husband. But for many years afterward he suffered from pains in the head, and from debility, which made him grieve the more over his situation.

The use of a certain bath in Virginia, which is called Frederick-spring,[44] was prescribed for him, and we accordingly journeyed thither. I believe that he increased his disorder by always wetting his head before bathing; and what was still worse was, that in spite of all we could do, his hair would remain damp. His fretfulness continued, and the thought of his imprisonment worried him more than ever. At night he could not sleep. I therefore hit upon the expedient of reading to him in a particularly drowsy tone. This was successful, for he always went to sleep. His hands and feet were constantly blue, and cold as ice. Whenever I thought that I might safely venture to lie down, his anguish would invariably wake him up. Every thing irritated him. One day a Virginian came into my room, and said that he was curious to see a German woman, eyeing me, at the same time, from head to foot. I was delighted at the idea of enjoying myself over something. But when, at his request, I brought him to my husband, the latter was so moved at the idea of his

[44] Frederick, or Berkeley, Springs was in Berkeley County in what is now West Virginia.

situation compelling him to be gazed upon at the whim of this or that man, that the tears came into his eyes, and I sincerely repented of having been so inconsiderate.

We made at Frederick-spring, the acquaintance of General Washington's family, and also of Madam Garel[45]—a very lovable woman—and her husband. She was an ardent American patriot, but reasonable, and we became great friends. She spent most of the forenoons with us. At such times Captain Geismar played the violin and I sang Italian airs, which gave her the greatest delight. One day, while thus engaged, a countryman, from whom we had endeavored by many kind words to obtain fresh butter, came in upon us. As the Americans, generally, are fond of music, he listened attentively, and when I had finished, asked me to sing it once more. I asked him sportively what he would give me for it? as I did nothing gratis. "Two pounds of butter," he at once answered. The idea pleased me, and I began to sing.

"Play another one," said he, as soon as I had finished, "but something lively." At length I sang so much, that the next morning, he brought me four or five pounds of fresh butter. He, also, had his wife with him, and entreated me to sing once more. I thus succeeded in winning their affection; and afterwards I lacked for nothing. The best of the joke was, that he actually believed I wished to be paid

[45] Mrs. Charles Carroll of Carrollton, Maryland.

for my singing, and wondered much when I paid them for the butter which they supposed they had already sold.

The Virginians are generally inert, a fate which they attribute to their hot climate; but on the slightest inducement, in a twinkling, they leap up and dance about; and if a reel—, an English or a Scotch national dance—is played for them, immediately the men catch hold of the women who then jump up as if they were possessed; but as soon as they are led back to their chairs they sit on them like blocks of wood. Regarding the practices of the people in this part of the country, one cannot give a pleasant description. For example, they informed us that two maidens had been got with child by their father; a circumstance, which, it is true, occasioned some talk, but which, nevertheless, remained unpunished. Another man also, who thought his daughter-in-law handsomer than his wife, proposed an exchange to his son, who consented, on the condition, that his father should give with the mother, two cows and two horses. The exchange was accordingly made, and the whole affair excited no farther comment.

The landed proprietors in Virginia own many negro slaves, and treat them badly. Many of them are allowed by their masters to run naked until they are fifteen and sixteen years old, and the dress which is then given them, is scarcely worth wearing. The slaves have an overseer who leads them out at daybreak into the fields, where they are obliged to work like beasts or receive beatings; and when thoroughly exhausted and burned by the sun, they come into the house. They are given Indian meal called hominy, which they make into pastry. But often they are tired and had rather sleep for a couple of hours, when they are again obliged to go to work. They view it as a misfortune to have children, as they in turn will become slaves and wretched men. As they have not the time to cultivate the little land which they have, they possess nothing, and are only able by the sale of poultry to scrape together sufficient money to clothe themselves. Still, there are also good masters, who can be easily told, by their slaves being well clothed and housed. Under such auspices, the negroes are also good servants, and are very faithful and much attached to their masters. That wicked masters have disaffected servants is not to be wondered at.

During our sojourn at this bath, my husband received news which gave us all much pleasure; namely, that he and General Phillips, with their adjutants, had permission to go to New York, in order to be exchanged. My husband, upon this, went back to Colle, to make arrangements for the maintenance, in his absence, of the troops, the command of which he handed over to Colonel Specht,[46] and to take measures for the sale of our superfluous

[46] Colonel Johann Friedrich Specht who commanded one of the infantry regiments under Riedesel.

things, and especially, our new house, which we had as yet not lived in—in which situation, indeed, we at various times afterwards found ourselves. We were often troubled in this way; for we would come to a place, expecting to remain for some time, but we would scarcely get our things to rights, at infinite pains, when we would receive an order, bidding us, instantly to depart. This time, however, every one was rejoiced.

IV. FROM VIRGINIA TO CANADA

I SET OUT from this bath, in the month of August, 1777, to join my husband in York-town, Pennsylvania. Madame Garel, the clever woman, whom I have already mentioned, had begged me to visit them at their country seat, in the province of Maryland, in case we should be in the vicinity. I, therefore, determined to do it now. Captain Freeman,[47] one of my husband's English adjutants, remained with us. Captain Edmonston had been exchanged through the intercession of his father. He was so devoted to the interests of my husband, and it gave him so much pain to leave him, that the latter was even obliged to persuade him to return to England. His departure affected us deeply, especially when he said, "I am certain that I shall never see you again."[48]

On our journey to the country-seat of Mrs. Garel, Captain Freeman saw a black snake—which, however, is not dangerous—licking a frog and swallowing him down. Crying out sportively, "I declare myself the Knight of the Frog," he drew his sword, and split the snake open, when lo! the frog hopped out of its stomach, thoroughly alive; at which we all were greatly amazed. Before we arrived, I was

[47] Captain Freeman had been assigned as an adjutant to General Riedesel.
[48] His premonition was right. He died of "consumption" on his voyage home.

overturned with my wagon, but without the slightest injury. I had advised Madame Garel of my arrival, and she sent a man on horseback to meet me. After I had passed through a very pretty hamlet, inhabited by pure negroes—each of whom had his garden, and understood some handicraft—we drove through a large courtyard, to a very beautiful house, where the whole family received us with a joyful welcome. The family consisted of an old father-in-law, eighty-four years of age, of a sprightly humor, and the most extreme neatness, upon whose venerable countenance, appeared happy contentment; four perfectly lovely grandchildren; and their kind, beloved mother, our amiable hostess. We were served upon silver, and entertained, not, it is true, with much display, but with taste. Nothing was wanting for our comfort. She said to me that, as she hoped I would remain with her a long time, she had received me as if I belonged to the family.

The garden was magnificent; and, on the following day, she drove us out to show us her vineyard, which was splendid, and displayed great taste, in fact exceeding my expectations. First, we went through a great fruit garden. Then we ascended the vineyard by a winding path, which led up to the top of the hill. Between every vine, a poplar-rose and an amaranth grew. The effect of this arrangement was to give a magnificent appearance to every part of the vineyard, to one looking down from the top, such a one, indeed, that for beauty, I have not

found its equal in any portion of America which I
have seen. The husband of Madame Garel had traveled abroad, and had gathered these ideas of the
laying out of grounds in England and France. In
other respects he was not very lovable, but rather
brusque, and niggardly, and not at all suited to his
wife, who, although she never showed it by outward
signs, nevertheless did not appear to be happy. Her
father-in-law she loved very much.

Not far from this estate, was a town, called Baltimore, which they told me was very pretty, and inhabited by many amiable families. We received a
visit from an intimate friend of our hostess. Both
these women reminded me of Rousseau's Heloise
and her friend, and the old father of the husband of
Heloise. Madame Garel was as full of tender feeling
as she, and would, I believe, have gladly had a St.
Preux[49] for a husband. We arranged for her a tem-
ple adorned with flowers, after the design of Captain Freeman, and dedicated it to Friendship and
Gratitude. She wrote me some years afterward, that
the family still continued to trim it with flowers.
The lovely, agreeable Madame Garel, is now dead;
and her family, but especially her children, have
met with a great loss. We remained here eight or
ten days, and our parting was very sad. They supplied us with provisions of the best quality, enough
to last for a long time. We, however, did not really

[49] St. Preux was a central character in Rousseau's senti-
mental novel *Nouvelle Héloise* (1761).

need them, as the royalists, through friendly feeling, and the others, through custom, welcomed us kindly, and furnished us with every thing needful for our sustenance. In this country it would be held a crime to refuse hospitality to a traveler.

Not far from the place where I was to meet my husband, we were overtaken in a forest, by a violent thunder-storm. A trunk of a tree broke and fell between the carriage-box and the horses. Here we sat fast aground, and could not stir from the place, as none of our servants were strong enough to move the tree from the spot where it had fallen. In the meantime, it thundered fearfully; the lightning struck in several places round about us; and another and larger tree threatened to crush us. I could only urge the servants to disengage us from the jam, but the coachman, who was completely bewildered, assured me, that it was impossible. At last, my little Gustava, who was at that time only eight years old, said, "Only unhitch the horses, and put them behind the wagon, and you can draw it backwards." This suggestion was immediately acted upon, and every one asked the other, why that idea had not occurred to them likewise? So finally we arrived happily at York-town, in Pennsylvania, where we found my husband, who had been very much worried about us, on account of the vivid lightning. We rode through a magnificent country, and passed, among others, a very well cultivated section inhabited by the Moravian brethren. One place is called

the Holy Sepulchre, and another district goes by
the name of the Holy Land,[50] in which is a town
called Bethlehem. We found a right good tavern,
where we waited for those of our party, who were
still behind. I had brought with me from Virginia,
some splendid birds. The male was scarlet, with a
still darker red tuft, as large as a jack-daw, and sang
magnificently. The female was gray, with a red
breast, and had also a tuft. As soon as these birds
are caught they become tame, and eat out of the
hand. This bird lives a long while, but if two males
are hung up in the same room, they become so jealous of each other, that one of them soon dies miserably. I saw also in Virginia, blue birds, just as large,
that constantly cried willo! This afforded us considerable amusement, as one of my husband's aids was
so named.

One of our servants found a whole nest of these
red birds, and trained them, and, as he knew I loved
them very much, he carried to me two cages full of
them from Colle, upon his back. But they all died
before he arrived, which gave us considerable sorrow. I had also made a collection of very beautiful
butterflies, and had packed them very carefully in a
trunk, but the wagon in which they were was overturned, and the trunk dashed to pieces. This happened to me twice, and entirely took away from me

[50] Apparently Madame Riedesel was given the wrong
name. One historian of the area questions the names "Holy
Sepulchre" and "Holy Land."

any further desire to make yet another collection.

After we all had once more got together and rested, we again set out and came to the house of a family who gave themselves out for royalists. Their name was Van Horn. They showed us much kindness, and begged us to recommend them to General Cornwallis, who, as well as General Clinton, was a friend of General Phillips and had brought about our return from Virginia.

We came to a very pretty place, opposite Staten island, called Elizabeth-town, where we found many royalists who welcomed us joyfully and treated us with hospitality. We were now so near New York and counted so surely on the exchange of my husband and the actual fulfillment of our dearest wishes, that, as we sat together at dinner, we confidently believed that we should cross over immediately to New York and be restored to freedom that same evening. But suddenly the door opened and an officer, sent by General Washington, stepped inside and handed to General Phillips a letter with an order to return again, as the congress had refused to ratify the exchange. The eyes of General Phillips, who was by nature very passionate, fairly scintillated with rage. He struck the table with his fist, and said, "This is pleasant! but we should have expected it from these people who are all rascals!" I was like one petrified, and could not utter a single word. He seized me by the hand, and said to me, "Now, my friend, do not allow your courage to fail you. Follow my example; see how collected I am!" "Every one," answered I to him, "shows his sorrow in his own fashion. I keep mine in my heart, and you manifest yours with passion. But it's my opinion that you would do better not to allow these people to see you in such a passion, who will only make sport of you, and may perhaps make you still more trouble." He acknowledged that I was right, thanked me, and assured me that he, like myself, would bear his sufferings with resignation. From this time he conducted himself perfectly quietly.

I was at this time with child, and in constant pain, so that the journey fatigued me exceedingly. I had hoped to find quiet, and be among people, from whom I could have received good nursing. Vain hope! After the single day's halt which was allowed us, we were forced to turn about again, and stop once more at the house of the Van Horns. This time we found there a nephew of General Washington,[51] with quite a number of other American officers, who within three days had wrought such a wonderful change in the sentiments of these people (they were among those who hang their cloaks to the wind),[52] that we not only saw the daughters of these pretended royalists on the most familiar footing with the anti-royalists, and allowing them all kinds of liberties; but, as they thought we would not now dare to remonstrate, we heard them singing

[51] Probably George Augustine Washington.
[52] Turncoats.

during the whole night, "God save great Washington! God damn the King!" Upon our departure the next morning, I could scarcely conceal my indignation. We now returned to Bethlehem, where my husband and General Phillips were allowed by the Americans to remain until the particulars of the exchange, which was yet unfinished, should be settled; and, as our former landlord in this place had treated us with kind hospitality, we all of us determined to board with him—"all of us" being sixteen persons, and four house servants. The latter received money with which to pay their board. We had, also, about twenty horses. Our host would make with us no definite agreement about the price, and, as none of us had any money, this was very convenient, as he would cheerfully wait for his pay till we received some. We supposed him to be an honest and reasonable man, and the more so, as he belonged to the community of Moravian brethren, and the inn was the one patronized by that society.[53] But how great was our surprise, when, after a residence of six weeks, and just as we had received permission to go to New York, we were served with a bill of thirty-two thousand dollars, that is to say, in American paper money, which is about four hundred guineas in actual money. Had it not been for a royalist, who just at this time chanced to pass through the village seeking to purchase hard money at any price, we

[53] This was the Sun Inn, operated by Jost Jansen, a Norwegian sailor.

should have been placed in the greatest embarrassment, and would not have been able by any possibility to leave the town. From him, we were so fortunate as to receive for one piaster,[54] eighty dollars in paper money.

My husband suffered greatly the whole time from constant pains in his head; and at night he could scarcely breathe. To obtain a little relief, he now accustomed himself to use snuff, a practice, which until this period, he had regarded with the greatest aversion. I first persuaded him to take one pinch. He believed that I was making fun of him; but as the very next instant after the trial, he experienced relief, he exchanged his pipe for a snuff-box.

My little Caroline was very sick, with a choking cough and, as I became continually further advanced in pregnancy, we all heartily wished to reach New York as soon as possible, in order to have near at hand the comforts of life, good nursing, and all necessary help.

In Bethlehem, as in all other Moravian communities, there were separate houses for the brethren and sisters. In the latter establishments they made magnificent embroidery, and other beautiful handiworks; we bought at these places several articles. A Miss Girsdorff,[55] a German and who afterwards resided at Herrnhut, had taught the sisters all these

[54] The Spanish dollar.
[55] Susanna Charlotte von Gersdorf supervised the house for "single women."

kinds of work. The houses of this community were well built, and there were at this place all sorts of manufactories. Among others, there was one that dressed leather, which was as good as that of England and half as cheap. The gentlemen of our party bought a quantity of it. There were also very clever cabinet-makers, workers in steel, and excellent smiths. We had very much wished to see Philadelphia, which is only twelve or thirteen miles from Bethlehem, and to which place there is a clear, good road. But as this was not allowed to my husband and the other gentlemen, and, as I wished to share with my beloved husband his joys and sorrows, I cheerfully gave it up. While at Bethlehem we often went to church, and enjoyed the splendid singing. The wife of the minister died while we were there. We saw her laid out in a separate enclosure, with bars, waiting for burial; for here they never keep a dead body in the house.

Finally, at the end of November, 1779, we again set out from Bethlehem. My dear husband, General Phillips, and their several aid-de-camps, had not, indeed, been exchanged, but permission was received for them to go to New York on parole. I did not wish to call again on the Van Horns, for I despise double dealing people; but we had the fatality of having our wagon break down before their very door, so that I was forced to tarry with them until the damage could be repaired. I did not, however, remain over night at their house; and when they again asked that we should recommend them, and assured us of their devotion to the king, in whose army the head of the family had served as a colonel, I answered coldly that I believed he did not need our recommendations; which reply he was welcome to take as he pleased. We came, also, once more to Elizabeth-town, where we were again kindly received, embarked upon the Hudson river, and reached New York very late in the evening, where my husband, who had gone on ahead of us, had already arrived before me. A soldier, who at the gateway, had been ordered to show us the way, conducted us to a very great and beautiful house, where we found every thing prepared for our reception, and better than all, a good supper. I was too much occupied in putting my children to bed, and too tired to inquire where I was, and supposed I was in a public-house. My husband, who had taken tea with General Cornwallis, came home late. The next morning a servant came in to ask me what I desired for dinner, and how many visitors I would probably have daily at table; I replied that as my husband did not dine at home, I should not need more than three dishes for six persons, namely: myself, my children, my women servants, and pastor Mylius,[56] the chaplain of my husband's regiment, whom we retained in our family, and who gave my children instruction in every thing useful. He was a man of piety and of excellent character, and good humor;

[56] Johann August Mylius.

and the children and we all loved him very much. I was then told that the order had been given to serve up on my table every day six large, and four small dishes. Being still under the impression that I was in a tavern, I decidedly forbade this profusion, as I dreaded the bill. But I soon discovered, that I was staying at the house of the governor, General Tryon,[57] who had forbidden them to tell me where I had been taken, through fear that I would not accept of his house.

This noble minded man, moreover, in order to avoid my thanks, crossed over to Long Island, where he had a provisional command.

All my wishes were anticipated, and I was only in continual fear lest I should abuse so much kindness. I also received a call from General Patterson,[58] the commandant of the city, who told me that they were still busy with the arrangement of the house which we were to have as our own residence. Lord Cornwallis and General Clinton likewise came to see me.

The latter offered me a country-seat, of which he had the disposal, where I might have my children

[57] William Tryon (1729–1788) had become royal governor of North Carolina in 1765. In 1777 he was appointed governor of New York. After New York City was taken by the British in 1776 he returned to the army and led several raids into New York and Connecticut. He returned to England in 1780.

[58] Major General James Pattison, British artillery officer, was commandant of New York City from July 5, 1779, to August 12, 1780.

inoculated with small-pox; an operation which
it would be dangerous to have performed in
the city, as that disease was raging there violently.
I accepted his offer with much satisfaction, and
so we made all necessary preparations. Cornwallis
went off soon afterwards upon an expedition.[59]
I gave our cook some ten guineas to purchase all
kinds of provisions. But when he very soon came
back and asked for more money, I learned to my
surprise that the money I had given him would
scarcely last for two days—so dear was every thing,
even the commonest thing. For example, one
pound of meat, reckoning according to our money,
cost twelve groschen;[60] one pound of butter, eighteen groschen; one turkey, four rix-thalers; a fowl
twenty groschen; an egg, four groschen; a quart of
milk, six groschen; a bushel of potatoes, two rix-
thalers; a half bushel of turnips, two florins; ten oys-
ters, eight groschen, and six onions, one rix-thaler.
But what was there left for me to do, but to bear it
with patience?

One day a general was announced. I received
him, and, in the course of conversation, he asked
me, among other things, whether I was satisfied with
my quarters? My heart was too full of thankfulness

[59] Sir Henry Clinton (1738–1795), commanding general of
the British Army in North America and Lord Cornwallis
(1738–1805), second-in-command, sailed for the southern
states which resulted in the taking of Charleston, South Carolina, May 12, 1780.
[60] A German coin of small denomination.

for all the kindness that had been shown me, not to give full vent to my feelings in this regard; and I at last expressed the wish to know personally my noble benefactor who had treated me with so much delicacy. He laughed, and just at that moment my husband stepped in and said to me, "That is the man who has shown us so much kindness!" I was so delighted at seeing him, that I could not find words to express my feelings.

Upon seeing my emotion the man was very much affected. I have invariably received from him the greatest proofs of his friendship.

The country residence of General Clinton, where we went, was an hour's ride from the city.[61] The grounds were beautiful, as was also the house; but the latter was arranged more for a summer residence, and, as we had come there in the month of December, we suffered much from the cold. Notwithstanding this, however, the inoculation was perfectly successful. Accordingly, as it was now completed, and we had nothing more to fear from the infection, we got ourselves in readiness to return to the city, and sent our cook and the rest of our servants ahead to prepare every thing for our arrival, which we expected would be upon the following day. During the night, however, we had such a terrible storm that we believed the whole house would be overturned. As it was, an entire balustrade actually fell down with a dreadful crash; and,

[61] This was the Beekman mansion, "Mount Pleasant."

on getting up the next morning, we saw that on account of snow having fallen during the night four or five feet on the level, and eight feet in drifts, it would be utterly impossible to venture forth without sledges. I therefore went to work to hunt up all that I could find for our dinner. An old hen that had been forgotten served us for soup, and some potatoes which the gardener gave us, with some salt meat that still remained over from our stock of provisions, made up the entire meal for more than fourteen persons, which number we then were.

While I was standing, the same afternoon, by the window, thoroughly perplexed, I saw our cook approaching on horseback. Filled with joy, I turned round to the rest of the company to announce the auspicious arrival. But upon again looking out, I could not see or hear any thing more of the cook! Terrified at his disappearance, the gentlemen immediately ran out, and found him, together with his horse, completely buried in the snow, from which position without their help he could not have got out, and perhaps never would have been able to extricate himself. Our people had been quite uneasy at our non-arrival, and, as they knew our larder was completely exhausted, the cook had brought us some provisions which supplied us with an evening meal. It was impossible to drive into the city in a wagon.

The morning of the next day brought us Captain Willoe with two large sledges, in which we seated ourselves. I was, however, not without anxiety, in regard to the children, whose pocks had not yet entirely dried up, on account of the terrible cold weather. The ride, however, did them no injury whatever. During the period of inoculation Carolina lost her whooping-cough, but immediately after it came back again and lasted a whole year.

On our return to New York I found, to my great amazement, our new dwelling fitted up throughout with mahogany furniture. I was at first frightened at the expense which this would occasion. But Captain Willoe informed me that the entire cost would be defrayed by the governor, and that the commandant, General Patterson, considered himself fortunate in being able to justify the confidence which I had placed in the English nation. To render this remark intelligible, I must here state that I had assured him, when he consulted me upon the arrangement of our house, that I would leave every thing entirely to the English, from whom, up to the present time, I had received sincere kindness and courtesy, and who certainly would still preserve towards us that full confidence, which they had shown towards us.

They overwhelmed us with distinguished marks of courtesy and friendship, for which we had, in a great measure, to thank General Phillips, who in New York was very much beloved, and was so strong a friend of ours, that he declared that whatever was done for us, would flatter him more than as if done for himself. I had also the good fortune during our stay to make many friends on my own account.

As the birth-day of the queen of England was approaching (which indeed really comes in summer, but as the king's birth-day also comes in that season, is celebrated in winter, to give more custom to the trades people, as every one upon those days appears at court in gala-dress) they wished to celebrate the day with a great fete; and as it was the general wish—partly to please General Phillips, and partly to make me forget my own sufferings—to confer on me a distinguished honor, they desired me to be queen of the ball. In order to bring this about they persuaded the wife of General Cornwallis's adjutant—who as an English lady of noble birth would have had precedence over me—to remain at home, on the ground that she was near her confinement.[62] When at length the great day arrived, all the ladies assembled at Governor Tryon's, where they received me with all ceremony.

The general introduced me to all the ladies, some of whom were envious of the honor which was shown me. But I immediately declared that I received this distinction only on account of the day, as they had conferred on me the honor of representing the queen, and that in future I would give place to those ladies who were older than I. As there were

[62] Probably Elizabeth, wife of Sir William Schaw Cathcart, aide to General Clinton.

quite a number present who were my elders, my explanation conciliated them. Their countenances, accordingly, very quickly brightened up, and I was soon upon a pleasant footing with the whole of the company.

At six o'clock in the afternoon I was obliged to seat myself in a carriage with Generals Tryon and Patterson to be driven to the ball, where we were received with kettle-drums and trumpets.

I wished, as I was far advanced with child, not to dance. But I was obliged to open the ball with one of the generals by a formal minuet. My situation as well as my bashfulness was the occasion of my thinking myself very awkward. In order, however, to remove my timidity, they all assured me that I did very well, and must dance once more; and the result was, that I danced several English dances.

At supper, I was obliged, as I represented the queen, to sit under a canopy, and drink the first toast. I was certainly much touched at all the marks of friendship I received, although extremely tired; still, in order to show my gratitude, I cheerfully stayed as long as possible, and remained until two o'clock in the morning. Not only on this occasion, but during the whole of my sojourn in this place, I was loaded with kindness; and I passed the remainder of the winter very pleasantly, with the exception of suffering very much from the cold, as the commissary had not had a sufficient quantity of wood cut. To save expense, he had this work done by his negro slaves; and the winter setting in earlier than usual, and it being impossible, as the river was frozen half over, to bring in wood either by boats or sledges, many of the garrison suffered for fuel. We, indeed, received an order for it; but how did that help the matter since there was no wood to be had? We were, therefore, often obliged to borrow wood of General Tryon for Saturday and Sunday, which we would return on Monday if we received any. The cold was so intense, that I frequently made the children lie in bed in order to keep them warm. Wood often could not be purchased for money; and if by chance a little was for sale, it cost ten pounds by the cord. I have myself paid one piaster (which is a crown with us) for a single stick. The poor were obliged to burn fat, in order to warm themselves and cook their meals.[63]

One day I was at the house of the lady of General Cornwallis's aid-de-camp, who had been confined, and complained bitterly of this lack of wood; whereupon, she promised to send me some coals, which I could return at my own convenience. I showed so much joy at this, that a certain major named Brown, who happened to be present and was attached to the commissariat, and who had already expressed much sympathy at our want of

[63] This was one of the coldest winters on record. The Hudson River froze solid from New York to Powle's Hook, a distance of about two thousand yards. A cavalry troop rode on the ice from Staten Island to the Battery.

wood, was so much affected that he immediately left the room.

The next day, as I was looking out of the window, I saw quite a number of wagons full of chopped trees standing still in the street. Each wagon contained two cords of wood. I went into the room where the pastor, Mylius, sat with the children before the fire-place in which the last stick was burning, and said to him, "Never before have I been envious, but now the distress and pain which these poor children suffer, make me so; for just now there has come to our very door four wagons filled with wood. How happy would I be if I only had some of it!" Scarcely had I thus spoken, when a servant brought me a message from Major Brown, stating that he had sent me these loads of wood with his compliments, and begging us to send to him whenever we should again be out of fuel. Imagine my joy, and my eagerness to thank our guardian angel. I had scarcely seen his face, as the lying-in chamber of milady had been so dark. Some days after I was at a ball where he also was expected to be present. He had been described to me as a man with a very prominent turned up nose. For such a person, therefore, I looked attentively; but I was obliged to look for a long time, because the excellent man kept continually out of my way, that I might have no opportunity to thank him. At last, however, I found him and thanked him right heartily. He then told me that up to that time he had known nothing

of our necessity, but that when he heard my story
he had not been able to go to sleep quietly the
whole night, through fear that the dispositions
which he had already made for our relief would not
arrive sufficiently speedy. These "dispositions"
consisted in giving the order to cut down some of
the trees in the great avenue in front of the city;[64]
and when this proceeding was objected to on the
ground that it would make considerable damage, he
replied, that it was much better to spare a few trees
than to have a family, who had served the king with
so much zeal, suffer from want. He further told me
that in future we must, under all circumstances,
whenever any thing was wanting that it belonged to
the commissary to supply, apply directly to him.
This acquaintance was of great advantage to us. My
husband was supplied with many kinds of provisions; with Indian meal, part of which we used for
bread and part for cake, and also with salted meat,
which latter article, however, was entirely useless to
us, as we received more than we could consume;
and it often was so uneatable that I gave it away to
get rid of it, especially since our servants were also
supplied with the same kind of food.

The major, accordingly, advised us to pursue the
same plan in this regard as the other generals, viz: to
exchange our meat for boxes of tallow and candles
of spermaceti (which burn better and are more
beautiful than those of wax), and also for butter,

[64] This may have been Wall Street.

which they did gladly, as they were obliged to supply the soldiers with meat. By this means, we saved considerable. We were now no longer troubled for the want of wood, for they broke to pieces an old and worthless ship in order to furnish us with fuel, and from this time we received weekly two cords of fire-wood.

A little while before my confinement I had a dreadful fright. One of our servants brought me something, and I noticed that his eyes rolled, and that he could scarcely speak. I was terrified, and attempted to run out of the room, but he ran ahead of me, fell down, slammed to the door in his fall, and immediately was attacked with an awful infirmity. As he lay directly in front of the door, rendering it impossible for me to escape, I began to call out and shriek.

The persons in the house endeavored to come in to my assistance, but the lock was sprung and they were obliged to break open the door. Even then the poor man had to be pushed aside to make room; and I was finally obliged to leap over him to get out, he in the mean time gnashing his teeth in a horrible manner, and beating himself with his hands. But I had been for such a long time accustomed to sad and dreadful sights, that this circumstance fortunately did me no injury in my delicate situation.

In the beginning of the month of March, 1780, an old acquaintance of ours came to New York, the

Hessian General Loos,[65] who had known me in my girlhood. "Why!" said he to me, as he looked at me from head to foot, "what has become of your slender waist, your beautiful complexion, and your fair white hands! They are gone, but in their stead you have seen many lands; and when you again return home you will be called upon by this and that one of your acquaintance to relate your adventures, and, perhaps, the very next instant, those very ladies, who first asked you, will out of envy, declare your narrative wearisome, and while playing with their fans, will say, 'The woman can talk of nothing but America.'" As I knew beforetime, that it was very much his custom to speak the truth, seemingly in jest, I answered that I thanked him for the caution, and would endeavor to guard myself against the weakness of talking constantly of this journey, into which fault I might otherwise easily have fallen. On my side, however, I counseled him, that when with other women, he should also guard himself against speaking of the perishability of their charms, as he had done in regard to mine, else he might find many who would not take it as good naturedly as myself.

On the following day, which was the seventh of March, I was brought to bed with a daughter. My husband wished very much for a son, but the little one was so pretty that we were soon consoled for its not being a boy. We had intended, in case it had

[65] Johann August von Loos was the godfather of the second Riedesel child born in America.

been a boy, to have named it Americus, which we now changed for the little girl into America. The baptism, however, was so hurried, owing to the fact that General Phillips, who, with the Hessian General Knyphausen, and Colonel Wurmb,[66] was the only sponsor, was obliged to leave town on a short expedition, that the name of America was forgotten; and we were obliged afterward to have it placed on the parish register. The same day, my eldest daughter was seized with a dangerous illness, called *asthma infantile*, and some days afterward my third child became also very sick; and, I, therefore, lay in bed between both my almost dying children. But if my heart suffered deeply, my body had by this time become enured to hardship, and I got along nicely, although I was in the first days of my confinement. Six weeks afterward, my husband persuaded me to accompany him to a dinner given by General Tryon. This had been concerted between them for a particular object; for while I was absent my husband had the child inoculated by an English physician, as the small-pox was raging violently in the city. He, therefore, had it done without my knowledge in order to save me anxiety, and he would probably have succeeded, had not his fatherly uneasiness betrayed him. But he was continually going every instant to look at the child, and in a little

[66]Baron Wilhelm von Knyphausen (1716–1800) commanded the Hessian troops in America. The colonel was probably Friedrich Wilhelm von Wurmb.

while, said, "Alas! how pale she is," or, "She is certainly sick;" so that I, wondering at all these expressions, at last, said, that he must most assuredly have a reason for feeling so uneasy, and asked him if he had had the child inoculated? Immediately I rolled back the sleeves, and there sure enough were two pocks on each arm. I must confess that for a moment I was quite provoked; still I appreciated the good intention of my husband. The child was so bad that we feared we should lose her. My poor husband was inconsolable, accusing himself of being the cause of this misfortune; and I had enough to do in keeping up his spirits. But God be praised it came out all right in the end. The experiment, however, did not terminate so happily with a nobleman who followed our example, for he was so unfortunate as to lose his child.

Throughout the whole winter, Generals Phillips, Tryon and Patterson were our constant friends and guests, and every week we gave a gentleman's dinner party. This was all that we could afford to do, as every thing was so terribly high in the city. At the end of the winter General Tryon sailed for England, but just before his departure, he sent to my house, unbeknown to me, magnificent furniture, tapestry, carpets, and curtains, besides a set of silk hangings for an entire room. Never shall I forget the many marks of friendship which I have received from almost every one of this excellent nation; and it will always be to me a source of satisfaction to be able at any time to be of use to the English, as I have learned by experience how pleasant it is to receive kindness from foreigners.

About this time our friendly relations began with our excellent friend General Clinton, who was the general-in-chief of the English army in the southern provinces of America. As is the case with every Englishman, it was at first very difficult for our acquaintance to ripen into intimacy. His first call upon us was one of ceremony; he came as general-in-chief, attended by his entire staff. As his general appearance and conversation were agreeable, I said to his friend, General Phillips, that I regretted that he treated us with so much ceremony, and that a more friendly manner would have better accorded with our feelings. Afterwards he invited us out to his country-seat to spend the summer, an invitation which was accepted. His country residence was magnificent, a most beautiful situation, orchard, and meadows, and the Hudson river[67] running directly in front of the house. Every thing was placed at our disposal, including fruits of the most delicious flavor; indeed, of this latter article we had more than we could eat. Our servants feasted on peaches even to satiety, and our horses, which roamed through the orchards, eagerly ate the fruit from the trees, disdaining that upon the ground, which every evening we had gathered up and given to the pigs to fatten them. It seems almost incredi-

[67] Madame probably meant the East River.

ble, but nevertheless it is true, that with nothing but this fruit we fattened six pigs, the flesh of which was capital, only the fat was somewhat soft. Peach, apricot, and other fruit trees, are raised here, without espaliers, and have trunks as thick as those of ordinary trees.

Not far from us were the Hell-gates,[68] which are dangerous breakers for those ships that pass through them up the river. We often saw ships in danger, but only one was wrecked and went to pieces during our stay at this place.

General Clinton came often to visit us, but in hunter's dress, accompanied by only one aid-de-camp. On one of these occasions, he said to us, "I feel confident that you look upon me more as a friend than a stranger, and as I feel the same toward you, you shall always be regarded by me as such. The last time he came to see us, he had with him the unfortunate—as he afterwards became—Major André,[69] who, the day afterward, set out upon the fatal expedition, in which he was captured by the Americans, and afterwards hung as a spy. It was very sad that this preeminently excellent young man should have fallen a victim to his zeal and his kind heart, which led him to undertake such a precarious errand instead of leaving it to older and

[68] The turbulent water passage between the East and Harlem rivers.

[69] This is the occasion when André went up the Hudson to negotiate with Benedict Arnold for the surrender of West Point to the British.

known officers, to whom properly the duty belonged, but whom on that very account (as they would be more exposed to danger), he wished to save.

We passed much of our time at this most agreeable place; but our contentment was broken in upon by a malignant fever,[70] that prevailed in New York, and of which, in our family alone, twenty fell ill; eight dangerously. Among these eight were my husband and my daughter Gustava. One can imagine my grief and apprehension; day and night I did nothing but divide my nursing between my husband and daughter. The former was so ill, that we often thought he would not survive the day; and Gustava had such violent paroxysms of fever, that she entreated me, when she was shivering with the ague, to lay myself upon her, at which times she violently shook me together with her bed, although she was only nine years old. It frequently happened that those sick of the fever died in these fits of shaking; and every day persons would tell me of fifty or sixty fresh burials, which certainly did not tend to raise my spirits. The heat which the sick suffered was so intense that their pulse beat one hundred and thirty-five times in a minute. All our servants were sick, and of course I was obliged to do every thing. I was then nursing my little America, and had neither opportunity nor desire to lie down, except while giving her the breast. At such times I laid

[70] This was probably an epidemic of cholera.

down upon the bed and fell asleep. At night I was often busied in making for my patients a lemonade of salts of wormwood mixed with lemon juice, sugar and water. By which means, as all the sick in the house had them, I used up in the space of two weeks, two full boxes of lemons, each box containing five hundred.

One day, we expected the physician from New York with the utmost impatience. My husband was taken with a severe diarrhea, and constant vomiting, and became so ill that our courage completely gave way. He slept continually, and when I wished to give him sago-water,[71] which I had been recommended to make him drink much of, he begged me imploringly to allow him to die in peace, as he could not hold out much longer. At this moment the physician came in, and I pressed him to tell me candidly if he thought there was still any hope. "Yes, surely," said he. At this confident answer, our two oldest children whom we had not observed (as, fearing that the opinion of the doctor would be unfavorable, they had hidden under the table to listen), when they saw the good news upon my face, suddenly sprung up, threw themselves at his feet and kissed his hands. Every one who witnessed this scene with me was deeply moved; and the doctor, himself, who was a man full of feeling, was affected to tears. Before this, he had visited us very punctually, but now he redoubled his attentions, and so

[71] Tapioca water.

managed it as to dine with us every day that he might lose no time, as he had many patients. He recommended to me strongly a drink made of sago-powder and water. At first he remained with my husband three minutes, then five, and then fifteen, and finally a full half hour. I had always a watch in my hand, and I was beside myself for joy at the increased length of his visits, a feeling in which every one that was with me shared. The pastor, Mylius, and our trusty yäger,[72] Rockel, both of whom remained well, assisted me by turns in watching at night.

Of thirty persons who composed our family, only ten remained in good health. The cook, cook-maid, etc., were all sick, and could work only on their alternate well days; and in addition to which, the weather was terribly hot. It is perfectly amazing what mankind can endure, and what I also went through. But I was well, and blessed with a cheerful happy temperament, which made me receive the smallest particle of hope with heartfelt joy. I do believe that, by degrees, the health can be undermined by repeated sufferings; still, I thankfully rejoice that I was able to be of use, and that without my attentions, I might, perhaps, have lost the dear objects of my affection, who now contribute so much to my happiness. At length all of our household who were sick were able to be restored to health, and not one died, a result that much more

[72] Servant, or footman.

than abundantly paid me for all of my own trouble.

We remained the entire summer of 1780, upon this lovely estate. Two Miss Robinsons came to share our loneliness, and enliven our little company. They remained with us a fortnight previous to our return to the city, when the news of the arrival of a ship from England bringing over the latest fashions, took them back again to the town. On our return to the city, I scarcely recognized them in their odd and actually laughable garb, which a very pretty woman, just over from England, had imposed upon them and the other New York ladies. This lady was with child and did not wish it to be known. Accordingly, she made them think that in England they wore bodices which were parted in the middle, whereby the points stuck upwards, hoops as large around as those of a hogshead, and very short cloaks tied up with ribbons, all of which they believed implicitly and copied after.

Upon our return to New York we were received in the most friendly manner; and our friends vied with each other in making the winter pass most pleasantly. My husband, General Phillips, and their aid-de-camps, were finally exchanged in the autumn of 1780; but the rest of the troops captured at Saratoga remained prisoners.

General Clinton, partly through friendship to my husband, and partly out of attachment to our present duke, wished to place General Riedesel in active service where he could serve to advantage. He, therefore, by virtue of the power which an English general has in his own army, appointed him lieutenant general, and gave him the corresponding English allowance; which, on account of the dearness of every thing (by reason of which we had had difficulty in making both ends meet), proved very acceptable to us. At the same time he gave him a command at Long Island, which island lies opposite New York, being separated from it by only a narrow channel called the East River. I was not able during the winter to be with him, as the house, in which he had his quarters, was not habitable for me, as it was possible to heat only a few rooms in it. My husband, accordingly, went back and forth, which he easily did all winter, as every thing was quiet. The autumn before he was appointed to this post, he had a severe relapse of his old complaint, caused probably by a cold which he caught by going in sea-bathing while heated. He suddenly became perfectly stiff and could not speak; and had it not been for friend Colonel Wurmb, who, fortunately, was in his room, it might, perhaps, have been all over with him. The doctor immediately opened a vein and rubbed him strongly, and God once more spared him to me; but his cramps, oppressions, headaches, and drowsiness increased. All the physicians gave it as their opinion that the climate thoroughly disagreed with him, and that he never would be any better as long as he remained in the southern provinces of North America. Still there was nothing else for us to do. My husband could not think of receiving permission to leave, and was, therefore, obliged to remain at his post.

In the spring of 1781, I also settled down on Long Island, where we, although pretty lonesome, might have lived perfectly contented if we only could have been without solicitude: but as the river was not frozen over, the Americans constantly attempted surprises in order to take prisoners. Major Maybaum was drawn out of his bed;[73] and we knew that they aimed to do the same thing with my husband. Our house was situated close to the shore and was perfectly isolated, so that if they had overcome the watch, they could easily have carried him away. Every one was therefore constantly on the watch. Throughout the entire night, at the slightest noise, he would wake up and place himself in readiness for an attack; and thus he lost considerable sleep. I also became so accustomed to watching, that day light would often surprise me, when I would lie down and catch a few hours sleep; for it was only when my husband believed that I was wide awake and on guard, that he would allow himself to sleep—so terrible was to him the thought that he might again be taken prisoner. We had from our house a magnificent prospect. Every evening I saw from my window the city of New York entirely

---

[73] The Americans concentrated on capturing officers so that they might arrange an exchange for their own officers who were held by the British.

lighted up, and, as the city is built close to the shore, I saw its reflection in the water. We heard also the beating of the drums, and, if every thing was particularly still, even the calls of the sentinels. We had our own boat and could cross over in it to New York in a quarter of an hour.

One day I saw out of a window of my room, a fleet of thirty-five ships approaching under full sail, and shortly afterward, from another window, I perceived them all lying at anchor between us and the city. My husband had many English under his command, and among others the light dragoons. Although the English troops are proud, and, as it is said, difficult to manage, yet they loved my husband, and were perfectly contented under his command. On one occasion, when the English officers were dining with us, my husband said to them that he would accompany them back to their camp; whereupon they very politely begged me also to go with the party. I, therefore, seated myself in a carriage, and reached the camp in advance of them. But I believe that they had sent word of my arrival ahead of me, for an officer came up, and, to my great perplexity, requested me to get out of the carriage and walk with him down the line. Upon my complying with his request, I was greeted with all military honors, even to the beating of drums, which still more increased my confusion. I remarked to the officer that this was not suitable to me, and that we German women were not accustomed to such distinctions. But he at once very politely answered that their whole corps could not sufficiently honor the wife of a general who, as their commanding officer, treated them with so much kindness; and more than all this, they would never forget what I had done for their comrades at Saratoga. Although not unmindful of all this, which was very flattering and agreeable, I welcomed the first favorable moment to get away.

During our sojourn in this place, I often saw people buried up to their necks in the earth; for in this manner they cure the scurvy.

We had a hospital in this place, in which were many wounded and invalid sailors. These good people replied to those who bewailed their fate: "We have fought for our king, and are satisfied, and when we are once in Chelsea, we shall be sufficiently rewarded." This is an excellent hospital for seamen, near London, where they are kept, clothed, and nursed in the best manner.

About this time, General Phillips was sent off on an expedition to Carolina. The parting on both sides was painful. We never again beheld this excellent friend, for he died there of an inflammatory fever, which he brought upon him by exposure. We have always mourned his loss. He was a very brave man, and a thorough friend to his friends.

As the health of my husband did not get any better, and his presence, moreover, was necessary to that portion of his corps which had remained behind in Canada, General Clinton was finally induced to send him thither, though he loved him so much that he parted from him with regret. This friendship continued between them—although separated—until the death of the former general.

As the time of our departure had been continually very uncertain, I had not wished to wean my little daughter America, and had accordingly nursed her the whole of the fourteen months. Finally, however, she became so large that I feared my milk would not hold out, and I therefore weaned her the beginning of May. But by this course I immediately brought upon myself a misfortune which occasioned me even more vexation; namely, an eruption of the skin to which most of the people in this warm climate are subject. Little pimples come out over the whole limb, which itches so that one has no peace whatever. They come with the hot and disappear with the cold weather: otherwise the person is perfectly well.

Our departure was determined upon for the month of July. I had for so long a time received my orders for wood, that during my sojourn upon Long Island, I had saved thirty cords; and I now wished to give them back to my excellent major of the commissariat, who had helped me so faithfully. But he would not receive it, but begged me either to sell it, or share it with the poor. "I know you," said the honest man, "you will take more satisfaction in alleviating distress." This was the view of the case that my husband and myself both took. We, therefore, gave twenty cords to a very worthy family of royalists, who had already lost much of their property and were afterwards obliged to emigrate. We then divided the remaining ten cords among other poor families.

Before going away, we desired to deliver up our furniture, but they did not wish to receive it, saying that it belonged to us, and that we had better take it with us to Canada, where we would certainly need it. We, however, did not wish to abuse so much kindness, and accordingly sent it back into the Royal magazine, except one English bedstead which we kept by way of remembrance. Nevertheless, I must frankly confess that I afterward somewhat repented of my decision, partly because we found nothing whatever in Canada, and partly because this beautifully furnished Royal magazine was subsequently plundered and burned by the Americans. At last we set out, or rather went, on board the ship,[74] for we remained at anchor within about an hour's sail of New York, for more than a week. General Clinton, desiring our safe convoy, had selected an agent (ship's agent) whom he supposed to be an active and skilled man, and desired him to seek out from among those ships that were to sail, one that should be comfortable and at the same time a good sailer— one that could run away from danger and not be captured along the way. But this furnishes fresh

[74] The name of this ship was the *Little Seal*.

evidence how the best of us are deceived; this agent was a corrupt, coarse and ignorant man, who either, through laziness, had not taken the trouble to examine the ship, or, as often happens, had been bribed by the ship's captain. But enough: we were placed on board one of the smallest and most miserable ships of the whole fleet, upon which, we were often in such danger from falling behind, that the captain of the second man-of-war, appointed to convoy us, was obliged to tow us, that is, to draw us along by a rope. For this purpose, one end of a great cable was attached to the towed ship, and the other was made fast to the man-of-war which drew us along. This, however, was very unpleasant, and often, indeed, dangerous; for if there was a calm, one ship would strike against the other, and if we had been so unlucky as to meet a ship of the enemy, we would have been obliged to receive the shock of battle. Besides, our ship had too few sailors, which would have been the cause of additional danger if we had been overtaken by a hurricane; in which case we should probably have been upset, as on account of the small number of men, we could not have taken in the sails quickly enough, especially as the ship was leaky and all the men would have had to be placed at the pumps. And to crown all, our ship was badly loaded, and lay so much upon one side, that we were obliged, while on the passage, to fill empty casks with sea-water in order to give the ship the necessary equilibrium, an emergency which ought always to be guarded against. In addition to all this, the company of the above mentioned agent, was in the highest degree unpleasant. We were obliged to defray his expenses, and have him near us, where he made himself exceedingly troublesome by his grumbling and whining yawns, by which he wakened all the men on the ship, and even ourselves, although we were in another room. Just as we were on the eve of embarking, we met with still another great vexation. Our faithful negroes, a man, his wife and a young kinswoman of theirs, were reclaimed by their first owner (from whom they had been taken on the ground that he was a rebel), under the pretense that he had again become a royalist; and he brought an order, that they should be delivered up to him, actually at the very moment in which the signal had been given for our departure. As they had served us faithfully, and the man was a bad master who treated them shockingly, the shrieks and lamentations of these poor people were very great. The young maiden (Phillis by name), fainted, and when she again came to herself, would hear nothing whatever about leaving us. She threw herself at my feet and embraced them with clasped hands so strongly, that they were obliged to tear her away by force. My husband offered her master money for her; but when the latter observed that we wished so much to keep her, he demanded for this girl thirty guineas, a sum which my husband did not wish to give. Had it not been at the very moment of our departure, I believe that we would have kept her notwithstanding. We made them a present of their clothing, and also the mattresses, which, in view of the voyage, we had had made for them. This very course, however, affected them still more, and Phillis cried out, "If I do not die, I will come again to you, even to the end of the world." This good maiden, also, afterward actually begged two or three persons to take her with them and bring her to me, adding at the same time, "My good lady will be very glad to pay my passage." She was perfectly right, but as none of these persons were confident in the matter, they were not willing to take charge of her. My husband had the money for this one purchase, but her greedy master, in order to compel us to buy them all three, refused to sell her separately; and as this would have been too much for our purse, we were obliged to relinquish the design. We afterwards, however, repented that we did not make the sacrifice, as we found that the female domestics in Canada were too simple and too clumsy.

The very first day of our voyage my eruption entirely disappeared, which rejoiced me exceedingly. This distemper, however, had rather an evil influence on my health the rest of my life, for three days afterward I was taken with such severe pains in my head and teeth, that I could neither eat nor sleep—and I had to endure this state of things day and night. The sharpness of the pain took hold of my very vitals; and my feet were so cold that they could not be warmed even with hot water. They gave me opium, which, it is true, stupified me somewhat, but gave me no sleep, as my pains were too violent; and I therefore suffered in this way during the whole voyage.

We had all kinds of mishaps on our passage. Among other things, a ship, during a calm, once came too near us and gave us a tremendous thump, and we were obliged to push it away with poles. At another time, also, a ship, with its stern, tore away our little necessary,[75] and it was very fortunate that no one was in it at the time.

One day, while we were enveloped by a thick mist, we thought we saw land. Most fortunately, however, at the same instant the mist, owing to a gust of wind, suddenly drew up like a curtain; and then the captain noticed with terror that we were at a place called Dusky-bay and close to a well known and dangerous rock, which, on account of its shape, is called the "old woman," and actually looks like one sitting there with bent back and bowed head. He immediately cried out to the captain of the man-of-war that had us in tow, who, making this voyage for the first time, did not know of this danger; and at the same moment a favorable wind fortunately arose, which we used to such good advantage that in less than an hour we had left this bay, which by the way is full of rocks, and on which ships are often wrecked. In the course of this voyage, we touched at

[75] The head, or privy.

Nova Scotia, where we landed for a short time. We were welcomed at this place in the most friendly manner. The governor and his wife (both amiable people) begged us at once to dine with them.[76] We accepted this invitation, and found assembled at their house, a very agreeable company, consisting of seven or eight families, who were continually exchanging visits one with another. The next day, they showed us, not only the city itself, but the country in the immediate vicinity, with which we were exceedingly pleased. One can live in this place very cheaply. Sea-fish, also, are found remarkably good here . It was remarked upon as a curious circumstance, that while, before the revolution, lobsters or large craw-fish had never been seen in this vicinity; yet no sooner had that struggle commenced, than numbers of them left the continent of North America and came to New Scotland. This gave rise to a standing joke among the people of this place, that the lobsters were good royalists, and accordingly wore the English (red) uniform. During our stay in New Scotland, I suffered so terribly with the tooth-ache, that I resolved to have the troublesome tooth extracted. In order however, to spare my husband and children all care and anxiety, I got up at five o'clock in the morning, and sent for our

[76] Sir Andrew Snape Hammond. It was also here that Madame Riedesel picked up the Hessian flags that she had sewn into a mattress and slept on them for the remainder of her voyage to Canada.

chirurgeon, who was considered very skillful in drawing teeth. We went into a remote room, where he made me sit down on the earthen floor, and with a coarse, dirty instrument gave me such a jerk that I certainly thought he had done the business, and asked him for my tooth. "Only have patience a moment longer," said he, as he made me again sit down, giving, at the same time, another tug at the tooth. Now, thought I, I have surely got rid of it; but by no manner of means, for he had, on the contrary, seized hold of, and loosened a healthy tooth, without, however, pulling it entirely out. I was exceedingly angry at this bungling: and, although he offered to pull this and the decayed one, I could not, and would not again trust myself to him. I have had good reason to repent this experiment; for this loosened tooth was so pressed upon one side, that for more than two years afterward it prevented me from shutting my teeth together; while, in addition, this experience made me such a coward, that I have never been able to bring myself to submit to a similar operation.

During the remainder of our voyage, we had a few storms, and just as we entered the river St. Lawrence, we met with the disagreeable mishap of losing two anchors. We anchored in this river every evening on account of the ebbing of the tide. Unfortunately an anchor was dropped upon a reef, which on account of the continual motion of the ship by the wind, parted from the cable. They then threw

out a second anchor, which met with the same fate.
We had now only one small anchor left. If we had
lost that we should have been at the sport of the
wind, and would have had to pass an exceedingly
wretched night. At the same time, also, our provisions failed us, a boat that we had sent ashore having brought back only some fowls and eggs. All
these *contretemps* made my husband resolve that we
should not remain another night on board the ship.
Accordingly, when the ship again came to anchor
the same evening, he ordered the long-boat to be let
down, and we, namely, my husband and myself, our
children, both the aids-de-camp, my maid servants
and two attendants, seated ourselves in it and were
carried to the land.

We chanced upon a pretty cottage occupied by a
peasant, where we were received in a very friendly
manner. The captain of the ship brought us hither,
together with our pilots. Some of these pilots come
on board, immediately upon the ships entering any
distance within the St. Lawrence. These people are
well paid, receiving often twenty guineas. As the
ships are all insured, every sea captain is bound at
his peril to take one. On the contrary, however,
every captain is released from all responsibility, the
moment the pilot is on board, who then takes the
entire charge, and is answerable with his head for
any danger.

My husband, with one of his aids-de-camp, went
on, the same evening, to Quebec, and I followed

him the next day, but did not arrive there until three days afterward. The country through which I passed, was exceedingly picturesque. Every inhabitant has a good house, which they take great pains to cleanse thoroughly once a year. This causes them to have a very neat look, and gives them, also, a glistening appearance in the distance. As their sons, and also their sons-in-law, as soon as married, build close to their parents, very pretty settlements soon spring up around them, on which account these people call themselves *habitans* (settlers), and not peasants. These dwellings, every one of which has attached to it a stable, orchard and pasturage, lie along the St. Lawrence, and present a splendid appearance, especially to those who sail up and down the river. To every house, also, an ice cellar is attached, which is made with very little trouble. A hole, for instance, is dug in the earth. This is then filled, first with ice and then with water, which, in congealing, fills up all the interstices, and makes the top as smooth as the surface of a mirror. Over this the inhabitants lay a very clean board, and place upon it various articles of food, which are thus kept with the greatest cleanliness. They take special pains to keep out of the ice-house any straw or hay, which they say causes the ice to melt more quickly. These ice houses are indispensable, particularly as each one kills his own cattle, nor would they be able otherwise to keep the meat fresh in summer when the heat is very great. As a general thing, these ice-cellars are made underneath their barns.

These people, also, keep in summer much cattle, which they kill at the beginning of winter, and bring into the city for sale. Some of the animals that they keep, for their own support—such as beeves, sheep and swine—they drive to the forest in the morning, and only in the evening give them provender in the stable. They have, also, in this part of the country, a little fish called small cod, which are caught under the ice. For this purpose large holes are made in the ice at intervals of six to eight hundred feet. In these openings they place nets which are made fast to great poles by strong cords. In this way they catch sometimes five or six sledges full. The fish are then thrown into the ice-cellars, where they freeze instantly, and they remain in this condition until they are needed. Then they are brought forth, thawed out, placed immediately in the kettle, and eaten. These fish, especially when fried in butter, taste very nicely.

The dwellings are exceedingly comfortable; and in them one finds remarkably good and clean beds. All the heads of the households have curtained beds; and, as the sitting-rooms are very large, they have their beds stand in them. They have, moreover, great ovens, in which they cook. Their soups are very substantial, and consist, for the most part, of bacon, fresh meat and vegetables, which are cooked all together in a pot, and served out at the same time with the entremets. The Canadians prepare a kind of sugar from the maple-tree which for this reason, is called the sugar-maple. They go in the spring of the year into the forest, armed with kettles and pots, in which the sap is gathered from incisions made in the trees. It is then boiled and that which is uppermost, and on that account the best, they keep especially for their own use. This maple-sugar has only one fault, that it is too brown; otherwise it is right good, especially for diseases of the breast.

The natives are hospitable and jovial, singing and smoking the whole day long. The women frequently have goitres. Otherwise, however, the people are healthy and live to be quite old. Indeed, it is not unfrequent to meet with very aged persons living with their great grandchildren, who take the greatest care of them.

We arrived in Quebec the middle of September, 1781, after a journey of eight weeks, and were welcomed in a very friendly manner.

Index

INDEX

List of The Lakeside Classics

The Lakeside Classics